Dearest Love —

Hope that you get the new boat soon and that lots of delightful hours are spent in fixing it up exactly the way you like it.

Love,
Wilma

BOAT REPAIRS AND CONVERSIONS

By the same author

COMPLETE AMATEUR BOAT BUILDING *(John Murray)*
BOAT MAINTENANCE *(Kaye & Ward)*
BUILDING CHINE BOATS *(Yachting Monthly)*
LIFEBOAT INTO YACHT *(Yachting Monthly)*

Boat Repairs and Conversions

MICHAEL VERNEY

C. Eng., M.I.C.E., M.I.W.E.S.

International Marine Publishing Company

CAMDEN, MAINE

Published in the United States of America
by International Marine Publishing Company,
Camden, Maine

This book is an entirely rewritten version
of YACHT REPAIRS AND CONVERSIONS
first published in 1951 (5th edition 1977)

International Standard Book Number 0–87742–031–9
Library of Congress Catalog Card Number 72–97994

Printed in Great Britain

Contents

To
DORA VERNEY
the secretary, crew and patient wife of an enthusiast

List of Illustrations

PLATES

FIGURES

TABLES

All illustrations are by the author.

Preface

When the original version of this book first appeared nearly thirty years ago, its purpose was to enable the enthusiast of modest means (who could not hope to buy even a secondhand yacht) to get afloat in a vessel close to the desired size and character.

The only way in which this position has changed since then is that due to rocketing labour charges and the high cost of living, do-it-yourself boat work is now even more worth while.

Another change has occurred, however, because the supply of working craft suitable for conversion has dwindled. Thus a higher proportion of practical yachtsmen now buy new standard hull shells mainly in plastics, steel, or ferro-cement, and complete the more expensive jobs of decking, accommodation, power installation and rig, by themselves.

The book is also intended to provide all the information necessary to enable owners to rejuvenate neglected boats (when such work would not prove economic if done professionally) and to modernize and improve the gear and comfort aboard sound but antiquated yachts.

Not only does any form of practical boat work pay great dividends financially, but it also creates immense satisfaction. Furthermore, in these days of mass-produced plastics boats the conversionist can become the most envied owner if his boat possesses that elusive quality, *character* – perhaps a gaff cutter with tanned sails; a steamboat; or a brigantine with bowsprit and clipper bow!

To equip this book for readers in the New World, the American equivalents of British terms and products are mentioned, while all dimensions are quoted in inch as well as metric units. The prices given in dollars represent average costs in America and have no connexion with the sterling rate of exchange.

April 1977 M.V.

1

Getting Afloat

The yachtsman of any age who simply must get a cruiser of his own has several ways of going about it. With time, space, and a little ability, building from plans is the most satisfying way and, taking the value of the finished boat into consideration, this is the best way.

When lacking the time and ability, but with a bit of capital, the amateur can buy a bare hull from a boatyard and complete the work in his leisure hours.

Carrying out a conversion is a similar process, but whereas there will probably be working drawings to cover the completion of a bare shell, the design work for a conversion will no doubt have to be done by the enthusiast himself.

Few naval architects would undertake the design work for a conversion nowadays, but if one could be persuaded, the cost would be in the region of £300 ($2000) for a 30 ft. (9 m.) lifeboat conversion and about £800 ($5000) for a 60 ft. (18 m.) M.F.V., depending upon the amount of detail required. Very few stock plans exist which can be purchased by the amateur for any type of conversion.

The economics of the business work out somewhat as follows. Taking a 30 ft. (9 m.) motor cruiser as an example, the value of a new boat might be £10,000 ($40,000) and a good secondhand craft £6000 ($24,000). Building from scratch could be done for £4000 ($14,000). A new bare hull would cost about £2000 ($8000) and the cost of completion another £3500 ($12,000), making £5500 ($20,000) for the finished job.

The value of a similar newly-completed professional lifeboat conversion would be £6000 ($24,000). Buying a hull for conversion should cost about £500 ($1500) with an additional £3500 ($12,000) required for deck, interior work and engines (equivalent to finishing a new bare hull), making £4000 ($13,500) altogether.

The economics of the work are more attractive when the latent item of interest on capital is taken into account.

If converting a 30 ft. (9 m.) cruiser takes three years, the materials used will cost a steady £15 ($60) per week excluding the occasional necessary capital outlays for such items as engines and fittings. Building from scratch over a five-year period would similarly amount to £12 ($50) per week. To pay off the loan or mortgage on a new yacht over a five-year period would cost about £50 ($200) per week. It can be seen that with a little patience, an absorbing practical hobby can be made to pay dividends.

Some projects for conversions or completing standard bare hulls fail because amateurs employ part-time workmen to accelerate the progress without realizing how this procedure can escalate costs.

The following figures illustrate a typical instance:

1. *No paid labour*	£	$
Cost of hull	500	1500
Cost of repairs to the hull	30	120
Cost of materials and fittings for cabins	420	1280
Total cost of conversion	950	2900

2. *One man employed full-time*		
Cost of hull	500	1500
Cost of materials for hull repairs	30	120
Labour on hull repairs for four weeks	250	1000
Cost of materials and fittings for cabins	420	1280
Labour on conversion for twenty-four weeks	1500	6000
	2700	9900

From this example we see that £1750 of a £2700 conversion is spent on labour alone. This is about 65% of the entire cost. When much work is done in a boatyard, this percentage naturally rises greatly. If the help of a shipwright or boatyard has to be obtained for some particular job which the owner is unable to do himself, he should be careful to get estimates for the work and see that his instructions are carried out.

Prior to 1950 the standard of design and workmanship on the

majority of boat conversions was often poor, chiefly because the enthusiasts who built them had very little data for guidance and the economics of the project would not permit the engagement of a professional designer. Since that time some useful books on the subject have appeared and the majority of modern conversions are pleasing in appearance.

There are other ways for the impecunious yachtsman to obtain a boat of his own. For instance, it may be possible to find a decrepit (though not necessarily very old) craft which can be bought cheaply enough to make complete rejuvenation worth while. Provided the vessel is of good design and likely to command a good value on completion of the work, rejuvenation of this sort nearly always pays. Needless to say one must strike a good bargain for the vessel initially, and minimize the use of paid labour.

THE QUEST FOR A HULL

To locate an ideal old yacht for rejuvenation on the above lines may take several years. Obtaining a modern hull for completion is a simple procedure, sometimes brought to fruition by conversations in the club bar or by scanning the advertisement pages in yachting magazines. Not all yacht builders producing standard boats will sell these in early stages of completion as a badly finished craft could prove detrimental to them. However, many yards will help the enthusiast in this respect.

When one has decided to adopt the cheaper alternative of a conversion, finding a suitable hull should not be too difficult once a choice has been made concerning the exact size and type.

Some of the most popular craft available for conversion (mainly in Britain) are listed below. As well as these it may also be possible to find a sound craft of earlier type which has been badly converted, neglected, or used merely as a houseboat. If the price is right, it may be possible to reconvert such a vessel into a first rate job.

(1) Ex-ship's lifeboats form the most readily available source of hulls for conversions. These (as well as R.N.L.I. lifeboats) are mentioned again in Chapters 2 and 6.

(2) The Navy constantly disposes of a variety of small boats varying from clinker pulling dinghies and the well-known whalers and cutters, to a range of double diagonal motor-launches with canvas spray hoods and larger motor tenders with one or more fixed shelter cabins.

The larger craft include pinnaces, harbour launches and motor fishing vessels, some of which can be converted into deep-sea cruisers or mobile homes. Many Admiralty craft lie derelict for long periods before being offered for disposal at scrap price, and so to avoid fruitless tours of inspection it may be advisable for the amateur to obtain one of these craft from a dealer.

Some dealers may also keep certain craft surplus to the requirements of the Army and Air Force. These may include pontoons, fast launches, landing craft, air/sea rescue boats, and motor personnel launches.

The Admiralty small craft disposals are advertised in the *Motor Boat and Yachting* magazine and any correspondence should be addressed to the Director of Navy Contracts, Ensleigh, Bath, Somerset.

(3) As fishing fleets are modernized, old boats can still be bought for conversion into motor or sailing yachts with plenty of character, see Plate 1. The structural condition of some of these vessels after fifty years of service may not be very close to the original any more but by limiting expenditure on converting the fish-well into a cabin with rugged joinery to match the hull, the economics of the job are frequently favourable. Few fishing boats built *to sail* can be found in British waters nowadays.

(4) For a really powerful seagoing conversion of large dimensions, hefty construction, and pleasing appearance, there is no doubt that the M.F.V.s (Plates 2, 42 and 43) being sold make most favourable propositions. Although these craft can be made to sail (as described in Chapter 2) the original single diesel engine can often be retained without alteration for a full power conversion.

These motor fishing vessels were built of oak framing and pine planking with cruiser sterns on typical Scottish fishing boat lines. The length varies between 45 ft. (14 m.) and 75 ft. (23 m.) with a cruising speed of between 8 and 10 knots.

Plate 1: Fishing boat suitable for conversion

Plate 2: Sea-going M.F.V.

(5) The barges, longboats, and lighters working on the inland waterways make good canal cruising conversions. Few Thames barges still sail but the ones that were motorized can sometimes be re-rigged for sailing.

A canal cruiser is about the simplest type of conversion one could contemplate and the traditional narrow-boat generally makes the most pleasing job. Some barge owners selling old narrow-boats for conversion cut them in half to make two short craft, one with outboard and one with inboard propulsion!

(6) Although the once numerous coastal ketches and schooners in Britain have now been sold out of service, there is no scarcity of these craft in Scandinavian waters and they are now being replaced with diesel coasters.

These vessels vary in length from 65 ft. (20 m.) to 160 ft (50 m.) and although large and slow they make most attractive ocean-cruising conversions for certain enthusiasts, while the less-sound craft can be turned into comfortable mobile homes.

(7) The supply of vessels for large conversions never ceases and as these are invariably commercial craft having regular Lloyds or Bureau Veritas condition surveys, they are not likely to fall to pieces shortly after conversion! Ferry boats, passenger launches, small coasters, trawlers, and drifters come into this category, most of them having steel hulls nowadays.

Some enthusiasts converting old Clyde Puffers or steam drifters like to retain the fascinating original machinery. Provided the boiler is sound this can be fired with free waste oil from garages. If a new boiler is required a modern monotube type (such as the Stone-Vapor) burning diesel fuel could be used, reducing the time to raise steam from three hours to three minutes.

(8) Ex-racing yachts can sometimes be converted into exciting auxiliary cruisers, though the accommodation may have to be spartan. A Dragon is about the smallest size normally adopted, but working upwards, outclassed 5.5, 6, and 12 metre yachts can all be made into satisfying cruisers for the connoisseur provided a suitable mooring is available.

APPEARANCE IS IMPORTANT

One fault with nearly all types of open hulls and fishing craft (except the M.F.V.s) is the low freeboard. A ship's lifeboat is well proportioned as a launch but when adding a deck and cabin, care is needed to arrive at a suitable amount of headroom avoiding an ugly cabin top. John Lewis in *Small Boat Conversion* advises one to be content with restricted headroom (see Plate 11). In contrast, *this* book suggests that before decking in a lifeboat, one should first extend the topsides upwards throughout.

Fishing boats often have low freeboard to facilitate the handling of nets and it usually proves impossible to raise the deck level. The cabin top coamings can be very much deeper than on a lifeboat, however, as there will doubtless be high bulwarks to mask the potential unsightliness and one can with advantage add bulwarks to these boats where none exist.

Modern yacht designs are masterpieces of how to get a quart into a pint pot, with appearance a secondary consideration. Except when a boat has to be exceptionally small for trailing, one is bound to conclude that owners who are limited with finance might be wiser to look for a second-hand yacht of larger size rather than give a naval architect ulcers trying to cram berths into the bilges!

The conversionist must forget the 'pint pot' idea or he will be disappointed with the results of his labour. Anyway, he is likely to be either the young hard-working type with insufficient leisure to spend months afloat when full headroom would be an advantage, or a retired person who will want to live aboard and must therefore have a large vessel with ample space

It may prove impossible to disguise the origin of a clinker ship's boat or an R.N.L.I. lifeboat but much can be done by adding a false stem, perhaps creating an attractive clipper bow. Double skin flush-hulled lifeboats can be converted into a pleasing Dutch appearance by fitting leeboards, the correct shaped cabin top, an

Plate 3: Lifeboat conversions with leeboards

ornate barn-door rudder, and the correct rig with curved gaff. An example of such a boat is shown in Plate 3.

Small motor cruiser conversions are always easy to design for pleasing appearance. The topsides can be raised for'ard to provide headroom and a full width cabin while a big cockpit with wheel-house shelter produces a vessel very similar to many standard yachts or fishing cruisers.

Headroom is normally adequate in the larger M.F.V. Oddly enough many ocean-going yachts have been designed on M.F.V. lines, so that there is never any difficulty in making a converted M.F.V. similar in appearance to one of these yachts.

THE SURVEY

Any type of hull chosen for conversion should be surveyed before the deal is clinched. This is not merely to ensure that a dealer is not diddling you, but also to make certain that a lot of time and labour is not wasted in converting a craft that will last only a few years.

The most knowledgeable amateurs might be able to avoid the engagement of a professional surveyor, but a preliminary survey by the amateur is always a good idea first, as any startling defects are then almost bound to come to light. If all appears to be well, then call in the surveyor for his thorough inspection, with the knowledge that he is not on a wild goose chase.

The survey of an open wooden boat does not take long and will not involve much expenditure if the surveyor lives nearby. Bigger craft with decks and cabins will require a much more extensive inspection. The surveyor will want to know exactly how far you want him to investigate, the usual categories being:

(1) Superficial survey as lying, including moving all loose sole boards, hatches, partitions and ballast.

(2) Structural survey involving boatyard labour to shift fixed sole boards, parts of lining or ceiling, and including blocking up to inspect underside of keel if necessary.

(3) Complete survey to include drawing (or X-raying) keel bolts,

some plank and floor fastenings, and perhaps unshipping the rudder. It may involve part dismantling of a big engine.

With a large craft, Method 3 would be required in any case before serious conversion commenced and so the expense is better utilized in the initial stages. The surveyor would know what to inspect first so that if he finds a serious defect at an early stage he will not proceed needlessly with expensive stripping work. The amateur cannot very well assist with stripping work, as the boat will not then be his property, and the owners will have to be assured that any parts or fastenings disturbed are correctly replaced by a competent yard.

The preliminary survey which the yachtsman can do himself should start with the outside of the hull. Make notes of any damage to the planking, stem, keel, or stern, and look closely at the plank ends to see whether they have shifted from the rabbets. Then get down on your back and examine the garboard planks and keel rabbets. If you can recognize where the floor fastenings are, it probably means that electrolytic action has loosened the stopping, so test with a spike or sharp knife point around the nails to find out whether the timber is soft.

Do not jab a knife into every bit of planking; tap it at close intervals all over, listening carefully. Sound timber will produce a metallic ring, while any soft places will react with a quite different dull sound. If you can find any such places, then produce the spike or knife to determine the extent of the damage remembering that the outside skin of timber may be sound with the rotten layer spreading from the inside.

Work similarly over the decks and any bulwarks, concentrating where stanchions or frame extensions pass through the covering boards. Probe around deck fittings or pads of wood for rot and examine any spars and rigging as far as possible.

On all small craft any damage to the rudder or wear in the gudgeons and pintles should be fairly obvious. Unless more than fifty years old, the rudder trunk on a large vessel is sure to be in the form of a metal tube housing a metal rudder stock.

To examine the trunk properly often entails removing the rudder heel bearing to enable the rudder to be withdrawn. Older craft, such as the Pilot Cutters and Brixham Trawlers had all-wood rudders and large diameter trunks lined with tapered strips of wood driven downwards from the top.

Once inside the boat, work will be much slower due to various obstacles and the need to check all faces of timbers and frames. Rust may have to be chipped from a few floors or bolt heads and flaking paint removed. All bilge water will have to be pumped out. If the bilge is oily, that is a good sign, as oily bilges rarely harbour rot. Take some rags and *Swarfega* with you to clean up afterwards! Watch out for loose fastenings, cracked timbers, and places where timbers or floors have pulled away from the planking. Any ballast should be shifted in panels and then replaced.

Away from the bilge, the most important region to examine is the gunwale of an open boat, or the shelf of a decked boat. Rain-water collecting in these areas can be disastrous, leading to very costly repair work. It should not be forgotten that a good look at the shape of a boat is often a clue to her condition. An uneven sheer line is not uncommon and a prominent seam often means cracked timbers or the result of crushing or dropping.

Do not write off a likely-looking hull because she has a few repairable defects. It may be possible to use this beneficially to lower the price, and the conversionist will normally be of the type who will learn to tackle most boat repair work himself.

METAL AND PLASTICS

Little corrosion may be found when surveying an aluminium alloy hull. The main faults are more likely to be fractured rivets and welds, dents, buckling, cracked plating and external scoring.

Reliable surveying of steel vessels is a specialized art, but a superficial examination is certain to reveal any serious or extensive rusting, enabling one to decide whether to proceed or not. The regions most susceptible to rust are in the bilges from amidships aft, especially where the frames butt against the shell plating.

Electrolytic corrosion may be either serious or non-existent. Deep pitting on the outside of the bottom plating is the most common result of this, but similar pitting may be found below the normal bilge water mark inside the hull.

A g.r.p. boat of reliable make is unlikely to have hidden faults unless she has been damaged. On the contrary, a badly moulded hull can have large patches of delamination when the outside looks perfect.

External chafe and abrasion is common on plastics, above and below the waterline. Unless this has been repaired speedily serious deterioration of the adjacent laminate could have occurred. This can often be checked by tapping the surface with a mallet while listening for the change from a high pitch to a low pitch sound.

Gel coat surface crazing is quite common, but is normally detrimental only if the hair cracks can be felt when stroking the surface with one's finger.

If a heavy object (such as a battery) has been dropped inside the boat, serious damage could have been caused to the skin. However, the resultant cracks may not show on the outside, especially where the bottom is coated with antifouling paint.

Inspect for trouble where timber engine bearers and other wooden inserts have been glassed into the main structure. Seepage of water at these places can cause failure of the bonding as well as latent rotting of the timber.

A similar type of trouble may be found around skin fittings. Be suspicious of parts attached by through-bolts as these may have worked loose in a thin laminate. If the bolt heads are deeply countersunk, high stress on the fitting could prove disastrous.

Few practical yachtsmen can undertake extensive welding repairs to an old steel craft, but g.r.p. repairs of most kinds can be tackled by the amateur and details of this work are given in Chapter 4.

2

Scheming it Out

Whether a new hull is to be completed or an old hull converted, it can be assumed that work on any craft smaller than about 40 ft. (12 m.) will be undertaken on dry land, while larger vessels will be kept afloat almost continuously.

PRELUDE TO CONVERSION

Assuming that a good hull has been located and successfully surveyed, on completion of the deal one has to arrange to shift the boat to one's home or to a nearby yard. Any firm having a low loader suitably licensed will undertake this haulage. Most of these vehicles have a winch and removable rear wheels to facilitate loading. Alternatively, many of the firms selling modern g.r.p. cruisers have a two-wheeled or four-wheeled trailer pulled by a Landrover that might handle the job. Your boat may have to be raised on chocks first, using jacks or levers, to enable the trailer to be rolled underneath.

When a big vessel has been laid up for a lengthy period, it may prove cheaper to await good weather and tow her to the new port rather than to arrange for a haulage contractor to shift her by road.

PREPARING DRAWINGS

While the inside of a hull is being prepared for conversion by removing unwanted fitments, cleaning, and painting, one can spend wet days or winter nights scheming out the proposed design, starting by taking accurate measurements of the hull. The same procedure applies when a new standard shell is obtained for home completion if fully dimensioned drawings are not available from the builders.

To make drawings, block up the keel of the boat so that the

waterline is level and set her dead upright athwartships. Draw five or six equally spaced vertical chalk lines from sheer to keel along one side to represent the sections of the hull to be drawn, shifting these lines if necessary to correspond with internal bulkheads or other important fittings.

Taking each section line in turn, from gunwale to ground set up a vertical batten which has been marked off in 1 foot (300 mm.) and 6 in. (150 mm.) intervals. Having taken a horizontal measurement between the batten and the hull surface at each of the 6 in. (150 mm.) marks, each half section can be plotted on squared paper and a mirror image drawn in, if necessary, to record the full width of the boat. With a hull clear of internal obstruction, it may be easier to take these measurements inside the boat. Further measurements may be necessary across the beam, fore-and-aft, and from the ground up to keel, waterline and sheer.

Armed with these dimensions, one can sit by the fireside and draw it all out to a scale of $\frac{1}{2}$ in. to 1 ft. (1:20 if metric) or larger. On one single sheet of paper lay out the views shown in Fig. 1,

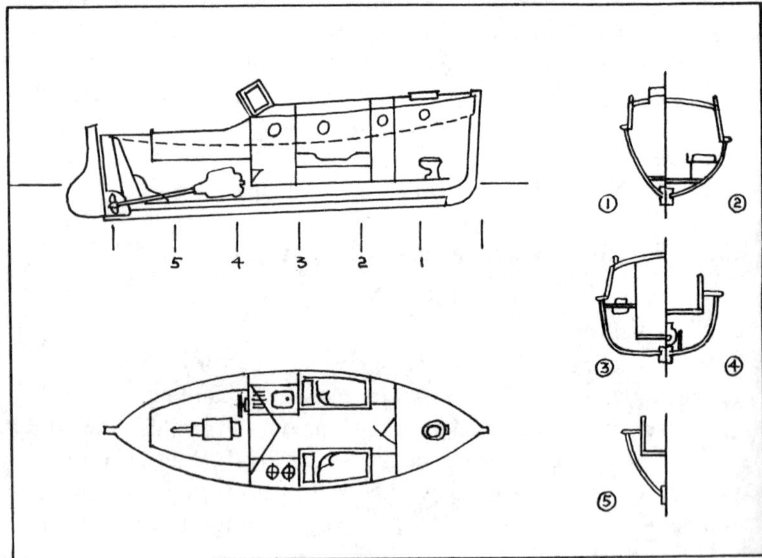

Fig. 1: Preparing working drawings

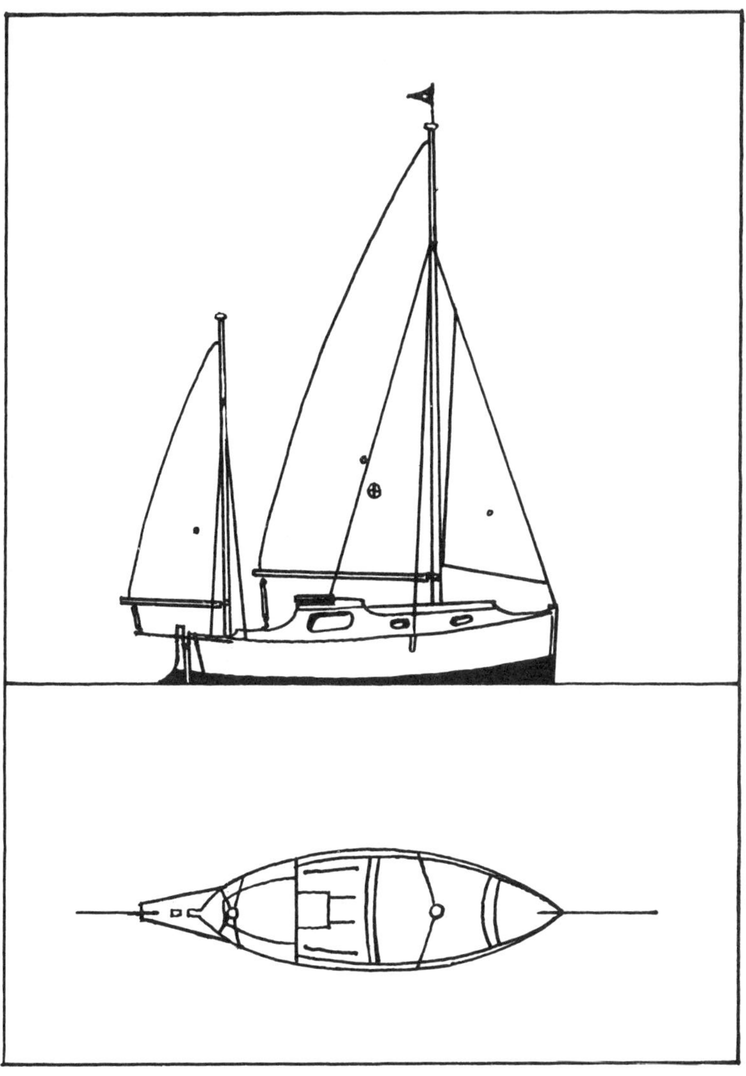

Fig. 2: The sail and deck plans

which will be used to sketch on the coachroof, accommodation details and engine. On a second sheet, a sail and deck plan should be drawn as in Fig. 2. These latter drawings can sometimes be made to serve at a scale of only $\frac{1}{4}$ in. to 1 ft. (or 1:40). A third sheet is handy for sketching various details such as raised topsides and coachroof construction, ballast keel, floor knees, hatches and skylights, steering gear, or sterntube.

ACCOMMODATION

The following factors should be kept in mind whenever an accommodation plan is being designed for a conversion or a new boat.

(1) Avoid splitting up the available space into small compartments or cabins except when essential.

(2) Keep the design fairly conventional as you might want to sell her one day and boats with queer layouts are often difficult to sell.

(3) Try to site bulkheads and partitions so that ventilation and natural light can be supplied to each compartment without the need for portlights and cowls in impossible places.

(4) Unless the cabin sole outline is marked on the plan accurately it may be found that the curve of the bilge projects into a cabin space and prevents the installation of doors or other fitments.

(5) Utilize to the best advantage such permanent obstructions as a centreboard case, mast or tabernacle struts and engine casings, to mask these with worktops, bulkheads and lockers.

(6) Try to utilize existing deck apertures for new hatches, skylights, coachroof, or ventilation, to avoid unnecessary structural alterations.

(7) Weight distribution must be watched. Arrange heavy weights (engines, tanks, gas cylinders and cooking stoves) evenly on opposite sides of the ship and away from the bows.

(8) The galley is best situated on the port side, making cooking easier when hove-to on the right-of-way starboard tack.

(9) Position the galley abaft the centre of the ship where the motion at sea is least. Try to have a window or large porthole handy to give the galley slave a pleasant outlook.

(10) Operation of the heads can cause disturbance at night. Insulate the toilet compartment by boxing it in with lockers, tanks, or storage spaces.

(11) Allow for plenty of locker space (especially when deep water cruising is contemplated) and position all essential lockers for maximum convenience, i.e. all food lockers close to the galley, the oilskin locker near to the main hatch.

(12) Unless the hinging of doors is detailed in the planning stage it may be impossible to reverse these later. Make cabin doors open in the direction of the main hatch to assist an emergency exodus. Arrange for locker doors to slam shut if brushed by a person making for the hatch. The direction in which sliding doors open is less important. No doors need be wider than 27 in. (680 mm.) and a width of 21 in. (530 mm.) is serviceable in many positions.

(13) Especially on large sailing vessels, some care is needed in siting the sail locker in relation to the fore hatch. There should be stowage racks for roughly folded sails and an adequately-sized hatch to pass them through, preferably placed so that a halyard can be led below to assist in the lifting of heavy wet sails.

(14) Avoid boxing in engines so that repairs and maintenance become troublesome and therefore neglected. On a big motor cruiser strive for an engine room with full headroom, preferably also equipped with a workbench and vice. An auxiliary engine offset from the centreline may be feasible with considerable benefit to the cabin layout.

(15) Calculate the sizes of fuel and water tanks before using all the available space for accommodation. Big tanks may upset the trim of the boat and any leakage from them could be serious. Otherwise big tanks are more convenient to fill and use than several smaller ones.

(16) Although diesel fuel tanks are normally safe in the engine compartment they will emit less smell if located in a cooler place. Petrol (gasoline) tanks should always be remote from the engines.

(17) Pipe cots are frequently only 6 ft. (1800 mm.) long but full size berths are best made 6 ft. 6 in. (2 m.) where possible. Single berths should average 2 ft. 3 in. (680 mm.) in width while a

Plate 4: Correctly ballasted sailing conversion

Plate 5: Unballasted lifeboat

double berth should be 4 ft. (1200 mm.) if possible. Some pipe cots measure only 1 ft. 9 in. (530 mm.) at the widest point and are still serviceable.

Six suggested sail plans and cabin layouts for sailing lifeboat conversions are detailed in Chapter 6. The design of a motor cruiser conversion is a far simpler matter, as one does not have the worry of ballast keels and sail area calculations. Plenty of ideas for conversions and completing a bare hull shell can be gained from perusing the designs published in yachting magazines. The only difficulty likely to arise is in creating a profile plan of good appearance coupled with adequate headroom and the desired number of berths.

MAKING THEM SAIL

For the most pleasing appearance, a sailing conversion based on a lifeboat should be ballasted so that the stern is at least 1 ft. (300 mm.) lower than the stem, producing the effect shown in Plate 4. This improves sailing qualities by inclining the keel, and serves to obtain good submersion for the propeller and rudder. The same idea is also advantageous in a motor cruiser, but difficult to contrive as there is no ballast keel and the engines are often rather close to amidships. A conversion with an unballasted stern is pictured in Plate 5 and even the propeller aperture in the stern post is visible above the waterline.

HEADROOM

For any lifeboat longer than about 26 ft. (8 m.) full headroom under the cabin top beams should be easy to attain without marring the appearance, but this cannot be achieved unless the topsides are raised throughout prior to decking. The neatest way to do this on a clinker lifeboat is to add two or three more strakes of clinker planking (as shown in Plates 6 and 36). If plywood or plain planking is used on a clinker boat the effect is not quite so satisfactory, as can be seen in Plate 4.

A rubbing bead can be attached at the original sheer level if desired. This is almost essential on a carvel hull to mask the joint between the old and the new planking, but a bead is unnecessary with clinker as the laps (or lands) automatically create seams identical to those on the original planks.

Lifeboats have a considerable amount of sheer, and by grading the plank widths to match the existing ones, i.e. about 5 in. (125 mm.) wide amidships and 3 in. (75 mm.) at the ends, the new sheer line will be automatically flattened slightly, the effect being obvious

Plate 6: Additional strakes improve a lifeboat

in Plate 4. A neater sheer is produced if the amount of the raising is greater at the stem than at the stern by 3 or 4 in. (75 or 100 mm.).

SIDE DECKS

There are several ways of building the coachroof sides, the simplest being to plant these on the inside of the gunwale as drawn in Fig. 42, giving splendid space below and creating the effect shown in Plate 7. The only fault with this is the difficult clamber for crew members going for'ard to attend to the jib in a seaway.

Plate 7: Coachroof sides planted on gunwale

Otherwise it proves cheaper to construct and stronger than any other method.

A conventional cabin top with side decks at least 12 in. (300 mm.) wide makes a safer ship to work aboard and in the opinion of most yachtsmen this makes a better looking job, though the fitting of half-beams and carlines involves additional work. Side decks do tend to allow leaks to occur if made in a shoddy manner, but they also permit one to fabricate a very neat cabin top (as in Plate 36) which could be built by the amateur as a single glass fibre lay-up or cold moulded from laminations of wood veneer.

All coachroof and wheelhouse sides must have *tumblehome* (sloping inwards slightly towards the top) to ensure good appearance. Raised topsides may not need this and can follow the original hull shape upwards, as described in Chapter 6.

BELOW THE WATERLINE

Having decided upon the accommodation, appearance, and rig, the essential underwater details of ballast and lateral resistance must be tackled. A lifeboat hull has almost no *deadrise* except towards the bow and stern, i.e. her bottom is almost flat with quite a sharp turn to the bilges. This gives her immense stability to withstand a good press of sail and she does not therefore need a great deal of ballast, rather like a barge yacht.

Plenty of conversions get by with internal ballast only. A 27-footer would need about 1 ton only, but such a design would require leeboards, a centreplate, or twin bilge keels to provide the lateral resistance necessary to prevent her from making excessive leeway.

Although bilge keels are popular and very effective, they cannot be used on a hull without deadrise unless a central ballast keel is also fitted. The full weight of a boat must not be taken on the bilge keels unless the hull was especially designed for such loads. If bilge keels of the requisite depth are fitted to a lifeboat without a ballast keel (or alternatively a deep false keel of hardwood) she will always sit on both bilge keels with her central keel in mid air.

One could argue that bilge keels would not be effective for lateral resistance unless they extended below the main keel, but this does not apply in practice especially as one bilge keel does fall well below the centre keel as soon as the boat heels under sail.

As a lifeboat requires plenty of extra lateral resistance and not a vast amount of ballast, concrete is the obvious choice for an external ballast keel. A cast-iron keel might cost twenty times as much as a concrete one, and so the extra work involved with concrete will not deter the keen conversionist. Furthermore, getting an iron keel into position under the boat and bolting it in place is far from simple, whereas a concrete keel can be cast *in situ* with the hull turned upside down as described in Chapters 6 and 8. A concrete keel can also be cast separately (with bolt holes cored through it) to be attached in exactly the same way as a cast-iron or lead ballast keel.

New internal floor knees are essential when external ballast is fitted to a whaler, cutter, lifeboat, or an old-type fishing boat. Extra floors are also advisable with additional internal ballast to prevent this from dropping through the bottom should the boat start bumping over a sandbank.

A MOTOR/SAILER CONVERSION

Although several sailing lifeboat designs are described in Chapter 6, power boat conversions are not included, being so much simpler to design and construct. A twin screw motor/sailer based on a 30 ft. (9.15 m.) lifeboat hull is shown in Fig. 3, representing the conversionist's answer to a very popular type of vessel having a fair performance under sail or power plus the enormous advantage over a pure motor vessel in that the sails can help to minimize rolling.

She has twin Wortham Blake Fisherboy petrol engines beneath the centre wheelhouse floor, and bilge keels of ½ in. (12 mm.) galvanized steel plate. These keels enable the yacht to stand upright when aground and are each 6 ft. (1830 mm.) long by 1 ft. 10 in. (560 mm.) wide with a toe-in of ½ in. (12 mm.) at the fore ends. They should be through-bolted to stringers of 5 in. by 2 in. (130 mm. by 50 mm.) timber inside the boat.

The ballast keel weighs 2600 lb. (1180 kg.) and an additional 560 lb. (250 kg.) of inside ballast (mainly well aft) will also be required. A new rudder hung directly onto the original sternpost is shown, with a skeg from the ballast keel supporting a bottom pintle. A short tubular steel tiller passing under the mainsheet horse allows a conventional wire rope steering gear to be installed

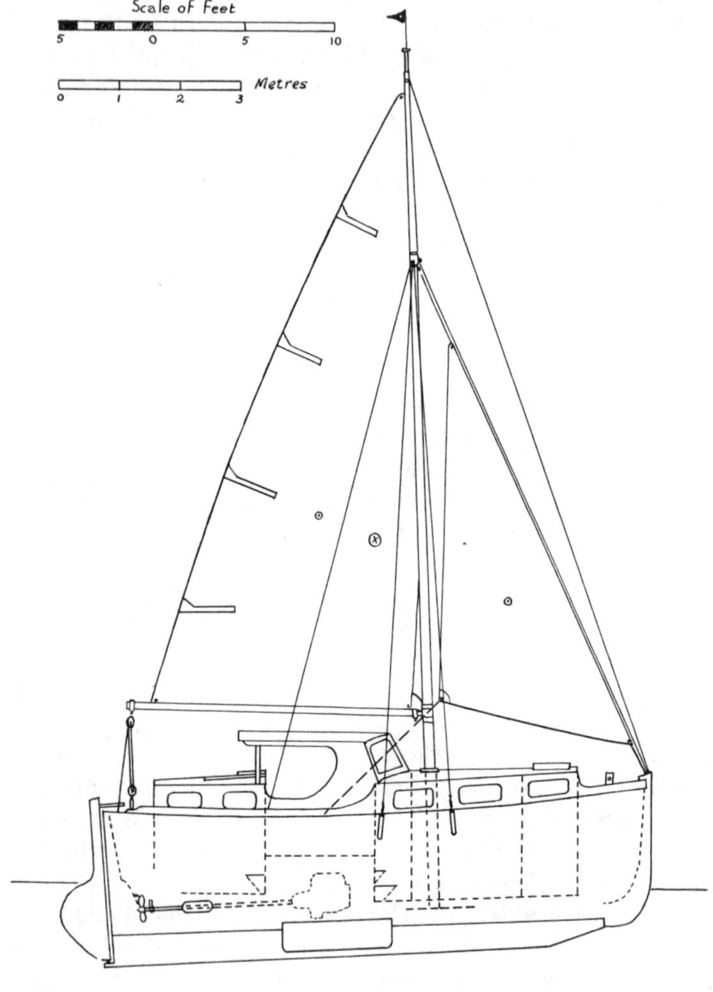

Fig. 3: Twin-screw motor/sailer on lifeboat hull

with a teak wheel on the port side of the main bulkhead in the wheelhouse.

The mainsail area is 240 sq. ft. (22 m.^{2}) and the working jib 110 sq. ft. (10 m.^{2}) both in 10 oz. (330 g.) Terylene. The boat is ballasted to allow the use of a large 6 oz. (200 g.) Genoa jib in winds under Force 4. Although runners are fitted, they would be required only in strong winds as the aftermost pair of shrouds provide good support.

The mast is set on the keelson and is a rectangular hollow spar. The dimensions are 6½ in. (162 mm.) fore-and-aft with 1¼ in. (32 mm.) walls and 5 in. (125 mm.) athwartships with 1 in. (25 mm.) walls. Above the forestay band the mast tapers to 4½ in. × 3 in. (112 mm. × 75 mm.) with the same wall thicknesses. All standing rigging is ¼ in. (6 mm.) diameter galvanized 7 × 7 steel wire rope. The boom is a round solid spar 3¾ in. (94 mm.) at the gooseneck and 5 in. (125 mm.) diameter at the outboard end arranged for roller reefing.

ACCOMMODATION

The main cabin coamings are fitted to the gunwales as in Fig. 43, with three additional strakes of clinker planking at the sheer. These coamings are extended into footrails the length of the ship and a pulpit and guardrails could also be fitted. The coamings for the wheelhouse and after cabin are set in to give a side deck 15 in. (380 mm.) wide.

There is full standing headroom throughout the accommodation including the wheelhouse. The after cabin has two berths with central companionway. Descending to the main cabin there is a wardrobe to port and an oilskin locker to starboard, followed by a dinette/berth to port with the galley opposite. For'ard of this, to the end of the coachroof, is a toilet compartment the full width of the ship, having a hinged wash basin discharging into the heads to port and a shower bath to starboard. Access to the forepeak is via a bulkhead door with the forehatch directly above.

Beneath the wheelhouse floor there is ample space for the batteries, and a charging set between the two engines. This sole should have very large hatches for easy access to the machinery, and removable panels should be incorporated in the centre of the shelter deck to enable an engine to be lifted right out.

The fuel tanks could be housed under the side decks abeam of the wheelhouse, insulated from the heat of the engines and high enough to provide gravity feed. Fresh water tanks could also be fitted into the 6 ft. (2 m.) long sponsons.

A mast stepped on the keelson is a great barrier to spacious accommodation. With a little extra labour it would be possible to fit a pair of internal frames fabricated from 2 in. × 2 in. × $\frac{1}{4}$ in. (50 mm. × 50 mm. × 6 mm.) galvanized steel (see Chapter 6) to allow the mast to be stepped on deck.

The four-berth arrangement would suit most families, but two extra people could sleep in the wheelhouse if roll down dodgers were fitted.

Such a conversion could cruise almost anywhere with safety and provide a family with a comfortable home afloat. For extended cruising many owners would prefer the economy of diesel engines, but for the average conversionist with limited leisure the low initial cost and smooth silent running of modern petrol engines are great attractions.

BIG CONVERSIONS

The following notes on the treatment of a 65 ft. (20 m.) *Motor Fishing Vessel* will serve as an example of a typical big conversion.

When converting an M.F.V. it usually pays to retain the original slow-revving diesel engine and its spacious engine room. This gives one somewhere to fix up a bench and vice, while the maintenance of all machinery, including auxiliaries and batteries, is so much more convenient with standing headroom. If the old engine must be replaced with a smaller high speed diesel, this should have 3 to 1 reduction gearing to enable the original large propeller turning at about 700 r.p.m. to be retained. Such an installation will prove more noisy, but it might be possible to reduce the size of the engine room and thus win more space for accommodation.

An M.F.V. can be given a really useful sail area with little addition of ballast. The rig would be used only for steadying purposes when going to windward, but when reaching or running, it should be possible to attain 6 knots in a Force 5 wind.

A typical ketch sail plan for a 65 ft. (20 m.) M.F.V. is shown in Fig. 4. The heeling effect is minimized by using a gaff mainsail, which not only makes for a cheaper job, but is also more efficient off the wind than Bermudan. A gaff sail looks right on a fishing smack-type yacht and is easier to lower with a wheelhouse in the way.

Roller reefing is essential where the boom is set high up to clear the superstructure and permanent gallows are desirable for the main and mizzen. A boomed forestaysail is not a good idea as very little tacking will be done.

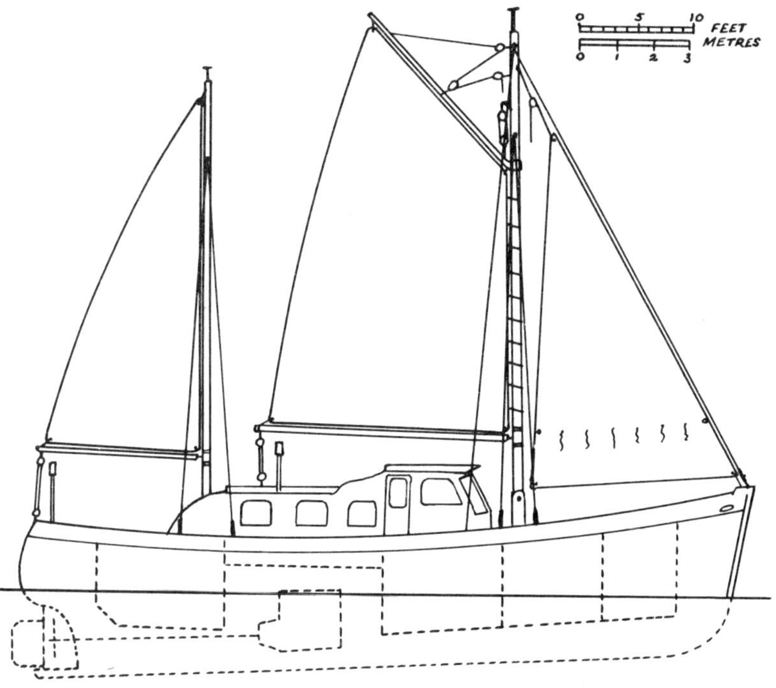

Fig. 4: M.F.V. Ketch conversion

The sail areas shown are mainsail, 500 sq. ft. (46 m^2); forestaysail, 230 sq. ft. (21 m^2); mizzen, 210 sq. ft. (19 m^2), giving a total of nearly 1000 sq. ft. (90 m^2). The masts are mounted in tabernacles on the original main deck. Owing to the method of construction, no support underneath is necessary in addition to strong bulkheads. Although the tabernacles might not be used for lowering masts during a cruise, they do minimize the length of the spars and facilitate unshipping them at laying-up time.

A further advantage of gaff rig is that the standing rigging need not be taut, reducing the compression load on the mast, and a simple solid spar is suitable. The mast is 9½ in. (240 mm.) diameter up to the shroud eyes, then tapering to 4 in. (100 mm.) at the truck staff. The mizzen is 7 in. (175 mm.) diameter tapering to 3 in. (75 mm.).

THE CABIN LAYOUT

A suggested accommodation layout for this 65 ft. (20 m.) M.F.V. is shown in Fig. 5. The deckhouse arrangement is detailed separately and comprises the wheelhouse at deck level with the galley and dining saloon sunk 2 ft. below the main deck.

A conversion of this size frequently has two companionways from the deckhouse to the cabin below, sometimes with a further two right fore and aft. This creates draughty accommodation and wastes space. Only one main companionway is required in the plan shown since a passageway has been built alongside the engine room.

The companionway is set athwartships and also serves the galley and saloon at the lower level. Emergency hatches would normally be fitted through the main deck at each end of the ship, but these should have vertical ladders which occupy little useful space. It will be noted that owing to the sunken deckhouse, the passageway would not normally have sufficient headroom, but this problem has been overcome by siting the saloon settee and galley worktop directly over the passage.

The after deck is large enough to allow a 12 ft. (3·5 m.) motor tender to be stowed to one side, while the mizzen boom is high

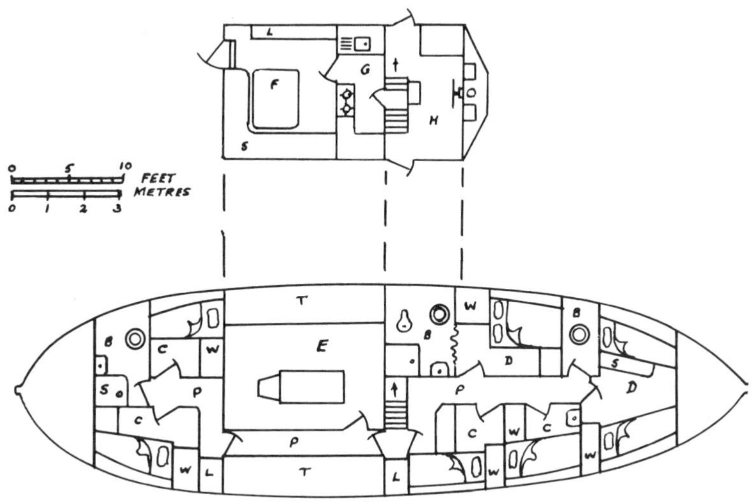

Fig. 5: Accommodation layout for M.F.V. Ketch

B — *bathrooms*	H — *wheelhouse*
C — *single cabins*	L — *lockers*
D — *double cabins*	P — *passageways*
E — *engine room*	S — *settees*
F — *folding table*	T — *tanks*
G — *galley*	W — *hanging lockers*

enough to permit the davits to be left standing. The mizzen boom gallows would be sited on one quarter to leave a clear space for the after davits. These details, and guardrails, have been omitted from the drawings for clarity.

A motor cruiser conversion could be devised on similar lines, but would normally have a squat funnel abaft the wheelhouse to take both the engine exhaust and a fan outlet from above the galley stove. The best solution to the exhaust problem in the ketch might be to feed this up a hollow lined metal mizzen mast!

If the exhaust is taken out to the topsides, fumes are bound to swill aboard at times, but it would be possible to lead the exhaust pipe under the deckhead to the stern. With water and fuel tanks housed alongside the engine room, convenient filling is assured via screw caps in the side decks. The engine shown is the 88 h.p. Kelvin K.4.

LIGHT AND VENTILATION

A deck galley has every advantage for a big conversion as ventilation is simplified, the cook has pleasing views through large windows, and can converse with other crew members in either the saloon or the wheelhouse. No details of ventilation are shown in Figs. 4 and 5, but unless a proper air-conditioning plant is installed, separate cowls must be fitted to serve the engine room, and further vents will be essential for the passageways.

Cabin doors can have louvred panels to avoid stagnant spaces, and there is no reason why opening portlights should not be fitted into the topsides to serve various cabins. Such ports, with curtains, are delightful assets to each berth and eliminate the need for a vast number of skylights and decklights to provide illumination.

Skylights are best kept to the centre of the deck coming mainly over the passageways. In this position they cause least harm should they leak, or when spray comes aboard before everything gets battened down. If leaks seem likely the sole should remain uncarpeted, of scrubbed teak with small holes or gaps to drain any water into the bilges.

Ventilation of the wheelhouse is simple, but a normal cowl vent should be avoided over the big chart table shown on the port side in case water should find its way through.

Clear vision aft is useful at sea or in harbour. Windows can be built into the after wheelhouse bulkhead above the galley, and the saloon can have aft-facing windows also.

Most M.F.V.s have engines like the K.4. which are designed to remain in place for the life of the ship, all types of overhaul being possible with the engine still on its bearers. If a high speed diesel (many of which are based on vehicle engines) is installed, removable panels should be left in the saloon floor and deckhead to enable the engine to be lifted right out.

BELOW DECKS

In Fig. 5 the two fo'c'sle berths would suit paid hands or youngsters, the small toilet compartment adjacent having a hinged wash basin discharging into the head. The fore hatch provides convenient access for the crew to the deck and also enables the sails to be transferred easily to the fore peak sail locker.

Although the owner's double berth cabin with bathroom would normally occupy the whole after part of the ship, an alternative arrangement is shown with this stateroom close to the wheelhouse companionway. The cabin has a dressing table and wardrobe, with access through a curtain to the bathroom with shower, basin, w.c. and bidet. This could be made into a communal bathroom by arranging access only from the passageway. In any case, all single cabins should have wash basins.

Right aft we have two guest cabins with adjacent bathroom. There should be a hatch over the lobby with vertical ladder and a separate hatch from the deck into the after peak store space, both hatches sited to avoid the tender when stowed on deck.

Although a big conversion on the above lines is an expensive project, the effect of this can be minimized if the owner intends to live afloat permanently and thus eliminate the customary expenses of running a house. If a big vessel is not used in this way, she will probably be owned by a syndicate of several yachtsmen, so that all costs will be shared between them.

Detailed information on ventilation and how to carry out the practical work of installing accommodation and other equipment is given in subsequent chapters.

3

Planking Repairs

With a little care there is no reason why any boat of wood, metal, plastics or ferro-cement cannot be repaired when damaged or rotten so that her value is not lowered.

Where such problems are extensive, repairs just might not be worth while, especially if professional assistance must be called in. Such work usually involves a large amount of labour with only a modest outlay on materials, so amateur repair work pays handsomely and can provide the enthusiast with much enjoyment and satisfaction.

Mystique surrounds the shipwright's work, but all the processes likely to be tackled by the amateur will be described in the ensuing chapters. Such work undertaken by a sensible amateur should be just as neat and strong as that done by a boatyard, but the amateur will, of course, take a much longer time to complete it. A shipwright operates instinctively most of the time and he has to make the job pay. The amateur has to think out each move most carefully and spend much more time over measuring and setting out as well as when using tools and finally shaping things to fit perfectly.

To avoid wasting good timber by mistakes, an inexperienced worker should make full use of templates made from cheap materials such as hardboard and tin plate. The expert may be able to save time by avoiding this process but the end product would be identical.

Remember that no bare wood should ever be used on a boat. All hidden surfaces should be *luted* (coated) with paint or bedding compound, while exposed surfaces can be given the same treatment as the original parts.

Especially when dry rot or similar fungi have been discovered, any new softwood (such as pine, spruce, fir or larch) used should be *Tanalised* or *Celcured* under pressure at a sawmill so equipped.

When this is not possible, and with most hardwoods, soaking in *Cuprinol* or *International P.C.P.* is advisable.

Note, however, that no treatment whatever should be given to surfaces to be sheathed with glass fibre or *Cascover* nylon. Most popular marine paints will adhere to proofed timber when sufficient time has been allowed for drying out, but P.C.P. is the most reliable fungicide in this respect.

CLINKER WORK

Good clinker boats need no more plank repair work than their carvel counterparts. Having no caulking, however, clinker boats can develop persistent leaks (perhaps only when underway) and with the exception of those dinghies with glued seams and plywood planking, clinker boats should never be allowed to dry out completely. Unnecessary shrinkage can put a strain on the fastenings and lead to troublesome repairs.

Replacing a single short length of damaged planking (on the lines pictured in Plate 8) is not much more difficult than for a similar carvel repair. Scarf joints at each end are ideal for clinker though they take some time to cut accurately. With carvel planking these joints may be made more simply by fitting backing

Plate 8: Scarfing a length of clinker plank

pieces (correctly called *butt blocks*) on the inside. Butt blocks could be used high up on the topsides with clinker planking but a truly leakproof job is difficult to achieve where plank seams overlap, and so the method is not advisable below or near the waterline.

If a piece of straight plank is used to fashion the new piece, it may need to be thicker than the original planking to allow for the making of the slight rounding or hollowing necessary to fit the curvature of the hull. It proves impossible to utilize the damaged section of planking (after being cut out) as a template for making the new piece where the length is very short. Depending on the quality of the job, several cardboard templates can be made to ensure a good first time fit. To do this precisely, four templates should be made. The first one should be rectangular to fit the opening you can see through, tucking up behind the next full plank above. The second one, also rectangular, would be made the full length to the end of the scarfs. The other two would be horizontal at right angles to the hull surface, picking up the taper of each scarf at top and bottom and the curvature of the planking.

To cut the new pieces of timber to the correct shape, the first two templates are held on to the face while pencil lines are drawn around them. Having cut to these lines, templates 3 and 4 are held along the edges of the piece and further lines are scribed from these. A little trial and error shaping will be necessary to enable the new piece to be pushed up behind the upper plank neatly and all *faying* surfaces (the surfaces in contact) marked for high spots, which are then shaved down to a good fit.

After this, fastening holes may be bored prior to permanent fixing in paint, glue, or bedding compound. After rubbing down and stopping, a good surface may be built up to hide all signs of the repair job.

In clinker planking the scarf joints would normally be fastened with copper nails and roves, the faying surfaces being luted with thick paint. Where roves would look unsightly on the inside (such as on an open dinghy) the scarfs may be screw-fastened and bedded in resin glue. Where butt blocks are preferred to scarfs, copper nails are usual in planking thinner than about $\frac{3}{4}$ in. (18 mm.) whereas screws are used in thicker materials.

When a large hole extending over two or more planks must be repaired, the effect is often as shown in Plate 9, the scarfs in adjacent planks being widely shifted for maximum strength. Up to a plank length of about 18 in. (450 mm.) a new piece can be shaped from thicker material to take up the accurate curvature of the planking, but in longer lengths, the timber may have to be steamed and given a slight permanent bend by clamping it to a temporary jig for twelve hours. Fitting trials can then proceed as described above.

Plate 9: Clinker repair covering several planks

In traditional clinker planking the fastenings through the *lands* (the overlapping seams) are always riveted copper nails, the only exception being in glued clinker plywood planking where no fastenings are used to augment the strongly-glued lands.

Repairing a single long length of planking differs from the above method because every effort should be made to preserve the old piece intact to serve as a template. This can save a lot of time, but leave a margin for final adjustment of the shape (and a little extra at each end) to allow for the discrepancies which sometimes creep in due to the fact that when marking out, the outer face of the template touches the inner face of the new piece or vice versa.

FASTENINGS

Before trying to remove the rotten plank from the hull by hammering it downwards to release it from the top land, care must be taken to ensure that every fastening has been removed. When removing copper nails, damage to the steamed timbers and adjacent planks must be avoided. An old wood chisel can be used to excavate around the nail heads on the faulty plank enabling the nails to be punched inwards as soon as the heads have been nipped off.

Along the upper land only, the stopping should be excavated from the heads enabling the nails to be punched outwards after filing away the riveted ends securing the roves or *burrs*. When punching in this direction keep an eye on the outside to make sure that slivers of planking are not broken away as each nail head moves.

A hand file may prove awkward to use inside the boat and sometimes an electric drill with a small grinding wheel fitted to an arbor in the chuck does the job more quickly and more neatly. Remember that an ordinary tapered nail punch will ream the hole in sound wood if driven too far, but as soon as a nail head has been punched free a pair of pincers (used in conjunction with a small block of wood to act as a fulcrum) can be used to prise out each nail. Similarly, a claw hammer can sometimes be utilized, while for really heavy fastenings special nail-pulling tools with pump action handles are available.

Sometimes the points of copper nails are turned over and sunk back into the wood instead of being riveted. This makes removal far more difficult and punching out is best done from the head end. Where this cannot be done a certain amount of damage to the inside surfaces is inevitable as the turned over nail point is prised out and cut off before a punch can be used.

The hood end fastenings which secure a plank to the stem and transom are frequently screws in large boats and copper nails in dinghies. Removing these is never easy, as screws frequently shear off and nails cannot be extracted until a lot of wood has been excavated from around the head. If screws shear off within the stem timber the old plank may be removed quite easily. When a screw shears close to the head, removing the plank intact may prove almost impossible.

There are two ways of dealing with this. In the first method, chisel a large hole around the screw (but not so large that the plank disintegrates), then find a short piece of steel tube which will just slip over the stem of the screw. Rock this to and fro to bend the screw, which will then soon break off in the stem rabbet. If you cannot find a piece of suitable tube, this can soon be made by boring a short way into the end of a piece of metal rod.

In the second method a similar piece of steel tube is required but instead of chiselling a large hole around the screw, prise away the loose head of the screw and drive the tube into the planking so that the screw stem is inside the tube. Now, with an electric drill and a Morse bit just a little smaller than the tube, drill into the end of the screw while securing the tube with a pair of grips. This will break up a brass or bronze screw quite rapidly. Fresh screw holes must of course be bored when the new plank is fitted.

Brass screws tend to disintegrate in sea water due to *dezincification* and so bronze screws should always be used in preference. These are harder and less likely to shear off when tightened vigorously. Barbed ring nails (such as bronze *Gripfast* or monel *Anchorfast*) are sometimes suitable for hood end fastenings and into sawn frames. They are much cheaper than screws and quicker to drive but they cannot be extracted if ever necessary. Copper nails tend to buckle when driven dead into hardwood. When the correct size pilot hole is used a smooth copper nail can work loose in time. To improve the grip, boat builders frequently twist each nail one complete turn while held between two pairs of pliers.

Detailed information about copper nails can be found in *Complete Amateur Boat Building*. This includes tables of standard lengths and gauges with correct sizes of roves to suit each gauge and the numbers of nails and roves for a given weight. Details of the correct size pilot hole to use, the tools needed and the procedure under various conditions are also given.

Countersunk heads are more commonly used than rose-heads and driving is simplified if the heads are left flush with the plank surface. In practice each head pulls below the surface slightly enabling a thin skim of stopping to be spread over it.

Two operators are needed when riveting copper nails. One drives each nail through from the outside and then holds a heavy hammer or steel dolly on to the head while the second operator forces a rove over the protruding point with a hollow punch and snips off the nail to leave only about 1/16 in. (1·5 mm.) beyond the rove. This stub of nail is then riveted over, using a few rapid light strokes with a ball pane hammer. Note that roves must be used with the concave side towards the timber. Riveting should not be vigorous enough to flatten the roves.

A rove punch may be made quite simply by cutting off a ½ in. (12 mm.) diameter bolt to the required length and boring for a short distance up the centre. It pays to make the hole only just large enough for the nail to fit into and so a separate punch should be made for most gauges of nail likely to be used.

Any short piece of round steel shafting will do for a dolly. Plenty of weight is an advantage. More weight is desirable for thick nails than for thin, but too heavy a dolly may prove tiring for the holder-upper! Note that where the heads of copper nails are sunk below the surface of the planking, a short stud of the requisite diameter must be fitted to the end of the dolly to keep in contact with the nail head.

Having made every effort to remove an old plank intact, this can be cramped to the new piece and scribed around to get the shape. Any odd pieces which split away from the old plank can be repositioned for scribing if necessary.

Next, mark the width of the lands by transferring the width from the old plank. Similarly, mark off any bevel along the lands and shave this off with a plane. The only problem likely to be encountered is at each end of the plank where the land bevel has to merge into a rebate towards the ends so that the planking becomes flush like carvel at stem and transom.

Three types of rebate may be encountered. The first method (see Fig. 6) is commonly used for dinghies. The second method (see Fig. 7a) is more robust and is used for larger vessels. The third

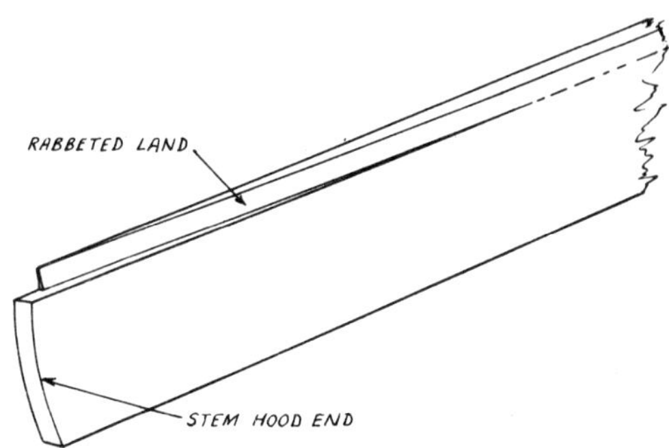

Fig. 6: Rabbeted land for dinghy plank

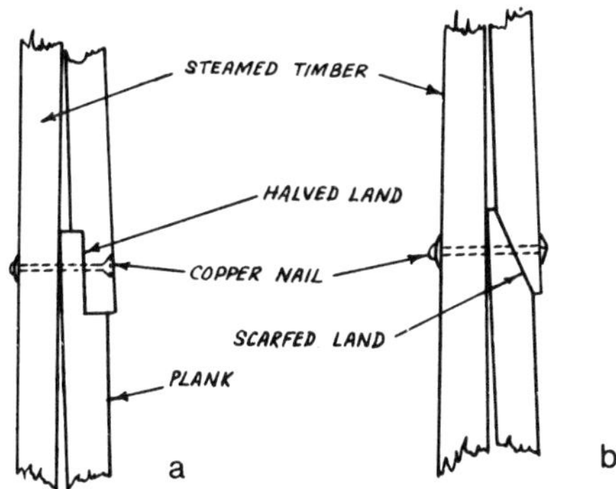

Fig. 7: Alternative hood end land joints

method (known as the *dory-lap* or *lap-strake* system) illustrated in Fig. 7b is the quickest and simplest method, but is more likely to cause leaks if the planking shrinks. Whichever method was used on the old plank will, of course, have to be used again on the new one to ensure a good fit.

Having shaped the new plank as described, offer up the stem end first. With a helper or a trestle to support the plank amidships it should be possible to trim the end and the land seams to a perfect fit without having to intermesh the plank correctly with its neighbours for the whole way. Having done this, the stern end can be fitted in similar fashion, but it will not be possible to get the exact length at the transom until the plank has been fitted properly.

STEAMING

Only on craft of very heavy construction will it be necessary to steam a plank for its entire length. In all other cases steaming is normally required only along about one-quarter of the plank length from each end. Softwood planking becomes supple after a very short steaming time while most hardwoods need considerably longer. Full details of times and steaming plants are given in *Complete Amateur Boat Building* but the amateur can get away with simple equipment for the odd planking repair.

Submersion in boiling water is generally easier to arrange than pure steaming. One can accomplish this by scrounging a length of steel tube larger in diameter than the plank width, sealing one end with a plug of concrete, standing the plugged end on the ground and supporting the other end at a higher level. When filled with water, a wood fire or a kerosene burner may be used at the bottom end to supply the heat.

Several other methods are possible. A horizontal open trough with a fire underneath is ideal if sufficiently long. Small portable steam generators are available from tool hire shops, as they are used for stripping wallpaper and de-greasing vehicles. A rough timber box can be nailed together and the steam fed in at one end while the plank is inserted at the other. The lance used for stripping wallpaper can be adapted to steam a plank while *in situ* on the hull. This latter method is not practicable for plank thicknesses greater than ½ in. (12 mm.) where steaming over a considerable length is necessary, but it has great value for secondary steaming and for applying additional heat locally to a plank while the cramps are tightened up.

When a new plank is offered up after steaming, great speed is essential. For planking ⅜ in. (9 mm.) thick, ½ minute is the maximum time for cramping. With $\frac{5}{8}$ in. (15 mm.) timber, 1 minute can be allowed, while for 1 in. (25 mm.), 3 minutes are available.

In view of this, when fitting a new clinker plank, if it will not slip readily under the upper land, do not waste time struggling with it but get the ends cramped back quickly so that further adjustments can be made at leisure the next day.

If the plank failed to pull right home in any one place, secondary steaming can be concentrated where required to prevent breakage. Once a plank has been steamed it will not normally fit back into the steaming box or water trough (due to its new shape) so if any further steaming is required for the final fitting next day, this will have to be done with a steam lance. Without this equipment, one can sometimes resort to rags soaked with boiling water. This latter method is frequently used when bending sheets of marine plywood planking into place.

Short lengths of planking (as in Plate 8) can be steamed to any slight curvature instead of carving from the solid. A jig to do this may be improvised quite simply by cramping across a thick plank with some strips of thin packing laid under the centre of the piece to be steamed.

Steamed parts always spring back slightly when the cramps are removed next day, and so an allowance should be made in a jig to permit a small amount of additional curvature. Some curvature may be taken out by pressure the opposite way when cold, whereas additional curvature cannot be applied without further steaming.

Some efficient means of holding a plank into position around the hull after steaming must be arranged beforehand to ensure a successful job. Where several planks are to be replaced, standard G-cramps may be used on all except the final (*shutter*) plank by hooking these behind the boat's frames. Where a single plank is concerned, struts from a wall or the floor may be feasible. Failing this, one may have to bore small holes through the plank to enable a tightening device to be fixed inside the hull.

Such a device could be a *Spanish windlass* (two parts of rope twisted together with a stick between them) to be fitted inside, or some other device comprising a rigging screw, long bolt, or rope tackle.

Alternatively, bridging pieces can be screwed to the two adjacent planks outside the hull and wedges driven between these and the new plank.

When struts are used, it may be advisable to tilt the hull over to provide the best strutting angle from a wall. Where a damaged plank comes below the turn of the bilge, careening the boat over is a more convenient working position and to make the inside of the boat more accessible.

When G-cramps are not available improvisation is simple if oddments of timber are bolted together to make jaws which slip over the plank and framing with sufficient space left to permit a pair of folding wedges (two ordinary wedges driven towards each other) to be inserted.

As described in *Complete Amateur Boat Building* many types of improvised cramps can be thought up utilizing scrap timber, bolts, chocks and wedges. A long jawed cramp may be useful when renewing a single plank on the topsides of an open boat, as the jaws can be passed over the gunwale to reach the plank.

A typical cramp of this type might be made from two legs of 2 in. × 2 in. (50 mm. × 50 mm.) oak each 4 ft. (1200 mm.) in length, strapped together with a length of light chain half-way along and forced apart at one end with folding wedges and chocks. A bolt of the requisite length passing through a hole in the centre of each leg could be used instead of chain, but keep the bolt diameter small as the hole through the leg (coming at the point of greatest stress) could cause the oak to bend or snap. To give a large range of adjustment for different jobs, *studding* (screwed rod) with a nut and washer each end can be used instead of a range of bolt lengths.

These improvised cramps may be difficult to control until in position, two pairs of hands proving almost essential. As the range of adjustment is small, other means (such as struts) may be necessary to pull a plank roughly into place before the cramps can be applied.

Instead of using wedges to tension such a cramp, a superior model can be made if a bar like a sash cramp is notched through the legs securing them at the desired interval by means of pins.

With a centre bolt made from studding, the nuts can have extended handles welded to them enabling the cramping action to be applied by turning these handles.

MINOR CLINKER REPAIRS

Many clinker hulls leak if allowed to dry out, but persistent seam leaks can often be cured by tightening the fastenings or riveting additional nails midway between the existing ones.

To tighten old copper nails, hold a dolly on the head and peen the riveted end as already described for a new fastening. If a plank is parting from the rabbet along the keel or at the ends, drive additional screws before attempting to tighten the original fastenings.

Where a seam has been open for a long time, dirt in the space may prevent the seam from pulling up closely when the fastenings are attended to. There may be enough space to allow sealing composition to be forced into the gap before tightening.

Seams that still leak can be cured in three ways. On dinghies, a fillet of sealer (such as *Polyseamseal*) can be run along the outside of the seam in a narrow continuous ribbon. Such materials are always elastic and long lasting where the movement is not too great. Nestling under the lands, future rubbing down need not cause any damage. To ensure good adhesion for paint or varnish the fillets of sealer should be kept as small as possible.

The second method is applicable to craft of all sizes. The surfaces on both planks are cleaned down to bare wood to allow a 1 in. (25 mm.) wide strip of finely woven glass-fibre tape to be stuck along the outside of the seam in polyester resin. When thoroughly impregnated with resin, a single layer of this tape is almost invisible even on a varnished surface. One layer will do for all except the larger clinker boats. The system has no elasticity and is therefore of most use below the waterline.

Whatever system is used, it should not be forgotten that although a boat may not leak while at moorings, with additional weight inside her (perhaps due to rain water) some leaky topside seams may come below water and cause her to sink.

The third method is used for large clinker boats, or where the planking is at least ½ in. (12 mm.) thick. A small rounded moulding is screwed to the land of the upper plank as shown in Fig 8, bedded

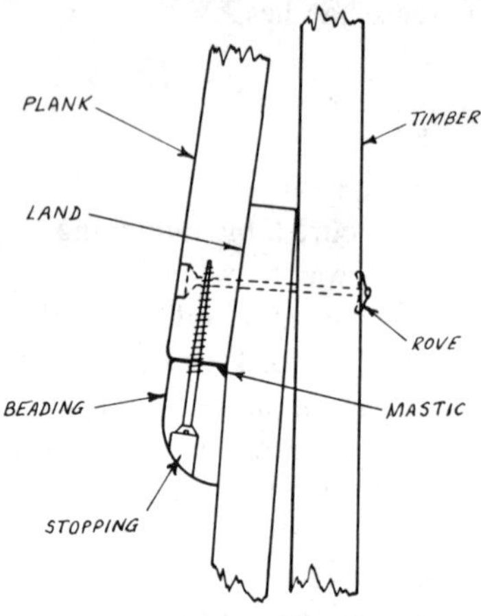

Fig. 8: Beading to stop clinker seam leaks

in *Evomastic* (or Dow Corning *Marine Sealant* in the U.S.A.) applied with a cartridge gun. This method has the advantage that shrinkage of the planking will not break the seal. The repair is inclined to look unsightly, especially where the lands have been damaged by chafe over the years. It would be used nowadays mainly on a large craft of workboat type.

Many racing dinghies are made with glued clinker plywood planking having no fastenings through the lands. When a short length of the glued seam fails, the wisest course is usually to drive one or two thin copper rivets through the joint and seal if necessary using the first or second method described above. If copper nails would look unsightly, small bronze screws can be used, the points being filed off flush on the inside if they come through.

When a long length of glued seam fails, re-gluing is usually worth while. Insert small wedges to open the seam to about $\frac{3}{16}$ in. (5 mm.) at the widest part ensuring that all moisture dries out and providing access for an old hacksaw blade to clean the joint down to bare wood.

Use resorcinol glue at a minimum ambient temperature of 50° F

(10° C) and cramp the joint (but not too tightly) using struts and wedges inside and out. Alternatively, small screws can be used from the outside, to be removed and the holes plugged on completion if preferred.

Failed seams in glued clinker plywood planking occur most frequently just beneath the turn of the bilge due to unfair stresses during trailing on the road. The most secure way of repairing this fault permanently is to fit extra (or stronger) slats glued to the planking on the inside of the boat to take shoe chafe. A hardwood such as mahogany or stained agba about $\frac{5}{16}$ in. (7 mm.) thick and $2\frac{1}{2}$ in. (62 mm.) wide is ideal for the slats. Screw fastenings can be used right through the lands and into the slats when the seam is re-glued, but if strutting is used instead of screws, it may be expedient to glue and strut each slat into position at a later time.

Clinker planking often shows longitudinal cracks which can spread over the years and cause leaks. Small cracks due to shakes in the timber can be opened out and filled with a mixture of resin glue and sander dust. Long cracks can be more dangerous and may need a backing piece inside screwed to the planking and set in bedding compound rather than resin glue.

The crack itself should also be filled with an elastic stopping such as Jeffrey's *Seamflex* (or Kuhl's *Elastic Seam Composition* in America) and a small hole should be bored straight through the planking at the endmost visible signs of the crack to lessen the likelihood of it ever extending further. Hard stopping such as window putty or trowel cement should be avoided. The crack may continue to open and close slightly, loosening any form of hard filling. Cracks may occur between the land fastenings on clinker planking and these are best filled with an elastic stopping.

When a hard stopping is suitable, use one of the polyester or epoxy resin car body repair putties, such as *Isopon* (or Kuhl's *Epotex* in America). These adhere well to timber and harden rapidly in any thickness. They are harder than the surrounding wood and are best shaved down flush by means of a Stanley *Surform* shaper, but they are ideal for use on plastics, steel, or alloy hulls. Similar putties can be made at home by mixing chopped-up glass strands with polyester or epoxy resin.

Resin glue is often more readily available and this can be mixed with sawdust to make a hard filler. Sander dust makes a better filler than sawdust, and other materials such as powdered chalk or pulverized coconut fibre can be used. *Cascamite* one-shot glue is ideal for making hard stopping though other glues that can be mixed into one liquid are suitable. The amount of dilution can be altered when the glue is one which mixes with water and that may be necessary to achieve a suitable consistency when a large amount of filler is added.

Hard stopping can be made at home in other ways when proprietary brands are not available. For instance, on big old boats, bolt heads and other gaps are sometimes filled with rich cement mortar containing one part sand to one part cement plus sufficient water to make a workable putty.

Permanently elastic stoppings are difficult to make at home, but a seam putty which remains slightly elastic for several years can be made as follows.

Mix equal weights of whiting and red lead powder. Add pure white lead paint in small amounts while beating and kneading the whole lot like pastry. Sprinkle whiting on the 'pastry board' to prevent sticking and use a smooth mallet instead of a rolling pin. After a few final vigorous blows the mass should be the same consistency as ordinary glazier's putty. The thickness can be altered by adding more whiting or more paint, followed by further beating. Goldsize may be added to speed the hardening time but this will also vitiate the elasticity. Make sure your hands and nails are cleaned thoroughly after using white or red lead.

CARVEL PLANKING

The term 'carvel planking' usually refers to any type of smooth surface wooden hull other than one planked with plywood. Technically, carvel planking consists of fore-and-aft strakes of solid wood similar to clinker except that the seams are flush instead of being overlapped, see Plate 10. Other forms of smooth surface wood hulls include double diagonal and the hot or cold moulded types.

Plate 10: Repairing a carvel plank

Carvel planking may be used on either hard chine or round bilge hulls but the hot and cold moulded skins are invariably restricted to the round bilge form. Plywood planking is almost exclusively found on hard chine or multi-chine shapes.

Carvel planking repairs follow quite closely the details given earlier in this chapter for clinker planking. Carvel is nearly always simpler as there are no lands, but for a given size of craft, carvel planking is normally thicker than clinker and therefore more difficult to bend where short lengths of planking are replaced. Use butt blocks screwed from the outside in preference to scarfs, provided the interior appearance does not matter. Make butt blocks at least as thick as the planking and big enough to overlap each adjacent plank by at least a plank's thickness.

Marking out a short length of plank is quite simple. Either the new piece of planking or a hardboard template can be held over the gap while a pencil line is marked around from inside. Cut out the shape slightly oversize and then plane down until a good tight fit is achieved. When this is correct, a slight bevel should be planed along the edges of the plank (and at the butt ends) so that a V-shaped open seam is formed to half the plank thickness as shown in Fig 9 to take the caulking. On completion, the caulking gap

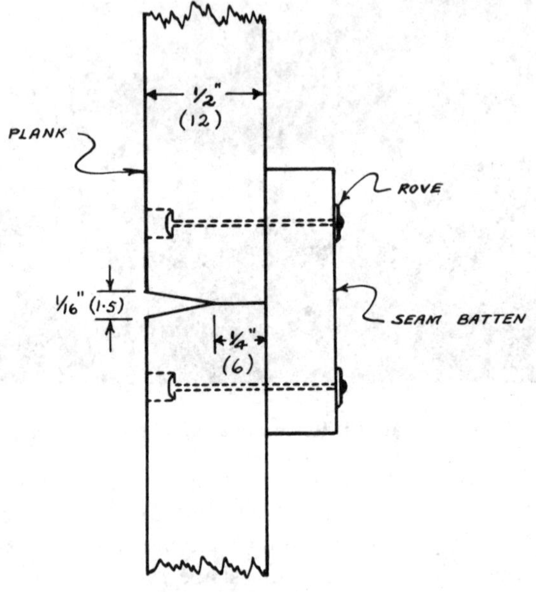

Fig. 9: Seam batten with caulked seam

appearing on the outside of the planking should have a total width of about $\frac{1}{16}$ in. (1·5 mm.) per $\frac{1}{2}$ in. (12 mm.) of plank thickness. Only one-half of the bevel should be planed from each plank edge as indicated in Fig. 9, the taper extending inwards for about one-half the plank thickness.

If a new plank is not made a good fit the caulking cotton may get forced right through the seam when driven hard. Details of caulking are given in Chapter 5.

Efficient caulking cannot be carried out with planking thinner than about $\frac{5}{8}$ in. (15 mm.) *Ribband-carvel* planking is often used where the thickness is less than this. Ribband-carvel is made with a seam batten covering the full length of each seam on the inside as shown in Fig. 9. This construction is mainly found in hard chine speedboats and light displacement sailing craft with widely-spaced sawn frames. The seam battens are usually notched into the frames. The external seams may be just a tight fit or sealed with a little stopping. Proper caulking is not normally necessary.

When repairing a ribband-carvel plank an effort should be made to leave sound seam battens intact. They are rarely important structural members and can be cut out if rotten, damaged, or glued to the planking. New short pieces can be inserted and screwed into the frame notches before the new planking is fitted. Where butt blocks are necessary these should be made a good fit between the seam battens and fixed all around with resin glue if leaks are to be avoided.

Seam batten-to-plank fastenings are usually riveted or turned copper nails, as there is rarely enough thickness to use screws. Turned copper nails have no roves. Instead, each nail is driven through until about $\frac{1}{8}$ in. (3 mm.) is protruding inside, then the point is dressed with a hammer to roll it over back into the wood obliquely across the grain.

A steel dolly is then held on the inside while the driving of the nail is completed from the outside using a hammer and a nail punch the same diameter as the nail head. Some boat builders turn nails by driving them to completion and then hammering the pointed end over to embed it into the wood. This is a rough and ready method and does not allow the nail to pull up tight. If turned nails must be clipped off to length an oblique cut should be used to create a crude sort of point. It usually proves wiser to use nails of the correct length; $\frac{1}{4}$ in. (6 mm.) longer than the pilot hole for 16-gauge nails, $\frac{3}{8}$ in. (9 mm.) longer for 12-gauge, and $\frac{1}{2}$ in. (12 mm.) longer for 8-gauge.

Any rubbery marine sealant may be used for luting between planks and seam battens, but Jefferey's *Hydro* (or in America Kuhl's *Avio*) are ideal and can be applied by brush.

HEAVY CARVEL PLANKING

The amateur may come into contact with a heavily-built converted fishing boat or a similar vessel with planking perhaps 3 in. (75 mm.) thick, with internal framing sawn from solid oak crooks. Plank fastenings are most likely to be *dumps*, which are heavy galvanized iron or bronze nails driven with a sledge hammer. Occasionally through-bolts may also be used, sometimes with nuts on the inside but more often iron or copper *clench bolts* which are riveted over a washer (like a rove) on the inside.

Dumps are sometimes very difficult to withdraw and a faulty plank may have to be chopped away. Old fastenings are easy to withdraw once the plank is out of the way but some may have to be cut off. Square galvanized roseheaded chisel-pointed deck spikes are available nowadays as replacement dumps in an iron fastened vessel of heavy construction. Iron clench bolts would have to be purposely made by a shipyard or blacksmith but copper clenches are easy to make from standard rod.

To form the *upset head* on a $\frac{1}{2}$ in. (12 mm.) bolt first make a former from a small piece of mild steel by boring a $\frac{1}{2}$ in. (12 mm.) hole through it and countersinking this to an overall diameter of about $\frac{3}{4}$ in. (18 mm.). Grip the rod in a vice and slip the former over the top so that about $\frac{3}{4}$ in. (9 mm.) of rod is protruding. It will be necessary to anneal the tip of the rod before starting and probably twice subsequently while riveting into the countersink. It may be a good idea to wedge a block of wood underneath the lower end of the rod to prevent it shifting in the vice while hammering. The former is pulled off the rod on completion to be used again on the next clench bolt.

SPILING

It may not be possible to hold a heavy plank against the hull to enable the shape to be scribed around from the inside and even on small craft there may be a lining or ceiling which prevents access from the inside.

Obviously a template is needed and the way to mark this out is by means of the process called *spiling* which is widely used by shipwrights to mark out weird shapes with curves, notches, tapers and angles, as used when fixing bulkheads, engine bearers, knees and shelves.

For planking, a *spiling batten* made from hardboard or thin wood is cut out roughly to fit into the space as shown in Fig. 10.

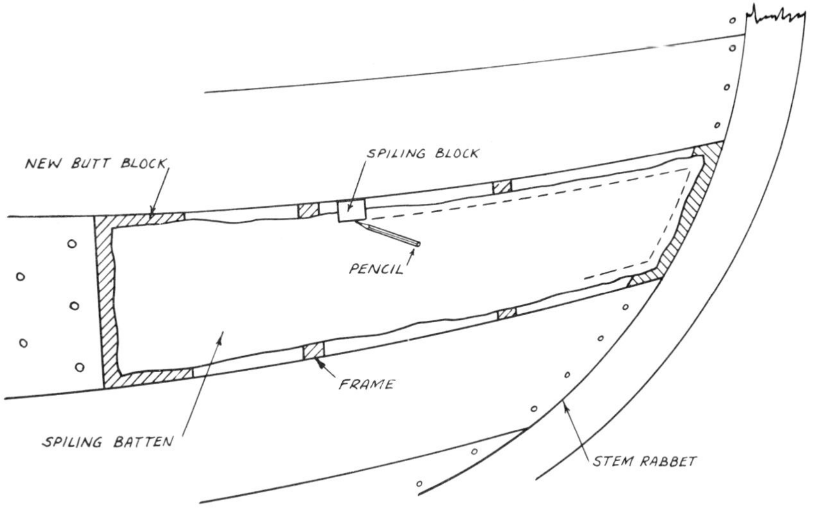

Fig. 10: Spiling batten and dumb-sticker

A small wooden block (a *dumb-sticker* or *dummy* to shipwrights) is prepared, its width just a little greater than the widest gap between the spiling batten and the surrounding timber. With a sharp pencil held against one side of the block, both block and pencil are moved along all around the shape leaving a pencil line on the spiling batten which is parallel to the true outline but smaller everywhere by an equal amount.

The spiling batten is then removed and tacked temporarily on top of the board to be used for the new plank. A plate of thin wood is now nailed to the dumb-sticker protruding beneath it by an amount equal to the thickness of the spiling batten as shown in Fig. 11.

By holding the block against the pencilled line at intervals of

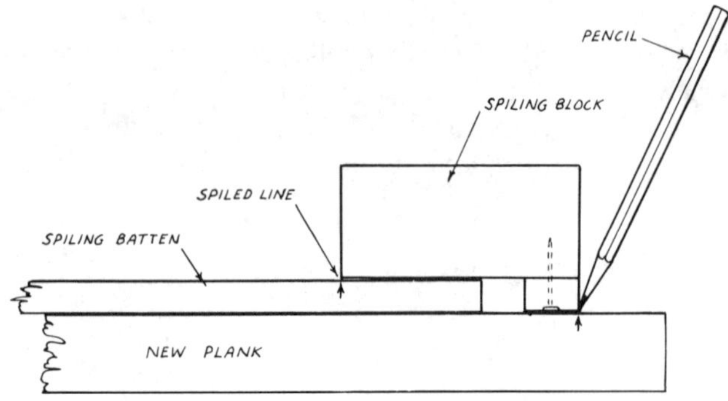

Fig. 11: Transferring the spiled line

about 2 in. (50 mm.) and making a pencil mark against the inside of the small plate, a series of points will be transferred to the new plank which, when joined up into fair lines, will produce a true outline for the new plank. A piece of springy batten (sometimes called a *spline*) may be used as a pencil guide where the points are in the form of a curve.

Instead of a dumb-sticker a pair of dividers may be used. To do this, draw a series of parallel lines across the spiling batten and the adjacent planks, open the dividers a little wider than the greatest gap and with one point of the dividers resting against the surrounding planking, prick the spiling batten at each line. Having tacked the spiling batten on to the new timber, transfer each position with the same divider opening, using a small square (as shown in Fig. 12a) to avoid the errors which would occur if the dividers were allowed to lean over as in Fig. 12b.

When spiling is used to pick up the shape of a bulkhead or similar large area the procedure is somewhat different, and is described in Chapter 11.

STRIP PLANKING

Another form of carvel planking which has proved most successful in thicknesses ranging from about 1 in. (25 mm.) to 2 in. (50 mm.) is *strip planking*, where narrow strakes of constant width (approximately equal to the thickness) are glued and edge-nailed

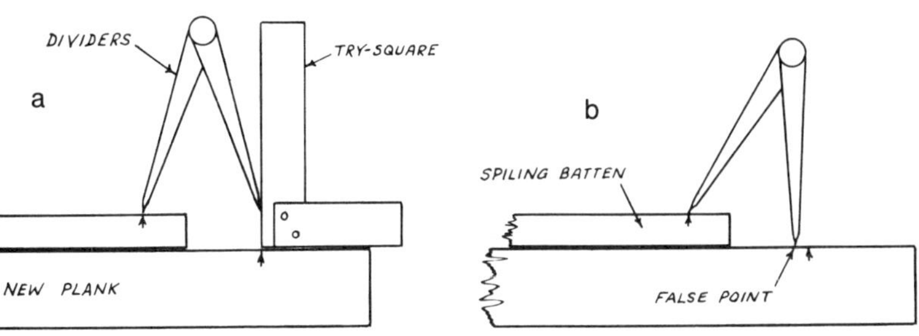

Fig. 12: Correct and incorrect use of dividers

together forming a seamless hull. There may be widely-spaced sawn frames or steamed timbers at close intervals. Collision or chafe damage is sure to extend over several strips in width, possibly extending over several frames or timbers in length.

The standard procedure is to cut out the strips in the fashion shown in Fig. 13. If the strips are glued to the framing and this is

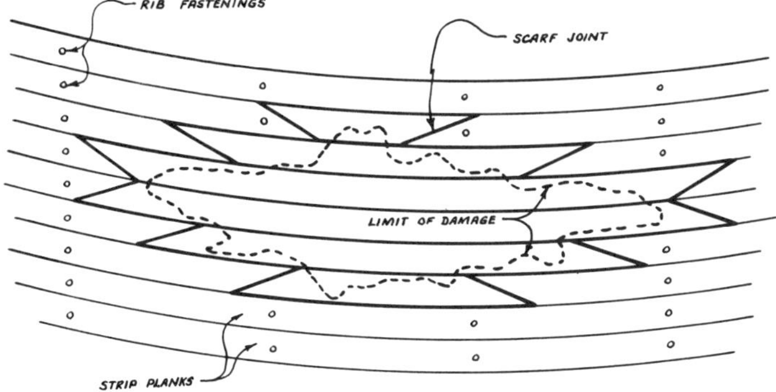

Fig. 13: Standard method of cutting for repair

sound, saw through the strips down each side of each frame and then split away the remaining pieces with a chisel and mallet. A hacksaw may have to be used to sever the edge nails encountered when sawing along the joints between the strips.

With the damaged panel cut out, any framing repairs can be completed; then new strips of a high grade stable hardwood (of the same dimensions as the original ones) can be glued into the spaces.

Start at the bottom so that new edge nails may be driven downwards.

Nearing the top of the panel where there is insufficient space to use a hammer, a piece of flat bar may be held on each nail head and struck with the hammer. Alternatively, each nail may be pressed in by means of a steel bar lever together with chocks of wood of different thicknesses resting against the upper planking edge to create a fulcrum.

Edge nails cannot be driven through the final strip but the necessary strength can be added by cutting the heads off copper or Gripfast nails and driving these pins through pilot holes bored obliquely upwards and downwards from the inner or outer face of the strip. Use the highest class resorcinol glue with an adequate ambient temperature.

When the frames are widely-spaced it may be impossible to bend the strips to the true curvature of the hull. This problem can be overcome by fixing a short additional frame between the others. If this frame can be left in permanently it will help to strengthen the repaired area. If unsightly on the inside it can be removed later. This idea of an additional frame can be most useful on chine hull repairs with ordinary carvel, double diagonal and plywood planking.

SURFACE DEFECTS

The hard stoppings described previously can be used to cover up most chafe and abrasion defects on wood and metal hulls, but where there is a hole right through the planking (perhaps caused by a dead knot) a more secure method may be necessary and on varnished finishes, a method which matches the natural grain of the wood more closely than any stopping.

The method normally used to achieve this is called *graving*. A thin plate of similar wood is inlaid into the surface of the planking, usually in the shape of a diamond, elongated in the direction of the grain. The thickness of the graving piece is generally about one-third the thickness of the plank.

The diamond shape is cut first, held in place and scribed around with a sharp knife. The inlaid recess is then routed to the knife marks by drilling holes with a depth gauge attached to the bit, finishing to the edges with a sharp chisel. The sides of the graving piece may be bevelled slightly to allow it to slip into the recess easily, secured with resin glue and brass panel pins. Enough wood should be left proud to enable the piece to be planed down flush. This form of repair may be used also on masts, coamings, decks, and rails.

Graving is difficult to use for long narrow defects but it may be worth while on a varnished finish. The options are normally to use resin putty or to renew a whole section of planking.

For emergency repairs a *tingle* can be used to seal a small damaged area or a potential leak. To apply a tingle, a sheet of 24-gauge copper is nailed to the outside of the planking on top of a patch (the same size) made from cotton sailcloth soaked in white lead paint. A well made tingle can be left in place for many years without harm but such a repair is used only below the waterline due to its appearance.

On yachts with varnished topsides all large nail and screw holes are filled with dowels (plugs) of matching timber. For painted surfaces any type of hard stopping may be used. Chandlers and hardware stores stock dowel-cutting tools nowadays which enable the amateur to cut his own dowels from offcuts of the correct type and colour of wood. Alternatively, any boatyard will cut dowels for you to standard sizes. Remember to bore the dowel cutter into the wood sideways (across the grain) and not the easy way along the end grain as used for the common beach dowelling stocked by handyman stores.

A dowel cutter normally provides one with plugs about 1 in. (25 mm.) long, so each plug will normally fill three or four countersink holes. Tap the plug into the hole after coating all surfaces with varnish. Then split off the plug by means of a wide wood chisel with its bevelled edge to the planking and propelled by a sharp blow from one's fist on the chisel handle. This should leave a small amount of the plug protruding which can be shaved down flush next day when the varnish has set.

To remove old dowels when repair work is necessary, scrape the surface down to bare wood, bore a small pilot hole through the centre of the dowel to enable a steel woodscrew of the appropriate size to be wound in. All being well, the point of this screw will press upon the fastening head and force the dowel out.

CAULKED SEAM PROBLEMS

On certain racing craft and launches with teak (or a similar high grade hardwood) carvel planking, the seams are *splined* instead of being caulked in the ordinary way. To do this, a single strand of cotton is driven into the caulking gap, then a specially prepared strip of the same timber as the planking is glued along one side only and driven tightly into the seam. Should the free side open up at any time this can be filled with a thin line of elastic stopping.

Similar splines can be used on old boats where the seams are too wide to caulk properly. The splines are laid in mastic and held in place with brass panel pins driven obliquely downwards.

When a short length of seam is too wide to caulk, this is often

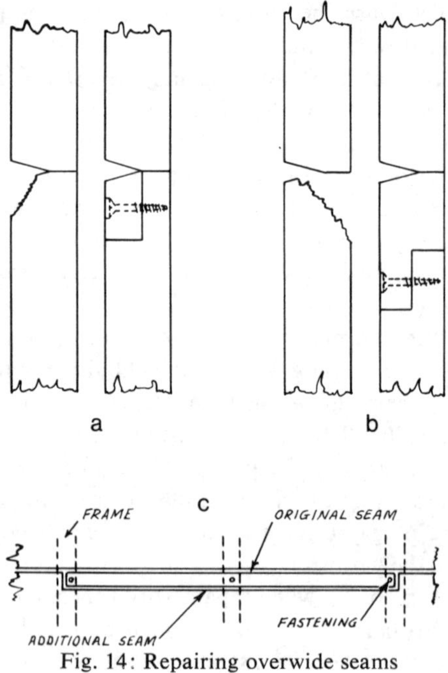

Fig. 14: Repairing overwide seams

due to the presence of sapwood on the edge of a plank which rots away when the remainder is perfectly sound. To repair this, a rebate can be cut along the plank edge to a depth not greater than half the plank thickness (see Fig. 14a) and a strip of new wood glued and screwed into place. Where a seam is similarly rounded on the inside, the repair shown in Fig. 14b is usually the best method. Difficulty arises where plank fastenings are encountered. The removal of a single one may not matter, but more than this should be replaced through the new timber.

When one plank is defective near to a seam between two sawn frames, it may be possible to cut this out and insert a new strip of timber overlapping the frame at each end sufficiently to ensure secure fastening, creating a caulked seam all around the new piece as shown in Fig. 14c. These types of seam repair can all be done from outside the hull.

Details of caulking plank and deck seams are given in Chapter 5.

MULTI-SKIN PLANKING

Double skin diagonal planking with a layer of calico between the two skins has always been popular for chine boats and was widely used for certain Navy craft. When fitted with sawn frames there may be numerous stringers running fore-and-aft between the frames and the planking.

Even the smallest repair job to the inner skin creates a great deal of work unless this can be reached from inside the hull. The outer skin is easy to repair as this can be stripped to any extent by removing the roved or turned nails that are used in the closely spaced pattern throughout. If the nails or screws into the frames are difficult to extract, the wood around them can be chipped away. The calico need not be replaced as the new wood can be laid in bedding compound and refastened on the original lines.

To renew even a small section of the inner skin means stripping a large number of the outer strakes. They need not be removed completely from gunwale to keel (or to chine) but they must be cut back in staggered formation so that adjacent ends are well shifted.

Frequently, as soon as any stripping work is started, unknown defects in the inner skin come to light. Repairing from the inside tends to make a botched job, but it does save an enormous amount of work. The usual procedure is to through-fasten a panel of thick marine plywood to the inside, set in bedding compound. If frames or stringers get in the way, less work may be involved in cutting these out and renewing them afterwards than stripping large areas of the outer skin.

Hot moulded multi-skin hulls (such as those produced by Fairey Marine) are built in similar fashion but the skins are resin-glued together creating a strong round bilge shell which requires no internal framing.

Cold moulded hulls are built in exactly the same way but they are not cured in an oven. Veneers of hardwood (frequently *Agba*) are commonly used for building moulded hulls, but thin marine plywood has also been used. Some of the largest craft have as many as five skins, some laid diagonally and some fore-and-aft.

The interior is usually easy to get at as there may be no framing and, perhaps, no fastenings. The difficulty when repairing damage is to pare away just sufficient of the inner and outer skins with well-shifted ends, so that new veneers of the original thickness can be glued back into place. If the damage extends to more than two plank widths it may be necessary to cut a series of templates from ¾ in. (18 mm.) floor boarding which can be fastened together with chocks between them to create a grid to fit exactly to the curvature of the hull, either on the outside or the inside. Fasten right through the new skin with veneer pins into the grid until the glue has set.

The outside shape is naturally more important than the inside and as external damage is usually more extensive than internal the templates are normally fitted to the outside of the hull, aligned and secured with temporary screws through the undamaged part of the planking. If the hull has a varnished finish the repair will always be visible and a change to enamel is usually wise.

PLYWOOD PLANKING

Before the advent of plastics, vast numbers of small yachts and dinghies were built with marine plywood planking. With careful

Plate 11: A neat lifeboat conversion

maintenance, this has proved a successful construction. Renewing the entire plywood skin of a neglected boat is by no means an insuperable task and stripping off the old plywood may prove the longest job. A saw can be run along clear of the rabbets to free the old panels of plywood, but try to prise the sheets away from the frames if glued there.

If a spiling line is run around each panel before sawing it out, the old sheet can be used as a spiling batten for marking out the new plywood. The pieces which remain glued into the rabbets can be chiselled away when as many fastenings as possible have been withdrawn.

A steam lance may be necessary to heat the forward topside panels when reskinning a chine hull and this proves a neater method than the more usual rags and boiling water.

To repair small areas of damage, cut away a regular-shaped hole, fix a patch of equivalent thickness plywood on the inside (overlapping all around) and glue in a patch dead flush with the outside surface. The patch need not fit precisely around its edges as knifing stopper can be used to make good.

Where a backing piece on the inside would look unsightly a different method is used. The damaged area is cut out as before, a rabbet is formed all around from the outside to a depth equal to half the skin thickness and the patch is prepared with a corresponding rabbet around it, then glued and screw-fastened into place. The job is simplified if some plywood exactly half the original thickness can be found. Two patch pieces are then prepared, one to just fill the aperture and one to just fit the complete area to the limit of the rabbets. However, the cruder method with a backing piece inside is considerably stronger.

4

Framing and Plastics Repairs

Some heavily built wooden hulls will continue to function quite satisfactorily when certain isolated parts of the framing show rot, cracking, or other defects. In lightly-built craft such as certain dinghies and deep-keeled racing yachts, even one broken member can put too much additional stress on the adjacent parts so that immediate action is necessary to avert costly trouble.

STEAMED TIMBERS

Some yachts have sawn frames with two or three steamed ribs between each. This has proved a very reliable system and, with the exception of rot or a collision, replacement of the steamed timbers is a rare necessity.

In a hard used craft older than about twenty years where all the timbers are steamed, some replacement is likely to be needed. Rot is rarely found in small open boats but these are the ones with thin bent ribs which are prone to cracking across the line of a plank seam. The steamed timbers in larger vessels may be as thick as 2½ in. (62 mm.) and these are more likely to be affected by rot than cracking.

Note that timbers between ⅜ in. (9 mm.) and ¾ in. (18 mm.) would have been fitted originally by springing them steaming hot into the newly-planked hull. Most thicker timbers (especially those between 1½ in. (37 mm.) and 2½ in. (62 mm.) in thickness would have been steamed and then bent on a jig before fitting, or perhaps bent *in situ* to the mould ribbands before planking.

When inside appearance is unimportant, *sistering*, or doubling-up with a *sister piece* (or short timber alongside the damaged one) is easy, and just as strong as removing the whole rib and inserting a new one. If a complete timber is replaced it should be impossible to tell the difference upon completion. Although the new piece should be made exactly the same width as the old one with rounded or chamfered edges to match, it may have to be a little thinner to permit passing it behind the shelf (or gunwale) and stringer or riser) without jamming.

In cases where broken timbers have been neglected for many years the shape of the hull in this vicinity may have changed. Where this has happened, careful inspection of the outside planking surface may reveal a seam which tends to protrude like a chine, usually at the turn of the bilge. To check this further a cardboard template can be made to fit the opposite side of the hull and held against the same position on the faulty side to show up the extent of the movement.

If one intends to get the planking back into its original shape, all caulking must be removed from the affected seams and the damaged timbers stripped away to allow the planks to move. Having done this, moulds of rough timber should be cut to the shape of templates taken from the opposite side of the hull and the planking pulled up to these with temporary screws while the ribs are being replaced.

On dinghies and other craft with a small amount of deadrise (rather flat hull sections near to the keel) each rib is continuous from gunwale to gunwale running over the top of the hog. For a complete re-ribbing when both gunwales and risers are removed, the new timbers can be made in exactly the same way. Otherwise, feeding a hot timber behind the gunwale and riser during the space of about one minute makes it advisable to terminate each half timber on the hog close alongside the other half.

Oak or American elm (Canadian rock elm) are the best woods to use for steaming timbers of any size. The grain must be true, running parallel to the planking when viewed on the end grain. Small defects can be accommodated normally towards each end of a rib. Steaming or submersion in boiling water should have a duration of not more than ten minutes for ribs $\frac{3}{8}$ in. (6 mm.) thick; fifteen minutes for $\frac{1}{2}$ in. (12 mm.); twenty minutes for $\frac{3}{4}$ in. (18 mm.) and thirty minutes for 1 in. (25 mm.).

The complete renewal of a heavy jig-bent steamed timber in one continuous piece is almost impossible with the fore-and-aft members still in place. Sistering with a short new timber fitted alongside the faulty one is the usual method of repair and such a piece can usually be forced behind a stringer after bending to shape over a jig and adjusting the shape with a plane or drawknife.

When a new timber is hot the copper nails may be driven straight through it (without need to bore a hole) for thicknesses up to about $\frac{3}{4}$ in. (18 mm.). The nail holes through the planking are bored beforehand, but where the original holes are used when fitting new ribs, it may be wise to fit nails a size thicker to ensure a tight fit.

By driving the nails through the hot rib without boring, work can be speeded up sufficiently to permit a timber to be pulled up close before it cools off too much. These fastenings should not be riveted or turned until the timber has hardened again unless the grip of the nails is insufficient to keep the timber close to the planking. It may pay to sharpen the point on each nail slightly with a hand file before starting to steam the timbers.

Bronze screws or barbed ring nails should be used to secure the heel of each rib to the hog. If there is a keelson, replacement timbers can usually be pushed underneath this with just sufficient space to get one fastening through the rib into the hog along each side of the keelson.

At the forward end of a dinghy the ribs may have to take a very sharp bend where the planking merges with the hog. If it proves impossible to do this without breakages, a fine-toothed saw may be used to slit the timber for a short distance as shown in Fig. 15. It

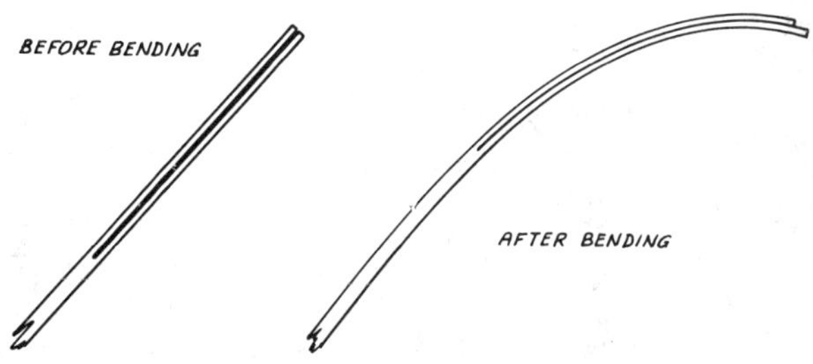

Fig. 15: Slitting ribs to facilitate bending

will then bend very easily. If nothing more suitable is available, an ordinary hacksaw may be used to make the split.

In similar fashion, when fitting a single replacement timber which is too awkward to get into place quickly enough after being steamed, it may be laminated cold in two pieces for the entire length. Ideally, the joint should be resin-glued to make it equivalent in strength to a solid steamed timber.

BENDING JIGS

Boat builders use jigs fabricated as shown in Plate 12 for cramping on any part to be steamed and bent before fitting in the hull. With a range of these formers, timber can be bent to any shape, using packing pieces on top of the slats to adjust the radius. Some ribs have reverse curvature in them and it may prove expedient to

Plate 12: Jig for preforming timber parts

steam one radius first, nailing a batten across it as shown in Fig. 16 on removal from the jig to hold it in shape while the other radius is being steamed.

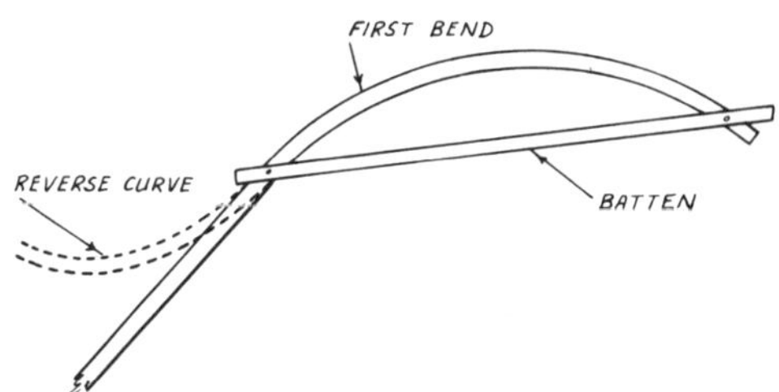

Fig. 16: Steaming a reverse curvature

Except with very heavy sections it pays to put a little extra curvature into the jig to allow for the usual spring-back which occurs when the steamed part is uncramped. If the bend is then too sharp, it can be flattened slightly by cramping cold in the opposite direction. When laminated parts (such as knees) have to be steamed, several parts can be bent in unison on a jig but the glue cannot be applied until the laminations have been uncramped and dried out completely.

Heavy steamed timbers may require bevelling on the side next to the planking. This can be set out quite accurately by holding the frame into position while the gap on the open side is measured at intervals with dividers and transferred to the opposite side as shown in Fig. 17. A pencil line joining all the transferred points

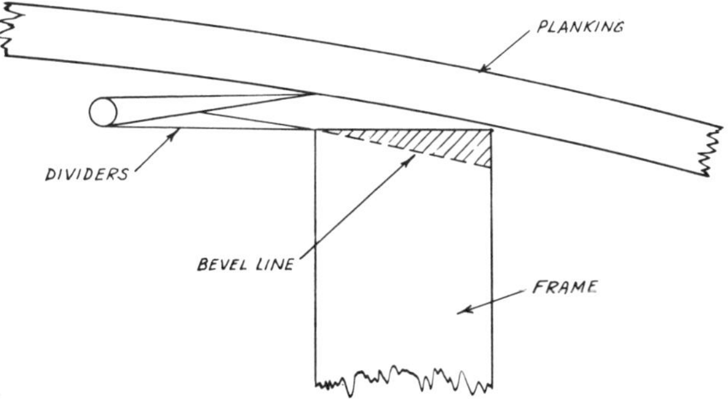

Fig. 17: Setting out a frame bevel

will now indicate the depths of wood to be planed off when making the bevel. Minor adjustments can be made after further offering up and marking.

Although every piece of timber in a boat should be painted or set in composition, this ideal is difficult to achieve when springing light section steamed timbers into place. However, the planking surface can be painted or varnished beforehand, the ribs can be treated against rot, and a certain amount of paint or varnish can be worked in behind each timber at the end of the job.

When it proves impossible to get a steamed timber behind the stringers, if the appearance is not detrimental, the type of repair shown in Fig. 18 may be adopted. The new frame is fastened on

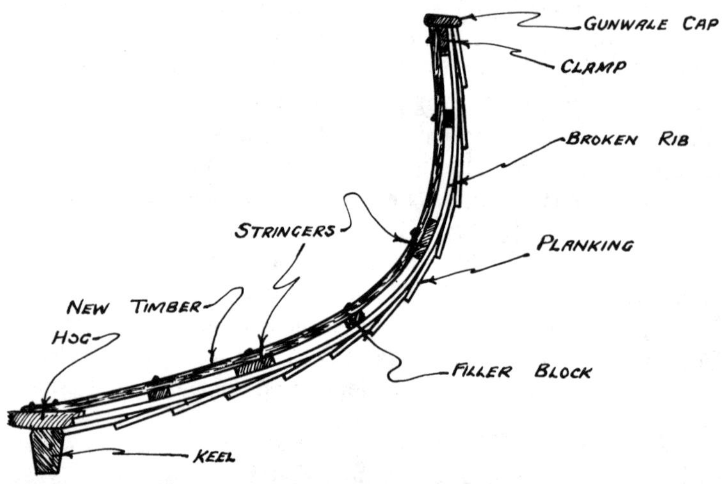

Fig. 18: New timber bent over the stringers

top of the stringers and gunwale with filler blocks between the old and new timbers (or between the new timber and the planking) to produce a girder effect with all fastenings right through.

Defective sawn frames are repaired as described for heavy deck beams in Chapter 5, while a complete futtock may be replaced to cure rot or damage in one side of a double sawn timber.

When fitting a new engine into a lightly timbered launch it may be unwise to use the conventional fore-and-aft bearers, for without adequate floor knees, many timbers could break in line with the bearers if the boat ever pounded, causing a plank seam to open widely, perhaps without warning.

To install a heavy engine into such a boat would mean adding athwartships frames (see Plate 13) welded up from angle steel and galvanized after fabrication. Two or three of these frames would tie all the planks together to give an old craft a new lease of life. The engine bearers should be fastened only to the steel frames.

Plate 13: Welded steel angle frames

Such frames cannot be made to look attractive inside the boat as they have to sit on top of the stringers with filler chocks between the frame and the planking all around, a through-bolt passing through each one. The steel frames need not be rolled accurately to the curvature of the hull as a shape similar to a multi-chine hull is just as good and easier to make.

STRINGERS

Nearly all round bilge boats have one or more pairs of stringers (called *risers* in dinghies) running fore-and-aft for the full length of the boat, fastened right through inside the timbers. Should these rot or break, they can be doubled up with a new piece alongside, with plenty of overlap at each end. Where the original stringers are almost square in section, the additional piece should be the same size. If the stringers are more like planks, it may look neater to fasten a doubling piece of almost equal size on top of the old member. Alternatively, two doubling pieces may be used, nearer square in section, one above and one below the original.

To repair a small defect in any but the smallest stringers, it may be possible to scarf a new piece in, as already described for a plank.

It usually proves easier to run the scarfs in the direction shown in Fig. 19. Sawing scarfs through the original stringers is not easy in a confined space, but a floorboard saw (sometimes called an electrician's saw) with arched cutting edge, is a big help. Awkward scarfs can be cut almost entirely with mallet and chisel when plenty of time is available.

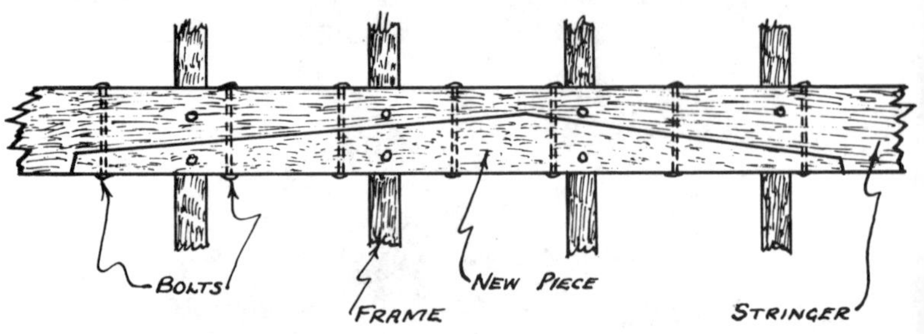

Fig. 19: Scarfing a piece into a stringer

STEM AND KEEL

Superficial wooden stem damage is easy to repair by inlaying graving pieces (see page 54) or by scarfing the cutwater after removing the stemband. Re-fastening slack hood ends is simple enough, but when a collision has sheared the old fastenings, or when the stem timber is soft, it may be necessary to fit an additional apron piece right across the back of the old stem or apron inside the boat. Fix this with through-bolts or coach screws, then drive new hood end fastenings into it abaft the original fastenings.

In most old boats faulty scarfs and hood ends have been filled by an ever increasing amount of stopper over the years. Although this may look neat, eventually the stem may become so weak that without warning, perhaps in deep water, it may shift and let in a rush of water.

Fitting a completely new stem or keel is not the kind of job that the amateur is recommended to attempt without skilled guidance, but it can be done. More simply, the outer part (*cutwater*) can be sawn right off flush with the planking ends, and new timber bolted into place.

However, although this appears simple, do be careful to replace adequately the original scarf and apron (inner stem) bolts which have to be sawn off. The new timber may need to be made in more than one length, and so any scarf joints should be shifted away from the remains of the original stem scarf.

Try to use T-headed bolts to secure the new cutwater and sink the heads into narrow vertical slots which will not be exposed when the stem is bevelled down to the usual leading edge covered by a metal band. Modern craft (and especially sailing dinghies) have a false stem beyond the planking rabbets fitted in the above manner when newly built and replacement may then be a simpler job.

A more common repair to an exposed stem scarf consists of fitting a specially shaped brass sheath as shown in Plate 14. This is recessed flush, secured with large bronze wood screws and set in bedding compound. For craft smaller than about 26 ft. (8 m.) in length 16-gauge (1.5 mm.) plate of naval brass quality is normally used; up to 39 ft. (12 m.) $\frac{1}{8}$ in. (3 mm.) will do and above this size $\frac{3}{16}$ in. (4.5 mm.).

Having recessed the stem to the plate thickness, take off cardboard templates from which a wooden former can be shaped, then bend and beat the metal to fit this former. Get a shipyard to do this job if the metal proves too thick to handle. Make the sheath slightly larger than the recessed area, trimming the edges down to a tight fit later by trial and error.

A similar job can be done in glass-fibre. On very small boats it may be possible to lay up two or three layers of cloth and feather off the edges after curing, but on larger vessels where up to twelve layers may be used, these must be recessed as for metal. After

Plate 14: Brass sheath for a stem scarf

curing, the moulded sheath must be drilled and countersunk for woodscrews (preferably of stainless steel) mainly around the edges but also criss-crossing the remainder.

External keels and deadwoods can be repaired quite successfully by scarfing in new timber provided adequate through fastenings are used. Woodscrews or coach screws are not normally suitable for this purpose unless there is a strong iron keel reinforcing the structure.

New timber can be fitted into fin keels without through-bolting if nut plates are inserted through narrow apertures morticed into the timber higher up, as described for engine bearers in Chapter 9.

Minor keel and deadwood damage can be repaired by inserting graving pieces (as described in the last Chapter) or by building up with *Mendex* (*Epotex*) or resin putty. A badly battered keel base can often be rejuvenated by fitting a new keel band of thick galvanized steel.

New keel bolts should be made from either bronze or galvanized steel as in the original construction. The heads of keel bolts must be caulked by winding a grommet of caulking cotton under them before insertion, all well soaked with bedding compound or a mixture composed of white lead paste and motor grease. Each head must be sealed over with resin putty before the keel band is attached with strong countersunk woodscrews of a compatible metal.

Details of how to treat iron and lead ballast keels and preserve steelwork of all types above and below the waterline are given in *Boat Maintenance*.

TRANSOM REPAIRS

It may take the amateur more than a year to completely replace the backbone of a 40 ft. (12 m.) yacht, but this might well be worth while if there are few other defects and when it might cost £10,000 (about $40,000) to buy an equivalent sound craft.

Provided one has the necessary facilities, steel boats are usually easier to repair than those of wood. Buckled skin plating can be pulled out with a small winch if holes are bored in the correct places. The holes can later be filled by welding. Gas welding is suitable for many small repair jobs to plating and frames but for long runs where the metal is of good thickness and not too badly corroded, electric arc welding has many advantages. Aluminium alloy is difficult to weld even with the correct *Argonarc* equipment and riveting or bonding with epoxy adhesive is often more suitable.

The majority of wooden yachts have transom sterns and these may demand more repair attention than either stem or keel. The flatness of a transom tends to make it weak when rammed, and water may get trapped between the transom frame and the plank ends, leading to extensive and sometimes hidden rot.

Once again the complete renewal of a transom (and perhaps also its frame) is by no means an insuperable task when the condition of the rest of the boat warrants it, but it may often be possible to scarf in a new section of framing or to replank part of the outer transom where a fault is localized.

Refastening the plank ends is usually the first step and it may be many years after that before any major work becomes necessary. If the softness is found during refastening, copious amounts of P.C.P. or similar fluid should be worked into the framing, if necessary boring holes through this into the inside to lead the fluid in.

Dinghy transoms may get disturbed by using oversized outboard motors. When repairing such damage, be sure to reinforce the transom so that similar trouble is unlikely to recur.

CHINE, SHELF AND GUNWALE

In certain plywood dinghies (such as the *Mirror*) and canoes, there is no chine member at all. The panels of plywood meeting at the chine are stitched together with thin copper wire and reinforced with layers of glass-fibre tape on both sides. Most other chine craft have a strong member running fore-and-aft along the knuckle usually formed by one of the systems illustrated in Fig. 20.

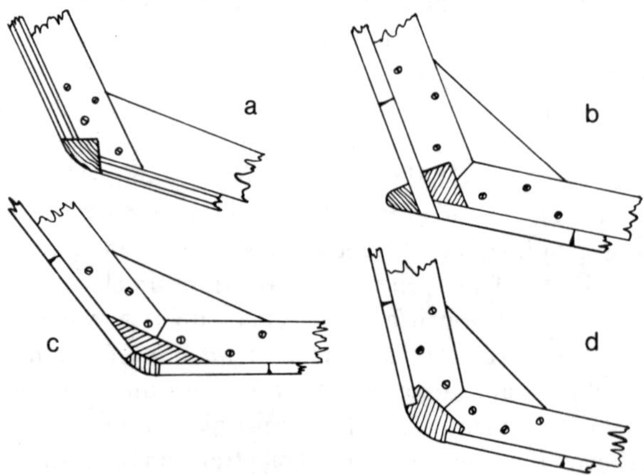

Fig. 20: Alternative chine joint structures

These chines are almost as important structurally as the keel. If they trap moisture and rot starts (or rusting in a steel hull) immediate drying out and application of rot preservative is essential. When deterioration or collision damage is serious, repair work will be necessary.

To do this over a considerable length means stripping off some planking and in the case of double diagonal planking this work can escalate alarmingly. An outer chine can be cut away quite easily and a new piece let in without disturbing the planking. Between frames, short lengths of inner chine can be renewed and reinforced with butt blocks at each end. Where longer lengths are concerned it may be quicker to strip out a frame than to disturb the planking.

Additional plank fastenings and recaulking will often cure leaky chines, but when coupled with external damage sheathing over with copper or glass-fibre may be expedient.

The internal fore-and-aft member at the top of the frames which also supports the deck beams is called the *shelf*. There may be two members, a horizontal shelf and a vertical *clamp*. In small open boats the same part is usually called the *gunwale*, or sometimes the *inwale*. Gunwale damage is most likely to occur when a dinghy gets crushed. Repair is simple as except for a capping piece to hide the ends of the steamed timbers in some dinghies the gunwale is exposed with one roved nail through the top of each timber and additional ones at the knees. Complete renewal (or neat scarfing) makes the best repair job, though doubling up is quicker with equally strong results.

The shelf and clamp on a decked boat are prone to rotting due to deck leaks. Whereas sea water is a mild fungicide, rain water creates a good culture for rot. This is the reason that experienced seamen always wash decks with sea water and not fresh. The shelf area is also more prone to damage by fire than many other parts of a boat.

Shelf and clamp repairs are normally much easier than similar work on a chine as the frames do not interfere – a doubling piece (sometimes referred to as a *flitch-plate* or *fishplate*) on top of the old shelf and notched around the deck beams can be used. Where this is not feasible a separate clamp piece through-fastened to the frames and planking below the shelf can be made to look an original part of the boat. A clamp is not interrupted by the deck beams and can be repaired by scarfing if necessary as already described for a stringer.

KNEES, FLOORS AND GUSSETS

Knees of various types are used in most craft of wood, metal, or plastics, to serve as stiffening brackets where constructional members meet at an angle in an otherwise weak joint. In traditional craft grown oak *crooks* with their grain following the radius of the knee are used, though certain other timbers, such as apple and cherry, may be suitable.

In an open boat quarter knees are used to tie the gunwales to the transom; a breasthook does the same job at the stemhead; a stern knee comes between the transom and the hog, while thwart knees form stiffeners between the planking and gunwale at the ends of each thwart. In larger traditional craft there are usually knees called *floors* at right angles to the hog, bolted to it and clenched or screwed to the planking and also sometimes to the frames. To stiffen the deck beams (especially in way of a mast) *hanging* knees are used from the beams down to the planking, while *lodging* knees lie horizontally under the deckhead fastened between the sides of the beams and the shelf.

Metal boats have similar knees made from flat plates (sometimes flanged along the edges) welded or riveted into place. Glass reinforced plastics hulls need few knees, but those having a ballast keel or carrying a heavy engine invariably have floor knees moulded in.

Chine hulls have additional knees called *gussets*, to tie each part of a frame together where they meet at the chine knuckle. The floors in such craft usually take the form of gussets on each frame across the hog, though additional floors, often of solid oak, are inserted between each frame to take the ballast keel bolts. Plywood gussets are sometimes double with a plywood plate glued and screwed to each side of the frame joint. Chine frames are sometimes made up with the deck beams attached. In this case, the hanging knees may also be plywood gussets.

Good quality marine plywood may be used to make knees of

any size or form. The thickness may be built up by gluing several plates of plywood together, as in Fig. 21. Cross the grain of each adjacent piece at right angles for maximum strength, especially if three-ply having a thick inner lamina plus two very thin outer skins is used. For best appearance when varnished, a strip of mahogany veneer may be glued around the exposed edge to hide the grain of the plywood.

Similar knees can be made with solid wood in three or four layers glued together with the grain crossing. Avoid straight grained solid wood in a single piece. This may look satisfactory with the grain running parallel to the hypotenuse but cracking along the grain at some future time is quite likely with most hardwoods. The usual through fastenings cannot always be placed in the ideal direction to ensure that the grain is cramped permanently everywhere, except with glued and screwed gussets.

The strongest type of laminated knee is pictured in Fig. 22, the strips running in the same direction as the grain of a proper natural crook. Use hardwood strips of the correct thickness (easily determined with a few trial pieces) to bend easily to the curve without steaming. Remember that several strips in unison will bend more readily when lubricated with glue than when dry.

Make all strips of the same length to make bending easier when cramped to a jig. When the glue has hardened, shave the corner chock to fit, then glue this to the laminated assembly. When working in winter, small glued parts should be brought into a warm room as resin glue may not harden properly when cold.

Cut out the shape of the knee from a template, using a bandsaw or coping saw. Plane the faces smooth *after* cutting out to reduce the area and save blunting the plane iron on rock hard resin glue.

A simple form of knee can be built up as shown in Fig. 23 with one thick steam-bent outer member glued to a system of filler chocks. Knees can be laminated entirely from thick steam bent strips, but the wood must be allowed to dry out completely before gluing.

Straight-grained ash bends well but it has poor durability when wet and needs impregnating with preservative. Oak and American

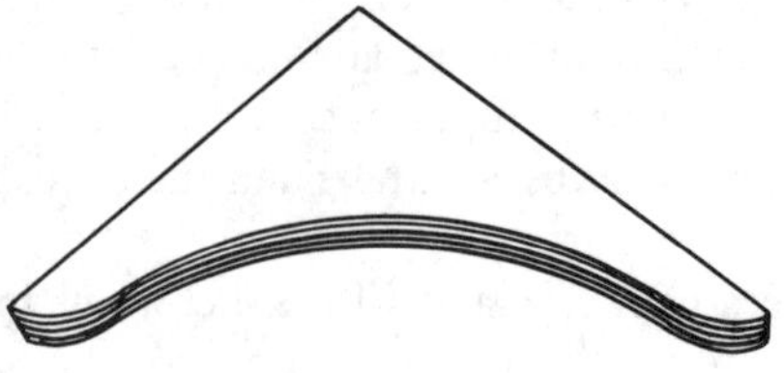

Fig. 21: Built-up plywood knee

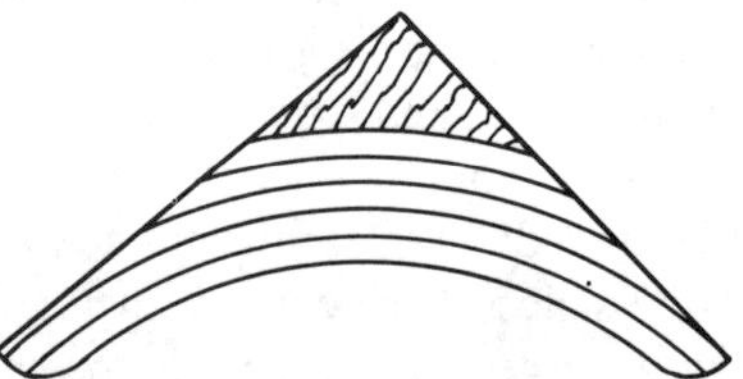

Fig. 22: Laminated hardwood knee

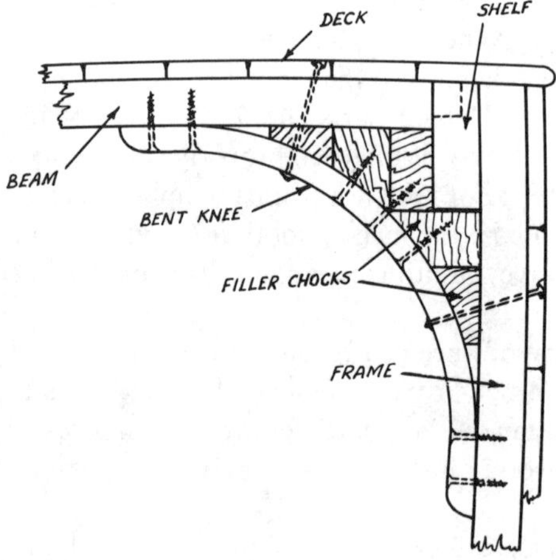

Fig. 23: Knee laminated with filler chocks

elm are generally better while agba is a durable hardwood which bends well.

Floor knees can be made in any of the ways so far described. Along the midship section of a hull with little deadrise it may be possible to use straight-grained oak, but then the *siding* (width) should be increased by at least twenty-five per cent over the normal for a natural crook.

Where old floors have cracked it may be possible to double up with a new floor fastened to the side of the old one, or a gusset of thick plywood may be attached to each side and through-fastened. Where a keelson is in the way it may be possible to strengthen a floor by fitting a new straight-grained piece across the top of the keelson as shown in Fig. 24, provided this will not obstruct the cabin

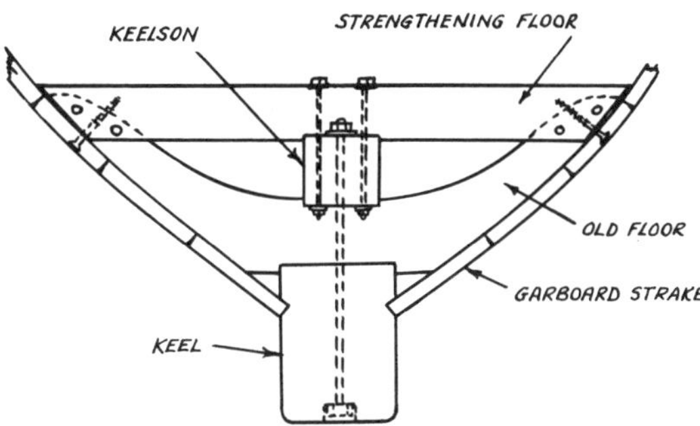

Fig. 24: Strengthening floor on top of keelson

sole or the stowage of ballast.

Excellent knees of all types can be made from metal and glass reinforced plastics. The best shape is usually a web (sometimes having lightening holes through it) with flanges along the edges, at right angles to the web, to give rigidity and to take holes for the fastenings. Such knees are simpler to install than wooden ones, but the angles and bevels of the edges cannot be corrected to make a good fit. To counteract this, metal and g.r.p. knees are often mounted on thin chocks of hardwood.

Knees of the above type when attached to wood are usually fastened with bolts. For neatness, the threads can be cut off close to the nuts and riveted over. Traditional or laminated wooden knees are best fastened with copper clenches. For small dinghy knees the shorter fastenings can be copper nails and roves, but for the long fastenings near to the throat of a knee, lengths of copper rod must be used. For dinghies $\frac{1}{8}$ in. (3 mm.) rod is common; $\frac{1}{4}$ in. (6 mm.) may be found in a four berth cruiser and $\frac{1}{2}$ in. (12 mm.) in a 50-footer.

An exact hole must be bored for long copper nails or rod. If only slightly tight the metal will buckle on driving and may shear off when extraction is attempted. Greasing, or coating the metal with soft soap before driving makes things easier.

Any length of steel rod can be brazed to the end of an ordinary Morse twist bit to enable long holes to be bored, but where an electric drill is available elongated bits can be fabricated by heating the end of a piece of silver steel rod of suitable diameter, hammering out a spade-shaped tip, grinding the end to a 120° arrowhead angle and hardening this as described in Chapter 5. Either type of drill may be ground down on the outside until test holes made by it make a neat push fit for the copper rod.

For rod up to $\frac{3}{16}$ in. (4 mm.) diameter, a standard rove can be riveted over each end. However, the hole through the rove may have to be drilled out slightly larger for roves cannot be forced on to rod with a hollow punch in the manner already described for copper boat nails which have square corners capable of reaming a rove hole. For all larger sizes of rod, plain copper washers are used at each end. These can usually be obtained from boatyards but tool shops sometimes stock the smaller sizes which are used for riveting leather belting.

Riveting over both ends at the same time is quite a tricky business single-handed and especially with the larger sizes of rod it proves best to form an upset head at one end as described on page 50 before driving the rod into the hole. Do not forget to slip the washer or rove under the upset head before driving!

CENTREBOARD CASES

Most sailing dinghies have a centreboard, centre plate or dagger board which houses inside an internal casing or trunk. Larger cruising yachts also use this device and their trunks can be very massive affairs with sides thicker than 3 in. (75 mm.), supported either side by large half-floor knees.

When such a structure starts to leak and the treatment of any caulked seams does not help, major reconstruction may be necessary.

When the plate is lowered under way the racking stresses on the case are very high and the requisite strength must always be built in when converting a lifeboat or other working craft to sail efficiently. The most damaging conditions occur when running aground unexpectedly.

Dinghy cases are normally made from solid wood as shown in Fig. 25, attached to the hog with large screws driven upwards, the joint being either resin-glued or sealed with bedding compound. Enormous strength is added by securing the centre thwart to the top of the case and this joint must always be maintained firmly.

The usual source of leakage is along the hog joint. This can be sealed quite readily by screwing fillets (beadings) of matching wood set in sealing mastic along each side (as shown in the drawing) and, if necessary, around the ends as well.

Such fillets are not usually fastened in both directions to stop any movement between the case and the hog, additional screws through the planking and hog into the sides of the case making a more secure job. However, if the screw holding is poor and the hog is wide enough, it may be preferable to fit oversized fillets and set them in resin glue with screws into the hog and into the case sides to arrest any movement. Leaks through the ends of the case are rare and are generally best sealed by inserting tight fitting strips of wood inside the case, nailed to the end posts and set in mastic.

Sometimes a side panel splits along the grain, often due to the shrinkage of unseasoned timber. Where appearance is important it may be possible to glue a spline of matching wood into the crack or to fill with resin putty. Otherwise, covering over with a thin batten set in mastic and secured with closely spaced screws as shown in Fig. 25 is generally better. If this looks unsightly, it may

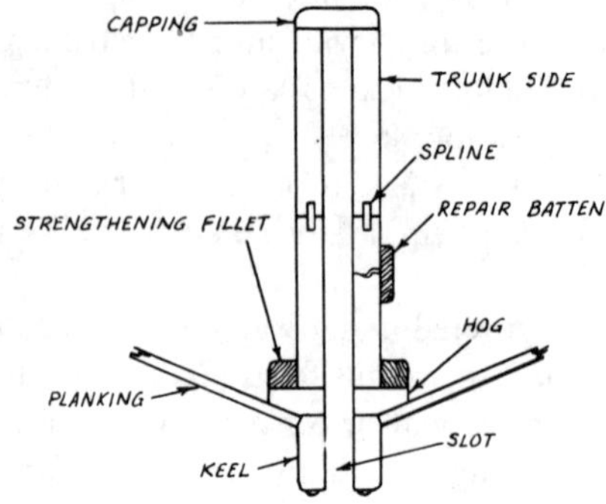

Fig. 25: Repairs to centreboard case

help to fit a similar matching strip on the other side of the case. Alternatively, a larger covering panel may be used, continuing right down to the hog.

Especially on cruising boats, an area of rot may appear in the side of the case. It may be possible to cut one plank right out and let in a new one with caulked seams top and bottom or perhaps using seam battens on the outside. Remember, where the sides are formed from planks the original seams may have been rabbeted or splined together. When cutting out such a plank, saw cuts may have to be made beyond the original seams to enable sound, new, caulked seams to be formed.

Some centre-plate trunks are made from mild steel galvanized after fabrication. These assemblies frequently last forty years without trouble but internal rusting may occur where the plate scrapes against the sides, while any leakage at the hog is difficult to cure without complete removal. If any strengthening by welding is necessary all zinc must be ground away from the old surface to ensure a sound job.

Most dinghy centreboards and dagger boards are made from solid wood, this being stronger than plywood or g.r.p. of equal thickness in the one direction required. Solid mahogany or similar hardwood may warp or crack and although more troublesome to make, a board laminated in two or three thicknesses (all with the grain running longways) makes a much sounder job. Any built-in weight or edge band should be carefully removed from the old board and re-used.

BIG BOARDS AND RUDDERS

Cruising yacht boards are sometimes built up from planks splined together and fastened with through bolts. Boring edgewise through each plank accurately is difficult for the amateur to do and sometimes straps are used across the board sunk flush with the surfaces, through-fastened to each other in pairs with copper clenches.

Rudders and leeboards are often made similarly but are likely to receive regular repairs being more readily inspected. A rudder made from one or two wide planks is prone to splitting along the grain and can often be strengthened by driving one or more *drift* bolts from the trailing edge well past the position of the split.

A drift bolt consists of a rod of galvanized steel with an *upset* head (or sometimes a screw thread formed on one end) and a vague point at the other end. If the correct-sized pilot hole is bored all the way, the rod can be driven into this and should never move.

A washer is placed under an upset head before driving and a special cap is screwed on before driving a drift bolt with threaded end. The cap may be made by drilling a blind hole into the end of a piece of steel bar and tapping the hole with the correct-sized thread. After driving, the cap is unscrewed, a washer is slipped on, followed by a nut which can be riveted over after tightening if required.

The correct drill size is important. If too small it may be impossible to drive to completion without buckling the head or splitting the wood. If too large, the rod will fail to grip properly. Normally, with standard size rod and standard size drills the thickness of the galvanizing is sufficient to ensure a tight grip.

Long-handled wood augers tend to make a slightly oversized hole and may wander off course if not of the bull-nosed variety with no point. The other types of extended drill previously described can be ground to suit. Withdraw the drill frequently to clear the swarf. Cramp two battens along the sides of the rudder or other piece to be bored, protruding beyond the edge to act as a guide for the drill.

Instead of using drift bolts for strengthening rudders and centreboards, ordinary screwed bolts can be used if a nut plate is fitted into a notch morticed into (or right through) the timber well beyond the weak place. Graving pieces can be glued into the notches on completion to create an invisible repair. Similar nut plates are widely used for engine bearer bolts (see Chapter 9) and for deadwood fastenings.

Whereas drift bolts must be of galvanized iron to hold securely and to be driven without buckling, with nut plates, bolts of bronze or stainless steel may be preferable. Studding (threaded rod) is available from some chandlery shops in these materials, and can be used for making the bolts by merely cutting to length.

If a galvanized centre-plate gets buckled there is very rarely any need to make a new one. Bulges and bends in steel plate can be removed by correct peening though it may be necessary to get an experienced man to deal with thicknesses greater than $\frac{3}{8}$ in. (9 mm.). A plate must be regalvanized afterwards or metallized with zinc to a thickness of 0·006 in. (150 microns).

Removing the centreboard of a sailing dinghy may be almost an annual ritual so there is plenty of warning about wear in the pivot bolt system. On cruising boats the plate is normally removed only when it jams, gets damaged, or has a broken chain.

It pays to have a look at the pivot bolt more frequently than this, as its failure under way could be critical. Abrasion continues even while a boat is swinging gently at moorings and a brass pivot bolt can wear through quite rapidly. Do not attempt to remove the bolt while the craft is still afloat as the spacing washers which align the centre-plate in its case might get lost in the drink. Furthermore, it will prove difficult to lift the plate to enable it to come clear of the recess which will have undoubtedly been worn in the pin.

The best time to drop a centre-plate is when the yacht is laid-up ashore. She can then be chocked up using jacks to give clearance below the keel or it may be possible to dig a trench beneath her.

REPAIRING PLASTICS

Full information on the mixing and handling of resins, tools for the job and tailoring glass materials are given in *Complete Amateur Boat Building*, while details of minor repairs, surface cracks and sheathing can be found in *Boat Maintenance*.

Big chandlery stores stock g.r.p. repair kits in various sizes (see Plate 15) and the use of these (often containing some tools and

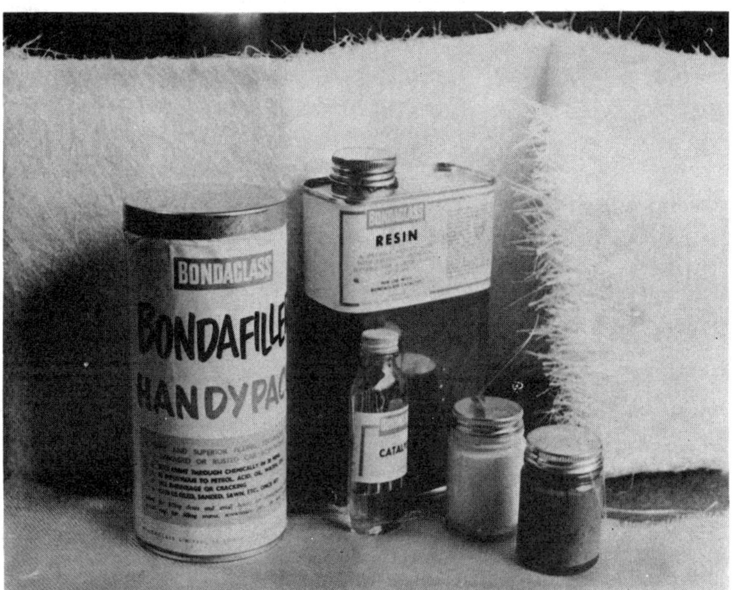

Plate 15: Typical g.r.p. repair kit

instruction sheets) simplifies work for the amateur tremendously. Check on the tools included, for you might need in addition a putty knife, a serrated Skarsten scraper and an old hacksaw blade (for roughing the surfaces), a Dreadnought rasp, Surform plane, coarse disc sander, masking tape and sheets of cellophane or polythene. The popular types of glass material in use are illustrated in Plate 16.

The most common damage to a plastics dinghy involves splitting of the skin due to striking a submerged pile or by dropping from a

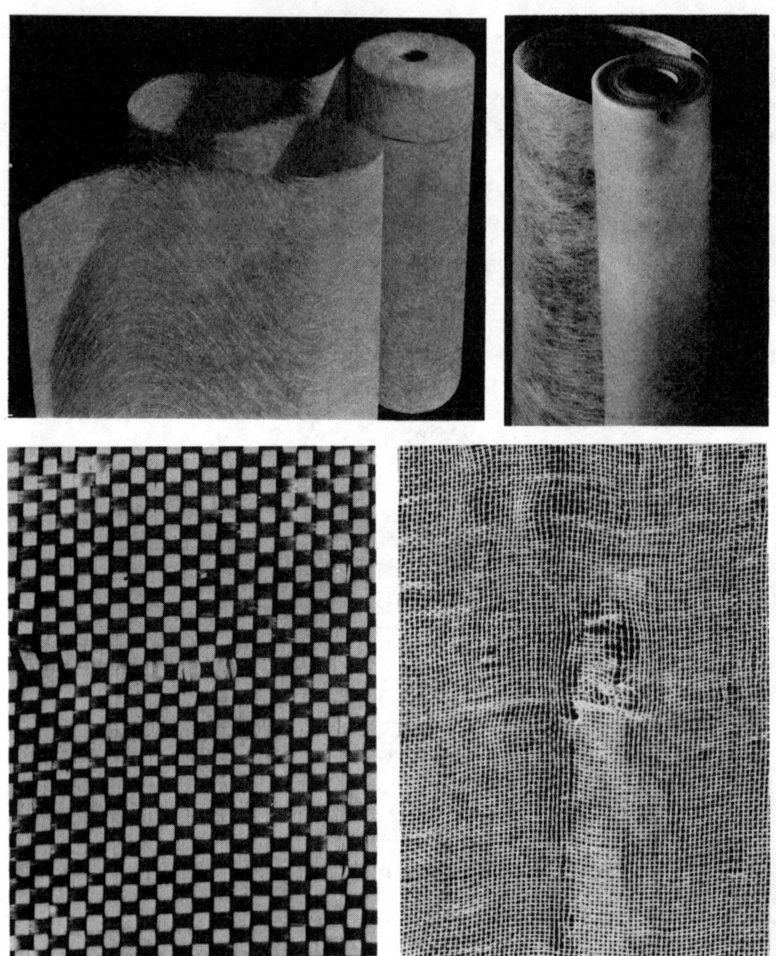

Plate 16. Commonly used glass fibre materials

Upper row: *chopped strand mat; surfacing tissue*
Lower row: *woven rovings cloth; scrim cloth*

height. If the internal appearance is not too important, repairs are easy to carry out by bonding two or three layers of glass cloth to the inside of the hull, then filling the crack flush on the outside.

It must be explained that fresh resin does not bond perfectly to old glass-fibre. Consequently, repair work must be done with great care to avoid disastrous failures. All surfaces must be dry, grease-free and dust-free. The atmosphere must be dry and the temperature preferably over 60°F (15°C). Bonding surfaces must be conscientiously roughened, with a generous overlap beyond any damage.

Epoxy resin is greatly superior to polyester (as used for all boat shells) where adhesion to old plastics is concerned and the extra cost is not too important for small repair jobs.

Cracks are treated as simple repairs, for, unlike large holes, they do not require an external mould to re-create the necessary fair curvature of the hull. However, some cracks do require support to ensure that the two parts keep in alignment.

The crack must always be opened out with a rasp to leave firm clean edges, allowing the outside to be flushed off with glass-fibre putty, rubbed down and polished. An attempt can be made to match the hull colour with pigment, but painting over afterwards will be found easier, especially for a large repair in a conspicuous place.

The patch should be the same thickness as the hull. The innermost layer of mat or cloth should extend at least 1 in. (25 mm.) beyond the damage, the second layer 2 in. (50 mm.), the third layer 3 in. (75 mm.) etc. The patch must always be inside the hull, unless some obstacle prevents this. The hull should be tilted so that the job is near to horizontal, but be careful to wipe away resin which runs through the crack. Alternatively, the outside can be covered with tape, and the crack filled (with a putty of pigmented resin mixed with chopped up glass-fibre strands) prior to laying up the patch.

BIG HOLES

Simple repairs can be completed in a few hours, but extensive damage may necessitate returning a boat to the makers, or obtaining from them a section of the hull laid up in the original female mould. In between these extremes, the amateur can undertake complicated repairs taking perhaps two or three days to complete.

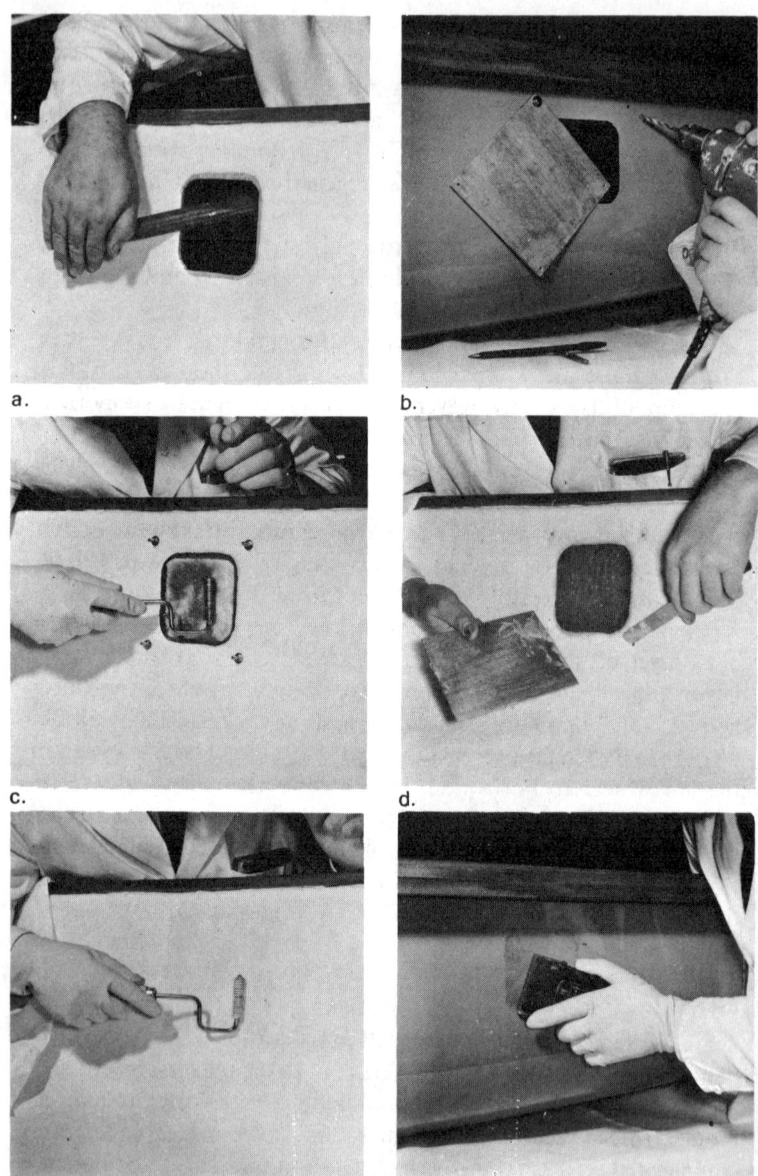

Plate 17: A plastics dinghy repair

Although a collision may not create a hole as big as your head, a large area may be delaminated. Some boatyards suggest that this bruise should be pushed out to its correct curvature and a patch laid up inside. This is a poor way to do the job. The outside surface rarely looks perfect, and moisture may get through the crazed resin to the fibres or between the two skins if bonding is not perfect.

The only proper procedure is to cut out a circular panel (or rectangular with well-rounded corners) at least 1 in. (25 mm.) beyond any of the damaged area. With a former bent to the outside surface, the hole is then filled to the original hull thickness with layers of impregnated mat, and additional layers are then continued inside with a generous overlap all around. The idea is shown diagrammatically in Fig 26a. For a cheaper and quicker job the method in Fig 26b is often quite satisfactory, but having no key, the patch could fall out one day.

Should the boat have moulded strengthening ribs inside, the Fig 26c method is essential. The rib is laid up over the same type of core as used originally (rope, polythene pipe, or aluminium top hat extrusion) and the final two layers of mat are taken over the rib.

Having cut out the aperture using an electric drill with jig-saw attachment or a metal working pad saw, the chamfers must be shaped using a disc sander, or Surform tool. The inner surface surrounding the aperture must also have proper roughening treatment.

If the bevels shown in Figs. 26a and 26c are made at about 45°, it should be possible to work the layers of mat under the lip fairly easily. Some people find this easier if each layer is impregnated

---

a. *Trimmed hole being chamfered on the inside.*
b. *After covering with releasing agent, a former is attached to the outside.*
c. *Following a gel coat, layers of mat are laid up in resin.*
d. *The bolt holes are stopped over on removing the former.*
e. *Covering the repair inside with a layer of surfacing mat.*
f. *The pigmented gel coat is flatted down prior to polishing.*

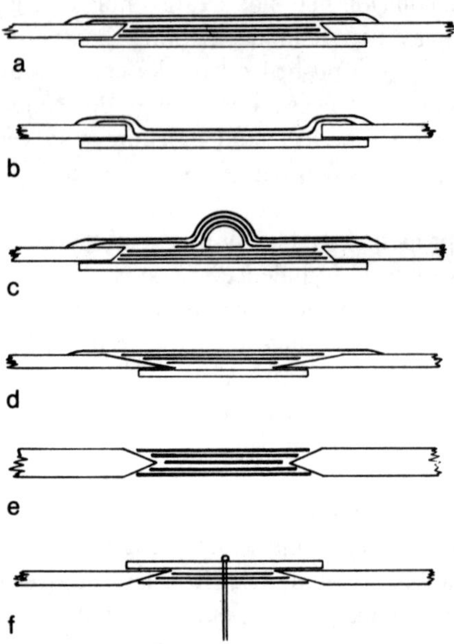

Fig. 26: Repairing holes in a g.r.p. hull

over a sheet of cellophane on the bench, stripping away the cellophane as the mat is pressed into the hole.

USING EPOXY RESIN

Taking advantage of the extra strength and bonding properties of epoxy resin, a different technique can be used. By cutting a wide bevel (3 to 4 times the laminate thickness) on the inside, the job appears as in Fig. 26d and only one layer is required overlapping all around. This method eliminates the problem of getting the mat into the undercut bevel, and results in a much cleaner external finish which requires little filler. Such a repair is illustrated in Plate 17.

On thick laminates where an internal patch would be unsightly, the double 60° bevel of Fig. 26e is permissible using epoxy resin. To obviate tucking mat under the bevel, the job can be tackled in two parts, provided both sides of the laminate are clear for working. A former is made to fit one side which is rebated to come through to the apex of the bevels. Having laid up the one half-thickness and allowed it to cure, the former is removed, and the other side completed.

Sometimes all repair work must be effected from the outside of a hull, due to tanks, etc., inside, or when construction is of the sandwich type. The hole must be cut oval or rectangular to allow a permanent former to be inserted inside, overlapping at least 1 in. (25 mm.) all around (Fig. 26f).

Such a former can be preformed g.r.p., or perhaps a sheet of aluminium. To hold it in place, two holes are drilled at its centre, and a loop of copper wire passed through, secured to a firm support outside. Lay-up is completed from the outside, and a sheet of surface mat is useful to get the best possible finish. The copper wire is cut off flush after curing, and sanded down with the new surface.

Plate 18: A rudder trunk sheathed with epoxy

Mixing epoxy resin (as with polyester) must be very thoroughly done. To ensure this, the resin supplied with some kits is coloured white, while the catalyst is black. For large jobs, it pays to use a paddle attachment on an electric drill for mixing. Special wooden mixing spoons are supplied with some kits.

Glass-fibre repairs can be made to plywood, cold and hot moulded, steel and light alloy hulls, using methods similar to those described above, and epoxy resin is generally considered the best choice. A leaky rudder trunk lined with lead (Plate 18) can often be sealed by sheathing with epoxy/g.r.p.

The external former shown in Figs. 26a to 26d, may be covered with a film of cellophane or polythene to ensure easy release, and it must be propped against the hull securely enough to allow for the pressure of stippling and rolling. On very small jobs one can sometimes get by with cardboard and adhesive tape. If possible, always roll the boat over to get the repair surface close to the horizontal position.

Any metal fittings affected should be removed before starting repairs and properly bonded in if this is how they were originally fixed.

FOAM SANDWICH DAMAGE

When rebuilding extensive damage, part of the core thickness must be sacrificed to increase the skin thickness – particularly around the edges of the repair.

Most hull damage produces a bigger hole through the outer skin than the inner. In this case, lay-up the smaller opening first, as in Figs 26a or 26b. Build back the core using pieces of the original material set in resin putty, or entirely from a mixture of resin and coarse sawdust.

Leave a gap between the core and the outer skin to enable a good thickness of new g.r.p. to be tucked behind it. Continue laying-up to a flush outer surface, then render smooth with resin putty.

With the increased thickness, chopped strand mat is suitable, though cloth would doubtless have been used originally.

(For details of finishing g.r.p. repairs see p. 301.)

5

Repairing Decks

Without counting metal and plastics constructions, many different systems of timber decking can be found, according to the age and size of a vessel.

Craft shorter than about 40 ft. (12 m.) traditionally have decks of tongue-and-grooved boarding covered with painted canvas. The modern equivalent have plywood decking covered with P.V.C. coated fabric (such as *Trakmark*) or sheathed with g.r.p. or *Cascover*.

Larger vessels traditionally had laid decks of solid timber planks with caulked seams. Teak was used in high class work while some form of pine found favour for fishing boats and other types of working craft. The teak normally had a scrubbed finish except for some varnished areas not often walked upon. Pine decks were sometimes painted.

The modern equivalent using teak has the same appearance as the traditional but consists of a base of thick marine plywood with thin planks of teak glued on top of it. The seams do not need caulking with cotton and are normally filled with one of the black synthetic rubber compositions. Timber fishing boats are still built on traditional lines and no better or cheaper substitute has been found for caulked solid pine decking.

On sailing yachts laid teak decking (including the modern type) is *swept*, the planks being approximately parallel to the covering board or outer edge of the deck. On motor cruisers the planks are more often laid straight fore-and-aft. Laid pine decking is usually arranged this latter way on all types of craft.

LAID DECK REPAIRS

Replacing short lengths of straight deck planking is much simpler than similar topside and bottom work. Butts are always made on top of a deck beam as butt blocks would look unsightly below and a short lipped scarf is made at each joint (see Fig. 27) to avoid

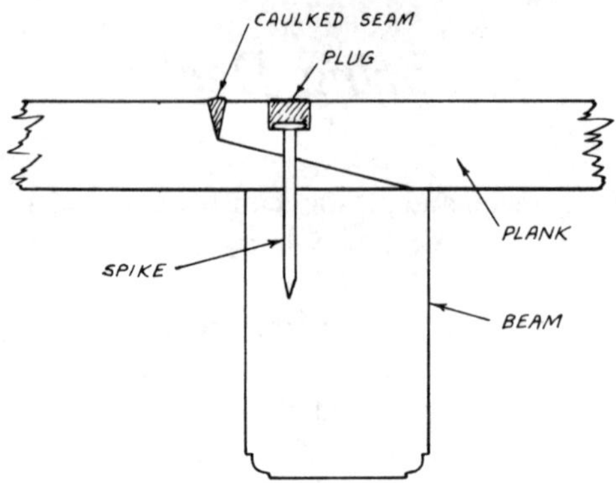

Fig. 27: Lipped scarf joint in deck repair

having two sets of fastenings close to the sides of a beam, possibly causing the beam to split. The exposed lip of the scarf is caulked and therefore looks exactly the same as a plain butt joint from the outside.

Replacing short lengths of swept deck planking is not always so simple, for although in a new deck the long lengths of planking may be wedged to conform with the curvature, short lengths prove too stiff for this treatment.

Sawing to shape from wider timber is the usual way to make short lengths and enables an exact fit to be achieved more readily than by steaming. A close fit is advisable to minimize any possible future leaks.

Although laid teak or pine decks of good specification are thick enough to withstand all likely deck loads,when long lengths have to be replaced by short ones (perhaps only spanning the distance between two deck beams), it usually pays to increase the thickness slightly on a short repair piece, making it flush on the outside surface but projecting slightly underneath. The usual V-joints along the deckhead seams will mask a fair discrepancy, but the new piece will need to be planed down to the original thickness just where the ends rest upon the deck beams.

If a plank does bend slightly under deck loads leaks will soon ensue. The laid decks on many old-type racing yachts were made as thin as possible to reduce weight, and strength was added by inserting bronze dowels across the seams just below the caulking Vee. These added strength in similar fashion to the spline between the joints of tongued and grooved boarding.

Planks with edge dowels cannot be removed without breaking them up. The usual way to do this is to make two saw cuts 1 in. (25 mm.) apart down the centre of the plank between the deck beams, remove the core piece, crosscut the ends, then prise each side piece in turn away from the dowels to freedom. To start the saw cuts, bore two 1¼ in. (32 mm.) diameter holes through the centre of the plank close to the beam at one end, chisel out between the holes leaving a long enough gap to get the saw through, and bore one similar hole at the other end of the run where the saw cuts terminate. This is the procedure often adopted for cutting the centreboard slot through a keel or hog.

As it proves almost impossible to fit dowels when the planking is renewed, the simplest alternative is to fit a pad of thick marine plywood underneath the deckhead, from beam-to-beam and fastened to the adjacent planks as well as the new one. If there are not too many of these pads they can be made to look shipshape and for some special purpose other than repairs! The plywood should be rot-proofed and laid in bedding compound.

It should be noted that all pine timber used for decking needs to be *rift-sawn*. This means that the grain, when viewed on the end of a plank, runs vertically or close to that direction. If the grain is almost horizontal (*slash-sawn*) splinters of wood are liable to break away from the surface and cause injury. Where a few slash-sawn planks must be used, lay them with the concave aspect of the end grain facing downwards. The grain direction is not so important with teak as with softwood.

CANVAS-COVERED DECKS

If well laid and maintained, decks of tongue-and-grooved boarding or marine plywood covered with painted canvas or

Trakmark prove highly satisfactory on small yachts and help to keep the weight down. Details of how to repair and re-cover such decks are given in *Boat Maintenance* and the following notes are intended to augment that information.

Small areas of rot commonly appear in this type of deck, the warning signs being springiness when walked upon and blistering of the paint underneath. A typical repair job in four stages is pictured in Plate 19.

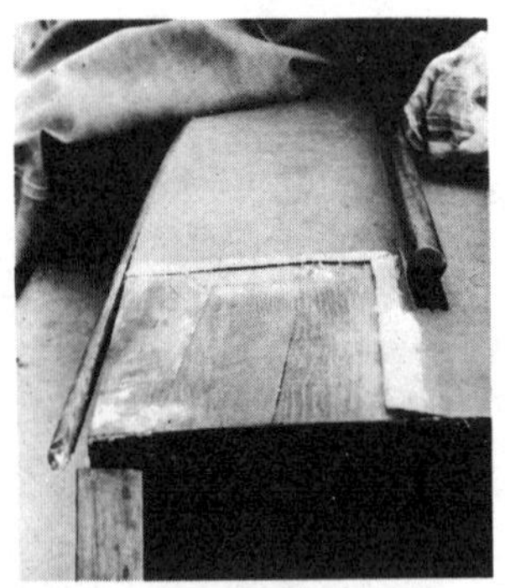

Plate 19: Repairing a rotten area of deck

The canvas is cut away neatly by running a sharp knife along a straightedge around it, the faulty timber is cut out to the midway point of the nearest deck beam, new timber is fitted in to fill the gap and the area is covered with new canvas, laid in adhesive or secured around the edges with closely spaced copper tacks.

As mentioned before, new planks replaced between two adjacent deck beams are much weaker than the original planks in long lengths and are further weakened if the tongues across the seams are cut away. Increased thickness or chocks underneath are therefore needed with canvas as well as laid decks. Where more than one plank is to be replaced, the tongues and grooves can be left on all except the outer ones.

The problems with plywood decking are rather different. Little strength is lost by replacing the original with a small new panel but the new piece will tend to be dead flat whereas the original will have assumed the camber of the deck beams and this curvature automatically makes the surface more rigid. To complete a perfect job it may be necessary to laminate the new panel from two sheets of plywood half the original thickness, gluing these together over a jig producing the desired permanent curvature. Alternatively, thicker plywood can be used, the upper surface at least being curved by planing.

To avoid the necessity for reinforcing pads underneath the seams, it may be possible to plane rebates to permit the joints to be half-lapped and glued. This can be done with T&G boarding as well as plywood. Rot-proofing treatment is advisable on all new softwood in addition to the luting of joints and surface painting.

Boatyards frequently use deck canvas weighing only 6 oz. per sq. yd. (200 g. per m^2), but it pays to use material of at least 12 oz. per sq. yd. (400 g. per m^2) for renewals, making a longer lasting job, especially when poor maintenance allows the paint covering to wear off.

Boatyards usually glue the canvas down with wet paint. This has the disadvantage that after some time the canvas may crack along the deck seams. Laying canvas in paint is a very messy job so it generally proves best to paint the planking thoroughly first and let this dry before canvasing. Side decks tend to lie hollow and it may be necessary to stick the canvas down onto such surfaces to keep it firm.

Although all canvas seams can be sewn by hand or machine to enable the whole lot to be tailored in one piece, most amateurs prefer to work in panels, driving closely-spaced copper tacks along each lapped joint. Folding the edge under before tacking is advisable with thin canvas, but this creates a hump with thick cloth; it proves better to leave the raw edge exposed, protected by arranging the tacks to almost touch each other. If a selvedge can be utilized along some of the laps, so much the better. Sealer between the parts ensures water-tightness.

All deck fittings must be taken off as well as the edge beadings before re-canvasing. Old canvas which was laid in wet paint may have to be burnt off as chemical strippers have little effect. Protruding deck nails should be punched down and stopped over, while any proud plank edges must be planed or sanded flush.

New beadings are usually necessary as the old ones may have been nailed on making it difficult to remove them intact. The angle between coaming and deck is rarely a true right angle so the backs of most quadrant mouldings will need to be planed to ensure a snug fit. Note that quadrant and half-round beading made out of lead is available to bend around corner posts and masts. Beadings are most satisfactory if attached with wood-screws, but barbed ring nails are cheaper and quicker if it seems that the beading will never need to be removed again!

Before laying canvas ensure that all sharp edges are well rounded. The life of the canvas can be increased tremendously if, instead of placing the half-round sheer beading flush with the deck as in normal boatyard practice, the beading is positioned $\frac{1}{2}$ in. (12 mm.) lower down the topsides so that the edge of the deck can be rounded off generously. The same method can be applied to a cabin top or wheelhouse.

The most frequent repair jobs to canvas decks are made necessary by cracking along hidden plank seams, accidental tearing or cutting of the surface, abrasion due to failure to maintain good paint covering and splitting along sharp edges.

All but the last trouble can be treated effectively by covering over with a smear of resin putty, or glass-fibre tape set in epoxy resin. Alternatively, it may be possible to utilize several thick layers of Dekaplex or a similar plastics deck coating.

Traditionally, small damage is repaired by fixing a patch of canvas over the spot, rather like the *tingle* on the outside of a hull. Such a patch is usually laid in thick paint, the edges are turned under all around and closely spaced copper tacks are driven as for a canvas seam. A much neater job results if the patch is glued down without turning the edges under. Impact adhesive such as *Evostik* works quite well if the old deck paint is rubbed down thoroughly to a clean smooth surface. If well-doped with paint this may last until a complete re-canvasing is necessary. Large glued patches are generally unsatisfactory as the edges tend to peel through shoe damage.

The fourth type of repair listed above is often the most troublesome, for to be effective the new material needs to be lapped *underneath* the old. The best procedure is to remove the sheer beading and footrail, trim off the old canvas to a line parallel with the deck edge and clear of the footrail, tuck the new canvas under the old (bedded in thick paint), secure with copper tacks close to the edge of the old canvas, apply undercoating and then replace all fittings.

Deck canvas should last for thirty years if made from the correct gauge of cotton duck, prestretched before use, further stretched during laying and laid over a fair surface with no sharp edges. Use sealer along all joints where future leakage might occur and make sure deck fittings cannot dig into the surface when under load, mounting them on wooden chocks if necessary. Lay canvas dry unless a hollow deck surface causes the canvas to pull away. In that case, bed in wet paint or special deck canvas glue. Dope canvas with coats of thin paint until the weave is filled and then use standard anti-slip deck paint.

PLASTICS DECK MATERIALS

Embossed P.V.C. coated synthetic fibre materials (such as *Nautolex* and *Trakmark*) are more permanent than canvas, being impervious to rot and very hard wearing, but they are more expensive and difficult to lay. The embossed surface has excellent anti-slip properties, but this may wear smooth in time and when the special deck paint is used to maintain a bright appearance, many coatings tend to fill the indentations.

Each maker supplies an impact adhesive with toothed applicator for easy spreading. A smooth well-primed deck surface is ideal. The glue is applied to both deck and covering material in accordance with the makers' instructions and as soon as the glue has set, the material may be laid and rolled down firmly.

All tailoring of cloth must be done before applying any glue. As the position of each piece cannot be adjusted once stuck, it pays to keep panels in easy-to-handle sizes, a few helpers being essential to enable the sheets to be lowered accurately to their marks.

To ensure easy handling, panels should not have any greater dimension than about 3 ft. (1 m.) for single-handed laying, 6 ft. (2 m.) with two operators, or 10 ft. (3 m.) with four people. All joints should overlap by about 1 in. (25 mm.). Butt joints look neat but always pull apart in time and are never entirely leakproof. Butt joints can be used if covered over with half-round aluminium strips laid in bedding compound and secured with countersunk aluminium woodscrews. Lapped joints can be made neater by rubbing down the embossed surface of the underneath piece. These glued joints should be hammered to ensure that the impact adhesive bonds firmly.

Trakmark is available only in rolls of 50 in. (1270 mm.) width. An imitation laid teak deck surface is marketed in this material, the seams being embossed in realistic fashion.

Instead of re-canvasing or laying Trakmark, an old deck may be given a permanent sheathing of glass reinforced plastics, or nylon cloth and vinyl paint as in the *Cascover* process. See later in this chapter.

BEAM REPAIRS

In wooden craft the deck beams may range from the thin strips of mahogany found in sailing dinghies and motor runabouts, through the delicate sawn, steamed, or laminated square sectioned beams of the average small cruiser, to the massive chunks of oak found in an M.F.V. or trading schooner conversion. In all cases, repairs are usually necessitated either by shakes or other defects in the timber or through rotting from prolonged deck leaks.

Repairs to beams which are not normally in view may be a simple matter of doubling up with a new piece fastened alongside. Where neatness is important the job can become a work of art necessitating the complete or partial removal of the old beam and scarfing in new timber. A sagging beam which is not rotten may be reinforced by bolting steel *flitch-plates* to the sides. If copper clenches are used instead of bolts the result of this method can be made to look neater than doubling up with timber.

Before any templates are made for cutting new beams, it may be necessary to jack up the old beam to regain its original shape exactly. This is much more likely to be necessary when several adjacent beams are damaged. A typical flitched repair is shown in Fig. 28a and scarfing a new centre section into a beam in Fig. 28b.

Beam ends are generally dovetailed into the shelves (Fig. 28c) and rot is not uncommon in these joints. Correct replacement is only possible by first removing the deck, but by gluing wedges at the ends as shown in Fig. 28d, a new beam can be inserted by placing it diagonally between the adjacent beams and swivelling it into position.

In most craft the shelf butts tight up under the deck, as shown for side decks in Fig. 42. In that case, you cannot poke both beam ends into place in unison, even forgoing proper dovetails. It can be done by scarfing the beam or by laminating from thin strips, but the strongest and quickest (albeit ugliest) way is to plant a chock firmly inside the shelf and dovetail each beam end into that. This method enables a rotted shelf joint to be cut out and re-made in sound timber without disturbing the original beam. Fitting is no more difficult with topside flare, provided one makes the chock notch to slide up over the beam dovetail. Assemble the parts close to the next beam where the boat is slightly wider. Slide the whole thing along to its correct location, then bolt (or glue and screw) the chocks against the shelves.

When nailing through the deck into the light section beams found on most yachts, struts should be erected from the beam to

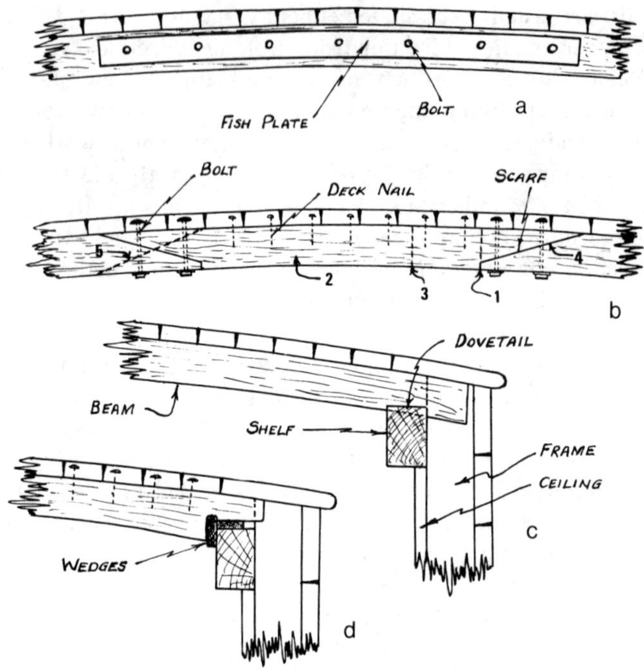

Fig. 28: Methods of repairing deck beams

the hog or frames to stop the vibration which prevents the fastenings from pulling up tightly.

Although full length replacement beams can be installed on similar lines by laminating flat strips *in situ*, great difficulty may be experienced when trying to plane down the sides flush and smooth. Another way to eliminate the need for wedges at each end is to laminate in two halves with vertical joint, one end only of each piece notching over the top of the shelf.

Scarfing a new beam section into place as shown in Fig. 28b is a true bit of shipwright's artistry which can be done quite successfully by the amateur if tackled in the right way. If well done, it makes a superior job to any of the previous methods where applicable and its success can be a source of lasting pride for the enthusiast!

First make vertical saw cuts (position 1 in Fig. 28b). A curved electrician's floorboard saw is the best tool to use for this as damage to the deckhead when nearing the end of the cuts is less likely than when using a tenon saw. Masking tape stuck to the deckhead may help to save scratching. Break away the damaged portion of the old beam (2) between the two saw cuts using a broad chisel and mallet. A further series of vertical saw cuts (3) along this length will speed up the chiselling process considerably. Beware of striking the deck fastenings with these tools, substituting old worn ones if there is any risk.

Next saw the scarf faces (4) making the length of each scarf about five times the depth of the beam. Mark out the lines carefully on each side, sawing accurately to simplify the later fitting of the new piece.

The new piece will be simpler to fit if the scarfs are cut in the direction marked (5), but this leaves a feather edge to the exposed part of each scarf which is not considered good practice. If the saw cuts are made erratically, one warped one way and one the other, it may be impossible to get the new piece into place with tight scarf joints. Scarfs cut as in (5) can be trued up using a sharp chisel or block plane after sawing, but when in direction (4) any adjustment is very difficult to make owing to the direction of the wood grain.

If the scarf has been cut accurately one hardboard template should be sufficient to enable the repair piece to be marked out. If the scarfs are mis-shapen, it may be advisable to make a template for each side of the beam. When accurate scarfs result after some time has been spent offering up the new piece, marking high spots and shaving down accordingly, resin glue (with good gap-filling properties) can be used on the scarf joints to augment the through bolts.

If only half the area of a joint meets accurately it may be worth while to use glue. Otherwise a dry joint (with the surfaces well primed or luted) may prove quite satisfactory when tightly fastened, any gaps being stopped over before painting to hide the imperfections.

In any case it would be impossible to get an accurate fit right into the pointed top corner of each scarf and it would be quite in order to saw off the feather edge on the new piece creating a gap to be stopped on completion.

The big advantage of cutting the scarf joints as marked (5) is that a true fit can be assured whereas with method (4), if a little too much wood is trimmed off the new piece becomes too short and may have to be scrapped. With the scarf splaying outwards at the bottom, by making the new piece slightly deeper than necessary, if too much is cut off one scarf face, the top of the beam can be planed down to put matters right.

Especially on small beams it pays to make good glued scarfs so that screw fastenings driven from underneath will suffice. This obviates the need to bore through the deck. On large beams through-bolts are always advisable and copper clenches make the neatest job, especially if the washers are countersunk into the underside of the beam.

Where nuts must be used, those in the thick part of the scarf can be sunk out of sight, but the use of thin stainless steel bolts is advisable to keep the nut size small. Remember that a small highly stressed bolt requires a washer under the head to spread the load, as a conventional sized head may chew into the wood. For all except the thinnest softwood decking there is no need to sink the head right down onto the hardwood beam. Where this is done, the large hole through the deck would need to be exceptionally well plugged with a glued dowel or resin putty to avoid leakage.

Where *carlines* notch into a beam, repair work is made more difficult. On small craft, carlines usually come into one side only of a beam, leaving the other side free for doubling up or flitching. The half-beams stretching between the carlines and shelf under the side decks of boats with cabin tops can be renewed quite easily if, instead of trying to dovetail the ends, lodging knees are fitted. The same idea is useful to augment the strength at the ends of any full length replacement beam and hanging knees of galvanized steel straps or welded T-section can also be incorporated with advantage. Tie bars alongside the half-beams (from carline to shelf) can strengthen a side deck greatly.

CAULKING

As described in Chapter 3, caulked seams are formed with a V-shaped opening to the outside. To prevent leakage, caulking cotton (or oakum) is forced into the seam to within about $\frac{1}{8}$ in. (3 mm.) of the surface and the remainder is then *payed* with some kind of stopping to enable a flush finish to be achieved.

Traditionally, the comparatively wide seams on working craft are caulked with oakum. This consists of strands of hemp impregnated with stockholm tar and pressed into 56 lb. (50 kg.) bales and is still obtainable through chandlers. To prepare oakum for caulking, random bunches are torn from the bale, teased out to the maximum length to create a loose diameter of about 1 in. (25 mm.) and this is then rolled tightly between the palm of one's hand and one's thigh to produce a twisted strand about $\frac{3}{8}$ in. (9 mm.) in diameter. The next length is overlapped about 3 in. (76 mm.) and rolled tightly so that a rope of considerable length can be made up and coiled down into a cardboard box to enable a continuous supply to be available when work starts on the hull or deck.

On the tarred hulls of working craft oakum is traditionally payed with hot pitch applied with a flat brush. Amateurs usually prefer to pay with tar putty, which is made by beating a mixture of whiting and coal tar until it reaches the consistency of ordinary glazier's putty. Any type of paying must be capable of clinging tenaciously to the oakum as well as to the planking edges. All the seams on a tarred hull (and below the waterline on any craft using black varnish) may be filled with *Fibrous Caulking Composition*, sold by K. M. Gibbs Ltd., a black putty containing chopped strands which fills the role of oakum and paying, simplifying caulking work tremendously.

Yacht seams are generally caulked with cotton and payed with hard or soft stopping. Caulking cotton comes in 1 lb. (500 g.) balls, each composed of one endless rope containing eight loose strands of soft white cotton. Before starting to caulk, a long length should be pulled from the centre of the ball, three or four of the strands (according to the size of the seam) parted from the remainder, and these strands made up into a tightly twisted rope.

Twisting may be speedily accomplished by tying one end to a post, while the other end is knotted and attached to a hook made from a bent wire nail fitted into the chuck of an electric drill. With the strands stretched out full length the drill is started and twisting is quickly completed.

To ensure that you lay up the right number of strands, a short trial length should be forced into each seam until, with hard driving, the cotton can be sunk to within the requisite $\frac{1}{8}$ in. (3 mm.) from the surface. The trial pieces should be raked out before proper caulking commences.

Before starting to caulk, priming paint (or a good white lead paint) should be brushed into the seams using a flat seam brush. On tarred plank seams a mixture of one part coal tar to three parts creosote is suitable.

CAULKING TOOLS

There are few modern aids to the operation of caulking and the tools have not needed redesigning for one hundred years. The most frequently used tools are illustrated in Fig. 29. Raking or clearing

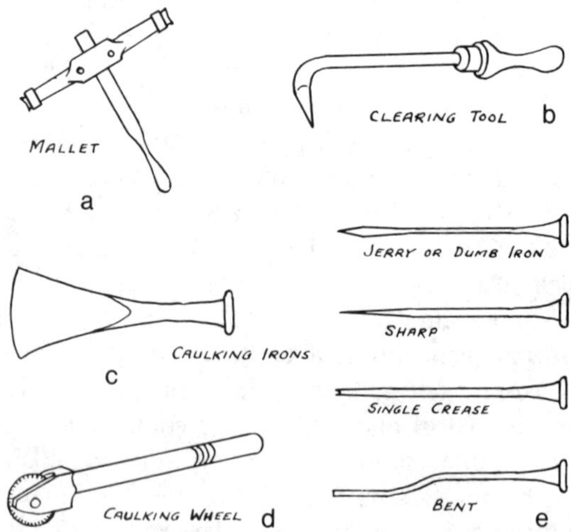

Fig. 29: Caulking tools

tools (for removing old cotton or oakum) are traditionally home-made by forming a hook at the tang end of a file. This is done by making the tip red hot, forming a hook with pliers or a hammer, letting this cool slowly, shaping the end with a file while in the soft state, making dead hard by heating to cherry red and quenching, then *tempering*.

Tempering is quite simple. Make a bright patch on the tang end with a fine file. Heat the metal a short distance away with a gentle flame and watch the colours travel along. When the bright patch changes from deep straw to pale blue, quench immediately. Quenching too soon at some shade of straw colour may make the tip too hard and brittle, while heating to deep blue may result in softness. Do not worry if the correct colour is missed. Return the metal to the dead hard condition, make another bright patch and temper once more.

Note that numerous tools can be made in this fashion from scrap pieces of tool steel (including certain car parts, lawn mower blades, etc.), but ordinary mild steel (as found in bolts, nails, fence pickets, etc,) is useless as it cannot be hardened or tempered.

Caulking irons of many different shapes may be required for one boat's seams and as these are not easy to make, it may pay to borrow them for the occasional job. Most caulking irons conform to the shape illustrated in Fig. 29c, while enlarged side views of the different tip shapes available can be seen in Fig. 29e.

The *jerry* and *reaming* irons are used to widen seams which have been damaged or are too narrow to caulk. Several *making* irons with different tip widths should be available for a big job but it may be possible to adjust the size of a single iron by grinding. Making irons are used to pinch the caulking cotton or oakum into a seam, while *crease* irons follow on to harden the caulking down to the correct depth. These may have single, double, or triple crease tips according to the size.

Bent irons are almost essential for caulking garboard seams where the keel gets in the way and also for working behind bilge keels, propeller shaft blisters, etc. For small carvel launch seams a *caulking wheel* (Fig. 29d) eliminates the need for making irons when placing the cotton.

The heavy traditional lignum vitae caulking mallet (Fig. 29a) is still preferred by professionals to any other type of mallet or hammer. The long head facilitates work below the bilges while the metal ferrules at each end help to create the correct weight for the job. An ordinary steel hammer should never be used as it makes a terrible noise and batters the head of the caulking iron, creating dangerous jagged edges.

Hold the caulking iron on the palm of the hand (Fig. 30), knuckles downwards, to minimize injury should the mallet miss its mark,

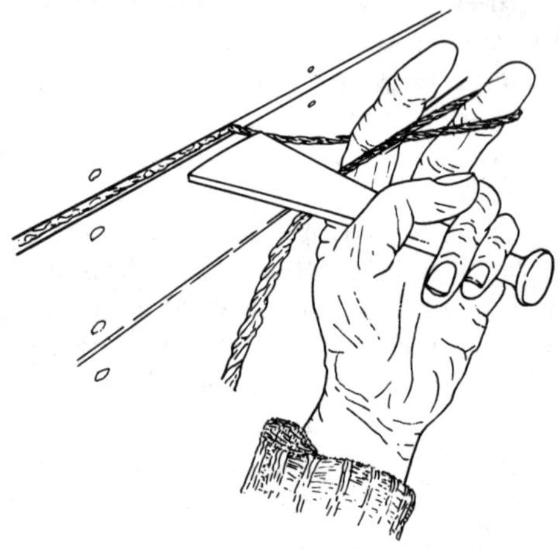

Fig. 30: The way to hold a caulking iron

and to keep the tip in view at all times. Professionals lubricate the tip frequently by keeping near at hand a shallow can packed with cotton waste soaked in linseed oil.

Caulking cotton should not need to be bunched into a seam to fill up to the correct depth. If the right number of strands have been twisted and the seam is of regular width, it should be possible to pinch the cotton into the seam with a making iron at intervals of about 2 in. (50 mm.), then harden down to leave the usual $\frac{1}{8}$ in. (3 mm.) space for stopping.

If the cotton sinks too deep after hard driving (and the driving must be hard to make a sound job) adding an extra strand or two on top of the other is bad practice. One can insert a single strand (or perhaps two twisted together) underneath the main caulking where a seam widens slightly for a short distance, but generally it would be better to twist the extra strands on to the main rope, or cut out some strands if the seam becomes *narrower* than average. For this reason it may not be wise to proceed too far ahead before driving to completion.

Being cheaper than cotton, oakum is frequently used for very wide seams, and to obviate having to stuff a great wad of it into place with a narrow making iron, the strand can be driven in a series of loops as illustrated in Fig. 31. Similar loops can be made with cotton where a seam suddenly becomes wider to obviate the need for twisting in extra strands.

A seam may be caulked in either direction, but most right-handed people prefer to work from left to right. After some practice one may be able to take the weight of the cotton or oakum strand on the first and second fingers of the left hand, as shown in Fig. 30 and so help to speed up the process of feeding it into the seams.

Caulking laid deck seams is an almost identical process, but due to the horizontal position work is much less tiring and the cotton or oakum can be laid along the seam instead of having to be lifted into it. However, it should be remembered that thorough deck caulking and paying is essential to prevent leaks. There is a good chance that slight leakage in underwater plank seams will take up a short while after submersion whereas deck seams never have the opportunity to do this.

Some kind of caulking may be necessary for purposes other than seams. A twist of cotton laid in white lead paste is essential under the head and washer of any bolt passing right through the hull to eliminate leakage. The rudder trunk in some old-type

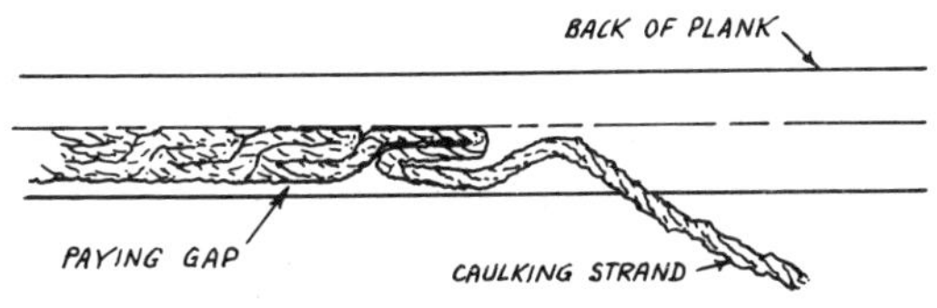

Fig. 31: Driving a wide seam in loops

trading and fishing vessels is a large cylinder passing through the counter, lined with staves of wood which are slightly tapered and driven downwards from the top. A few yarns of oakum stuck in white lead paste onto the edges of the staves helps to prevent leakage. In all cases where white lead paste is mentioned one would nowadays probably prefer to use bedding compound or one of the synthetic rubber mastics.

PAYING AND CAULKING COMPOSITIONS

The *paying* (stopping) which seals the caulking into a seam and fills it flush with the surface plays an important part in the leak-proofing of the hull as well as aiding its appearance. Very rarely is the traditional hot pitch paying ever used nowadays as most paint makers produce stoppers which do not require heating but will adhere to the caulking and the planking equally well. Traditional black marine glue is still used for deck seams and proves the quickest and cheapest method. Only the best quality marine glue should be used for yacht deck seams. Where long runs are to be made, a continuous supply of hot glue must be assured with never less than two ladles (see Plate 20) in use.

Marine glue must not be allowed to boil as it may then lose its elasticity when set. Few people bother to keep the glue at correct maker's temperature but this is usually about right when smoke starts to appear. A cast-iron pot large enough for the ladles to be dipped into is ideal for heating the glue, using a wood fire underneath, or preferably a portable bottled gas burner which can be turned to a low flame as soon as the glue is up to temperature.

A ladle not previously in use should be pre-heated before filling with glue. The amateur may have difficulty in pouring from the ladle to fill a seam completely in one pass. Pouring in two passes is much simpler and is quite satisfactory with most makes of marine glue if the two passes are made within a few hours. The work must always be completely dry to ensure good adhesion and if the glue thickens during pouring the operation should stop immediately until the ladle has been refilled.

When a perfect job is made, the hardened marine glue lies flush with the deck surface or very slightly hollow. Most amateurs

Plate 20: Paying a deck with black marine glue

tend to over-pour and the surplus glue can be scraped away quite easily for the amount normally encountered. A bent file scraper with the blade tip rounded is the best tool for this job, well lubricated with water and undertaken on a cold morning when the glue is in its most brittle condition.

As a general rule, elastic stopper is used for paying underwater seams where some swelling and shrinking of the planking is inevitable annually. Hard stoppers are used for the topsides (which always remain relatively dry) to enable the surface to be rubbed down to perfection, ensuring a fine glossy paint finish which completely obliterates all trace of the seams.

Most paint makers supply suitable stoppers which are compatible with their paint, but it should not be forgotten that only a resin putty should be used to pay hull or deck seams when the surface is to be sheathed with glass fibre or *Cascover*. Nearly all resin putties set hard and they are ideal for filling nail and screw holes. They are readily available from car accessory stores, being used for repairing rusty car bodies. Some are air hardening while others are two-can products requiring the addition of a catalyst before use.

Similar substances can be improvised by mixing ordinary polyester moulding resin with powdered chalk or chopped glass fibre strands, but well-known putties (such as *Isopon* in Britain and *Evercoat Formula 27* in America) are the correct consistency for use, thus saving much time and trouble.

The makers of Cascover sheathing kits supply a resin putty specially formulated for use under their materials. This must be used when filling depressions other than seams, though it may be possible to economize where many fastening countersinks are to be filled on a large vessel by using a skin of resin putty over rich cement mortar.

Nearly all seam stoppings are best applied by means of a broad-bladed pallette knife as used for stripping wallpaper and when burning off paint. The broad tip should be kept parallel to the seam, handle downwards. With a little practice, a good speed can be achieved leaving the surface of the stopping slightly humped to allow for shrinkage of the material and ensuring that the surface can be rubbed down flush without leaving a depression. If the blade is wider than the mouth of the can, it may be necessary to spread the stopper on to the tip of the blade with one's fingers or with a smaller knife. For stopping screw holes and small blemishes a glazier's putty knife (or an old dinner knife) may prove more convenient.

Although a sealer gun could be used for paying, only elastic stoppings are normally packed in the readily available cartridges for these tools. Whatever method is used to apply stopping, the amateur may not be able to get a good finish without resort to much rubbing down and secondary filling. Stroking the stopping with one's finger at a certain stage during the hardening process often helps to produce an almost perfect finish requiring very little subsequent rubbing.

SYNTHETIC RUBBER COMPOUNDS

On all modern laid decks of high specification caulking and paying is carried out in one operation by filling the seams with a black or coloured synthetic rubber mastic, extruded in a creamy consistency from the nozzle of a gun, later curing to a permanently firm but elastic filler of a high tenacity.

These substances are expensive and demand care in use for ideal results. Adhesion to the timber is the main possible weakness necessitating the use of a special primer and clean wood surfaces. If such a material is to be used on seams from which all the old caulking has been raked, it would be almost impossible to clean up the wood surfaces thoroughly enough using scrapers or abrasive paper. The most effective tool for the job is a small electric router with a special tapered spindle cutter to enable all seams to be reamed slightly as the tool is passed rapidly along.

Priming should follow immediately in accordance with the maker's instructions. The whole job is best done in a shed to avoid the need for drying out seams or postponing work due to weather. Alternatively, it may be possible to rig some kind of shelter, transparent polythene proving best for good illumination.

Some of the best synthetic rubber caulking compounds are two-part catalyst preparations such as *PRC*, *Polycast*, *Caulkodek*, and *Kuhl's Seam Stopping*. However, air hardening versions such as *Calfa*, *Bondite* and *Decolay* have proved most successful and have the advantage of instant availability from a cartridge without the need for mixing prior to use.

Achieving a good flush surface direct from the gun is not always easy and some operators use a pointing trowel to stroke the surface smooth.

Much time can be wasted trying to remove irregularities in the surface after curing. Various tools have been tried for cutting down rubber compositions, including a smoothing plane, Stanley shaper, disc and belt sanders. Deck paying does not need to be exactly smooth and flush, but synthetic rubber composition can be used for caulking hull seams above as well as below water.

This means that a good flush surface is essential.

Most types of paint adhere quite well to the composition, but if the surface has to be rubbed down by hand or power it will become slightly roughened, taking several coats of paint to obliterate. A good trowel finish is therefore advantageous. White composition would normally be used for topside work. One alternative would be to keep the composition below the surface and finish flush with a skin of ordinary hard white trowel cement which rubs down much more easily and takes paint better.

PLASTICS SHEATHING

Even on new wooden craft, the deck and all or part of the hull surface may be sheathed with g.r.p. or a similar process. Many amateurs think of g.r.p. sheathing as mainly of use in preventing leaks on an old boat. However, this is really a fallacy because it would be unwise to rely on a g.r.p. sheath to add strength to a weak hull and even if the sheathing does not crack the bond is sure to fail, letting water get between, leading to hidden rot.

All types of sheathing provide permanent protection against marine borers (such as *Teredo* worm) when kept in good condition below the waterline, while on topsides they provide a considerable degree of protection against abrasion, a special advantage where thin plywood hulls are concerned.

Glass-reinforced plastics sheathing has an advantage over *Cascover*, *Samcolastic* and various other sheathing processes, in that it may be given a permanent anti-slip surface when used on decks, while on topsides the outer coat of resin may be pigmented to eliminate the need for annual painting for several years.

Glass cloth produces an even finish, but to simulate the

mirror-like finish of a good wooden hull, much rubbing and re-coating with pigmented resin or paint is necessary.

Time can be saved by smearing resin putty thinly over the whole surface, followed by a normal painting program after careful rubbing down – a method often used on the surfaces of foam sandwich hulls. Cascover sheathing takes a good finish with adequate painting, but the overlapping seams are difficult to obliterate completely.

Details of how to apply g.r.p., Cascover and Samcolastic sheathing processes are given in *Boat Maintenance*, including the relative costs of five different processes. The material suppliers invariably publish instruction sheets and these should be studied carefully to avoid costly mistakes.

A good sheathing process is far from cheap, so the possible benefits should be evaluated before making a start. Although some of the liquid rubber sheathings are cheap to apply, they are not normally as permanent as the more sophisticated methods. *Black Rubber Sheathing* (K. M. Gibbs Ltd.) is particularly suitable for very old craft that leak under way (or have been out of water for a long time) but this may require an additional coat every two years.

Processes using any type of cloth are difficult to fix to clinker planking, but it can be done and many clinker lifeboat conversions have been sheathed successfully.

Cloth may be laid fore-and-aft, diagonally or vertically. Fore-and-aft is generally used for dinghies and small hard chined craft; diagonal for clinker boats of medium size; vertical cloths for most round bilge craft and all big vessels.

It pays to start sheathing, if possible, with a deck, as the operation is so much simpler on level surfaces than working overhead on the bottom planking or even vertically on the topsides. Work on a hull is much simplified if the boat can be turned over and chocked up at the most convenient angle for sheathing each side. The cloth required for each length can be handled most conveniently if wound on to a cardboard roller. Drawing pins (thumb tacks) are handy to keep the material in position when cutting to size or when impregnating with resin. One should tailor the cloth approximately to shape well ahead of the laying up operation allowing for overlaps of about 1 in. (25 mm.).

Working with Cascover nylon cloth is similar to the g.r.p. procedure except that resorcinol glue is used to stick the material to the wood instead of polyester resin. One other difference concerns the stretching of the material. Cascover nylon is sufficiently elastic to enable it to be stretched around all corners and curves without

Plate 21: Stapled battens holding stretched nylon

cutting. To make maximum use of this property, nylon cloth is normally stretched continuously as work proceeds, thus ensuring a smooth wrinkle-free surface, a minimum quantity of expensive glue being used.

This stretching is achieved with nylon by stapling thin battens of pine across the panels of laid material (see Plate 21) using a small piece of hardboard, scraped across the nylon to stretch it and squeeze out the glue. These stapled battens also enable the material to be firmly secured into corners and into any concave curvature of the hull.

The resin glue may ooze partly through the material, but

generally the work can be carried out (even on overhead surfaces) without too much dirt on the hands. On completion, the cloth is doped with a special vinyl paint and repeated coats are applied until a good finish is built up.

Woven glass cloth has a certain amount of elasticity (especially in the open *mock leno* weaves) enabling it to be formed around compound curves but stretching is only possible by securing the cloth beyond the wetted area, as additional resin must be stippled or rolled into the weave to ensure thorough impregnation. Working on overhead surfaces is therefore more difficult than with Cascover and even when using a proper thixotropic (non-drip) resin it may prove difficult to control the thickness of the laminate accurately, resulting in a wavy surface and perhaps some resin getting on to the operator's face and hands.

Whenever any form of cloth is used for sheathing one should endeavour to strip off all skin fittings, rubbing bands, zinc anodes and other metal attachments to allow complete sealing of all planking. Any recesses for metal fittings should be enlarged and deepened to allow for the thickness of the sheathing.

Parts such as rudder, propeller shaft blisters, bilge keels, (and any similar protrusions made from wood) should be sheathed separately before work proceeds on the major planking areas. This makes for an uninterrupted flow of work and enables a beginner to practise on small parts. The same idea is normal for copper sheathing also.

Although only a single layer of Cascover nylon is used on large and small vessels, several layers of g.r.p. may be necessary on the bottoms of large vessels, high speed craft, and on some decks. A table giving the number of layers and weight of cloth (and whether surface tissue is necessary) for various duties is given in *Boat Maintenance*.

Sheathing can add significantly to the weight of a racing craft. Most forms of sheathing are costly and they make it difficult for condition surveys to be carried out.

6

Converting Lifeboats

Lifeboats have always proved attractive for conversion to yachts of various types as completely sound hulls are nearly always available in a range of sizes at prices around one-tenth of the new value.

Wooden hulls are the easiest to convert, though they are rapidly being superseded by steel, alloy and glass-fibre types. Clinker and double diagonal planked ship's lifeboats can be bought from most shipbreaking firms, but alloy and plastics hulls are sometimes kept by the owners of the scrapped parent ship for installation on a newly-built vessel.

Most of the larger surplus lifeboats have inboard motors nowadays, making them worth more than the older designs intended for rowing and sailing.

The following table gives the basic dimensions of the most popular sizes of standard ship's lifeboat hulls in feet and metres. The depth measurement is taken amidships from the gunwales to the top of the keelson.

LENGTH	BREADTH	DEPTH
32.00 (9.75)	9.75 (2.95)	4.00 (1.20)
30.00 (9.15)	9.00 (2.75)	3.75 (1.15)
26.00 (7.90)	7.75 (2.35)	3.25 (1.00)
24.00 (7.30)	7.50 (2.30)	3.00 (0.90)
20.00 (6.10)	6.75 (2.05)	2.60 (0.80)
18.00 (5.50)	6.25 (1.90)	2.40 (0.73)

Some small clinker-built Navy boats similar to lifeboats are still to be found. The most common are the Montagu-rigged whalers measuring length 27 ft. (8.2 m.), beam 5 ft. 11 in. (1.8 m.) and the cutters which are 32 ft. (9.8 m.) by 9 ft. (2.7 m.). Both have centre-plates and can sail quite well. Various inboard motor launches are also sold out of service.

Ships' lifeboats are available in most countries where there are shipbreaking yards. In the U.K., the following breakers could be approached:

The Hughes Bolckow Shipbreaking Co. Ltd., Blyth.
Pollock, Brown & Co. Ltd., Southampton.,
Thos. W. Ward Ltd., Albion Works, Sheffield.
W. H. Arnott, Young & Co. Ltd., Dalmuir.
R. Blair Ltd., Barnlake Point, Milford Haven.
H. G. Pounds, Southampton Road, Paulsgrove, Portsmouth.
Husband's Shipyards Ltd., Marchwood, Southampton.

Various dealers buy up lifeboats, ex-Navy craft, and other vessels suitable for conversion, and some of these advertise in the practical boating magazines. Two useful ones are:

The Belsize Boatyard, Priory Road, Southampton, and
F. J. Watts, Parham Road, Gosport.

The procedure for purchasing a surplus R.N.L.I. vessel is different. One writes to The Secretary, Royal National Lifeboat Institution, 42 Grosvenor Gardens, London S.W.1, asking to be placed on the list of prospective purchasers. Whenever a craft becomes available all persons on the list are advised of the details and are invited to tender for the boat concerned.

These vessels are replaced by more modern types after some twenty to thirty years' service, and the ones sold are normally in sound condition, being built to an extremely high specification and meticulously maintained.

The number sold each year generally varies between two and eleven. Most of the older ones are of the 35 ft. 6 in. (10.8 m.) *Liverpool* type with 10 ft. 8 in. (3.3 m.) beam, see Fig. 32. The larger ones being sold include the 41 ft. (12.5 m.) *Watson* type with 11 ft. 8 in. (3.6 m.) beam, and the 46 ft. (14 m.) Watson with 12 ft. 8 in. (3.9 m.) beam. All have twin screw diesel propulsion with the propellers housed in tunnels.

Such craft are most suitable for motor cruiser conversion, but

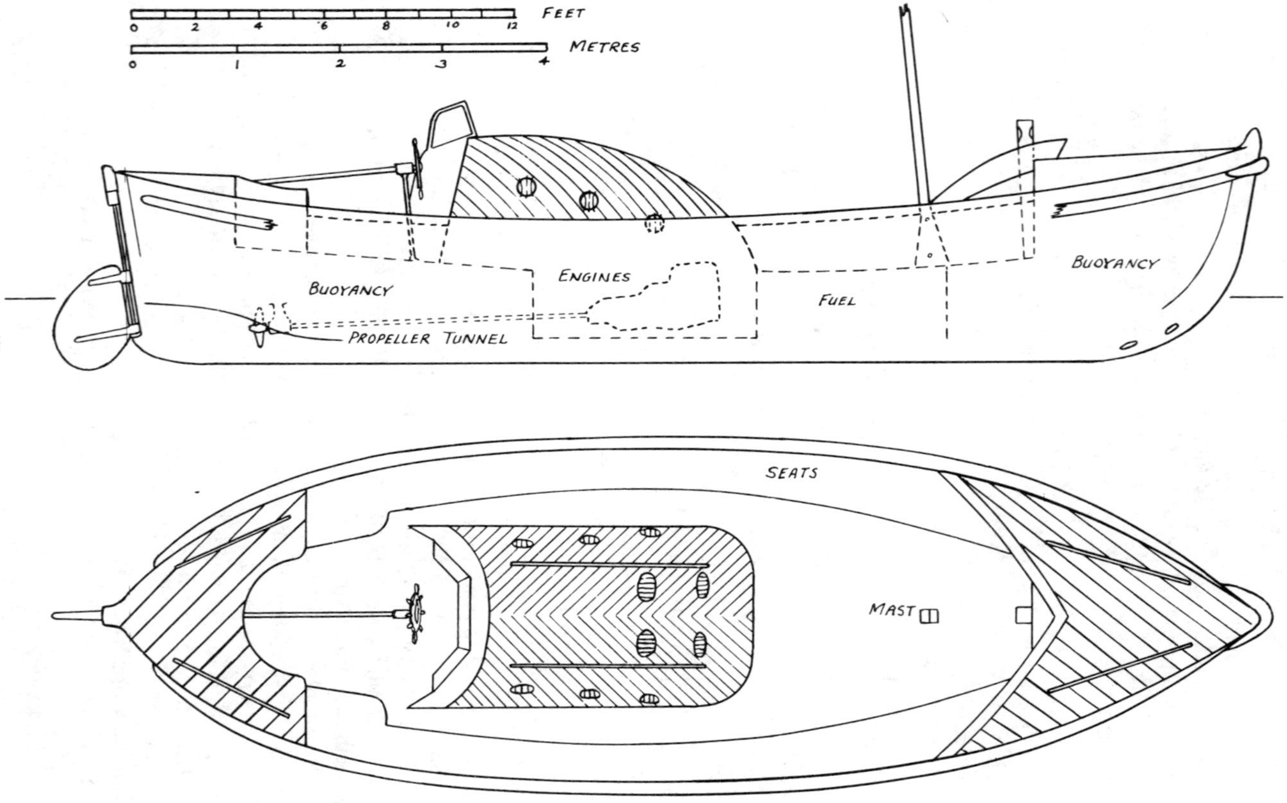

Fig. 32: The *Liverpool* type RNLI lifeboat

many have had ballast keels fitted to permit the addition of a respectable sailing rig, if only of auxiliary or motor/sailer proportions, as in Plate 22.

Plate 22: Motor/sailer lifeboat conversion

Although the sails sometimes sold with a ship's lifeboat do not prove of much value for a yacht conversion, it may be possible to utilize them as additional storm sails, while the mast can sometimes be fashioned into a boom.

Montagu whalers and Navy cutters have respectable sail areas and many yachts based on these craft have proved successful with the original rig retained.

Six suggested lifeboat conversions are illustrated in Figs. 33 to 38 and each one will now be described.

(1) *An 18 ft. (5.50 m.) Gaff Sloop*

A sail plan and cabin layout for this boat are shown in Fig. 33. A 5 h.p. outboard motor shipping on brackets alongside the cockpit is the intended form of auxiliary power.

The gaff mainsail measures 137 sq. ft. (13 m^2) while the jib area is 42 sq. ft. (4 m^2). A larger overlapping jib could be added for light airs.

The mainmast, mounted in a tabernacle, should be of 4 in. (100 mm.) diameter solid pine. A hollow spruce mast of the same diameter with walls a minimum $\frac{3}{4}$ in. (18 mm.) thick would help to reduce weight aloft. The simple standing rigging consists of one pair of 7 mm. diameter 1 $\times$ 19 galvanized wire rope shrouds and a 6 mm. forestay. The bobstay should be of $\frac{1}{4}$ in. (6 mm.) galvanized chain.

An L-shaped centre-plate of $\frac{1}{2}$ in. (12 mm.) galvanized steel is shown, controlled by a winch just inside the companion way. There is no external ballast, but 1100 lb. (500 kg.) of inside pigs would be necessary. The original rudder has been retained with an enlarged blade area.

It would be foolish to try to get standing headroom under the cabin top in such a small cruiser, but the cook would be able to stand at the galley when the main hatch is open. A forehatch would only clutter the fore deck and would be inaccessible from below. A strut would be needed from the tabernacle to the keelson, perhaps removable when in harbour to improve access to the fore peak.

A bucket head appears between the berths just abaft the mast strut where there is sitting headroom and the anchor cable locker is situated as far aft as possible to keep this weight away from the bows. There are no interior bulkheads, reducing weight and cost and giving an illusion of spaciousness.

Note that the cockpit seats are to port and starboard only, with a space between them and the main bulkhead. This arrangement makes room for four occupants while the spaces are convenient for anyone standing up or reaching overboard.

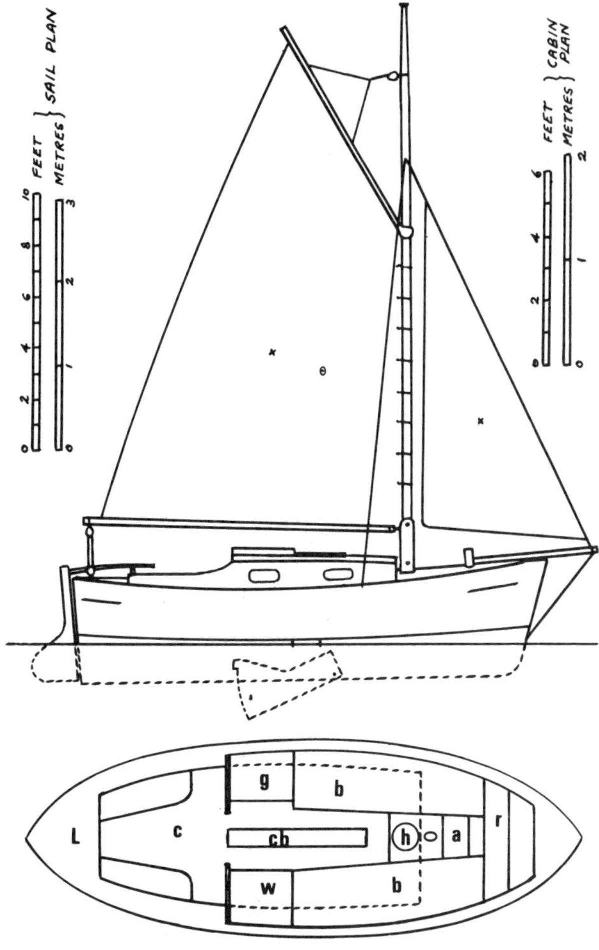

Fig. 33: 18-ft gaff sloop lifeboat conversion

a — *cable locker*
b — *fixed berths*
c — *cockpit*
cb — *centreboard case*
g — *galley*
h — *heads*
L — *stern locker*
r — *storage racks*
w — *hanging locker*

(2) *A 20 ft. (6.10 m.) Gunter Sloop*

Illustrated in Fig. 34, this design has the coachroof coamings set along the gunwales, eliminating side decks and making a roomy interior.

Sail areas are 150 sq. ft. (14 m²) in the mainsail and 41 sq. ft. (4 m²) in the working jib. The stubby mast can be to the same specification as for the 18-footer, while the Gunter yard could be of bamboo. Shrouds and forestay are 6 mm. diameter.

An external ballast keel weighing 1680 lb. (760 kg.) eliminates the need for a centre-plate or bilge keels, only a few pigs of inside ballast being necessary to correct trim. Structural details of such a keel are described in later pages.

To improve rudder efficiency, a steel drop plate is attached to the original rudder. This can be triced up to avoid rudder damage when the boat dries out.

As startling windward sailing performance is unlikely from such a design, a small inboard auxiliary engine fitted below the companion steps and driving a quarter propeller would be an advantage.

The accommodation here is unusual just to show what can be done. Because there are no side decks, an athwartships dinette/double berth is possible against the solid forward bulkhead. This is a specialised arrangement to suit a couple who never quarrel and who do not intend to sleep when under way!

The toilet compartment is isolated in the fo'c'sle, with sitting headroom under the hatch. A big galley is possible in the best location near the companion way and the spacious oilskin locker opposite would prove a blessing at times.

(3) *A 24 ft. (7.30 m.) Bermuda Sloop*

Here we have a conventional modern conversion (Fig. 35), with good sailing performance, having 189 sq. ft. (18 m²) in the mainsail with a 66 sq. ft. (6 m²) working jib. Having no overlap, this jib can be fitted with a boom for single-handed sailing.

A light alloy mast would be ideal, but a hollow rectangular spruce spar stepped on the keelson can be made quite easily by the amateur. Its dimensions should be 5½ in. (138 mm.) fore-and-aft

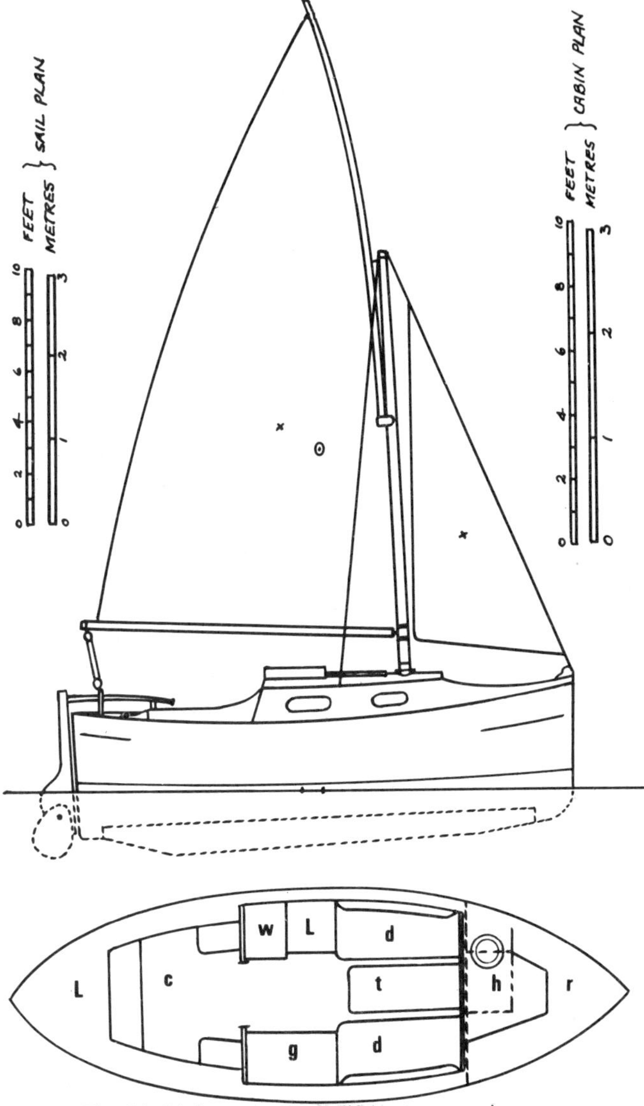

Fig. 34: 20-ft gunter sloop lifeboat conversion

c — *cockpit*
d — *dinette/double berth*
g — *galley*
h — *heads*
L — *lockers*
r — *sail racks*
t — *table*
w — *wardrobe*

with ¾ in. (18 mm.) thick walls and 4½ in. (112 mm.) athwartships with 1 in. (25 mm.) walls. Above the forestay band, tapering can be applied down to 2½ in. (62 mm.) fore-and-aft with ⅝ in. (15 mm.) walls by 2 in. (50 mm.) athwartships with ¾ in. (18 mm.) walls at the masthead. An alternative solid round mast should be 5¾ in. (144 mm.) in diameter up to the forestay band. Refer to Chapter 7 for spar building details.

Standing rigging is to be made from 6 mm. galvanized 1 × 19 wire rope in the forestay and forward shrouds, while the after shrouds are 7 mm.

The external ballast keel weighing 2462 lb. (1120 kg.) extends right aft. A false sternpost has been added to create a propeller aperture. A new rudder of increased size is intended, hung to the new sternpost.

The coachroof coamings have been kept low for attractive appearance, but to increase headroom, the cabin top deck should be of elliptical section with a big camber.

As in the previous design, the fo'c'sle is a completely separate compartment served by the fore hatch and containing a pipe cot. The saloon has two full length settee berths with a folding table attached to the mast. The galley is placed in the most favoured position with the oilskin locker and heads behind curtains to starboard.

In all these drawings minor details such as small lockers and shelves have been omitted for clarity. Details of cabin joinery are given in Chapter 12.

(4) *A 26 ft. (7.90 m.) Gaff Ketch*

The profile and accommodation details for this boat are illustrated in Fig. 36. Another centre-plate design with drop plate added to the rudder, this craft carries 1680 lbs. (760 kg.) of inside ballast only.

The sail areas are mainsail, 176 sq. ft. (17 m^2.); mizzen, 62 sq. ft. (5·8 m^2.); foresail, 67 sq. ft. (6·2 m^2.). The mainmast is to be 5 in. (125 mm.) diameter solid, or with 1 in. (25 mm.) walls if hollow, stepped through the cabin top to the keelson. The mizzen mast is solid 3 in. (75 mm.) diameter stepped at the for'ard end of the

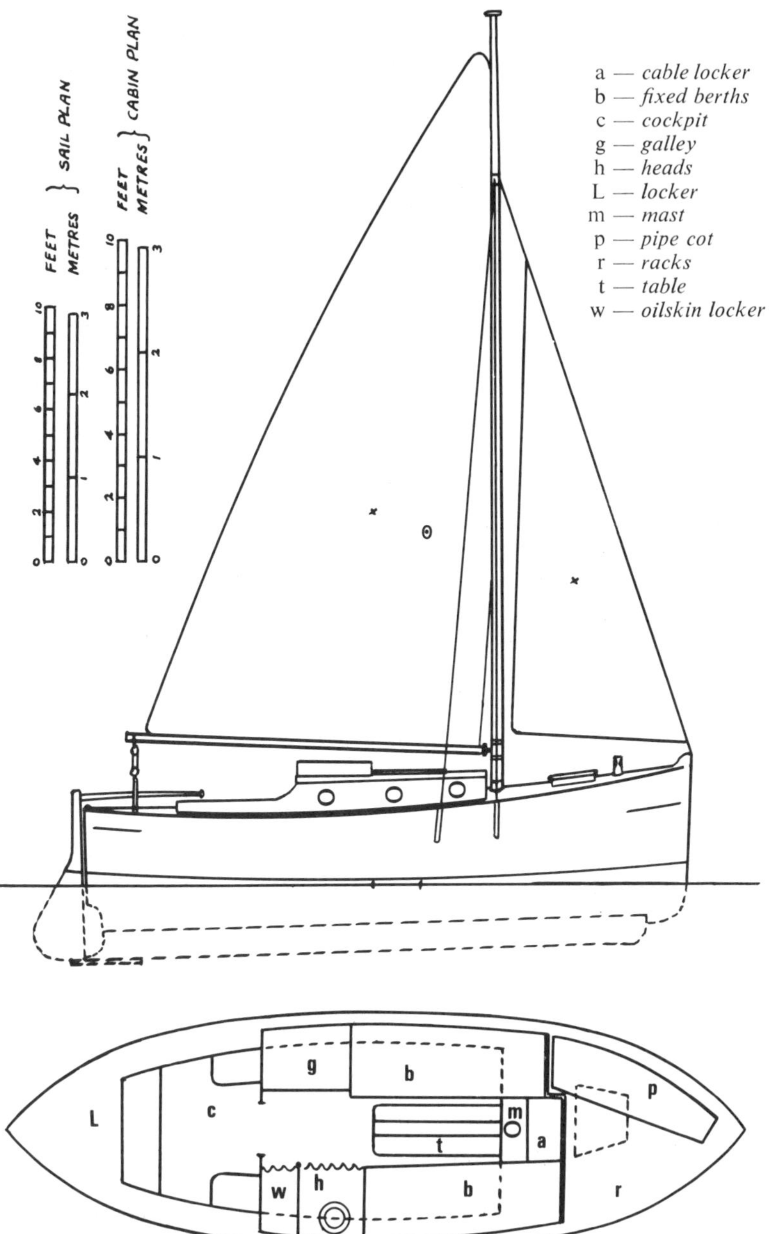

Fig. 35: 24-ft bermuda sloop lifeboat conversion

cockpit against the bulkhead. Rigging diameters are main shrouds 8 mm.; forestay, 7 mm.; mizzen shrouds, 6 mm.; bobstay, $\frac{5}{16}$ in. (8 mm.) chain.

Note that the sheer has not been raised in the manner previously recommended. The deep cabin top coamings of varnished teak come direct from the gunwales, the top deck having a big camber to give headroom, and with 2 in. (50 mm.) high footrails set about 2 in. (50 mm.) inboard from each side.

When the coamings are set this way, work is simplified by eliminating side decks. However, do not carry this process too far by making the cockpit also the full width of the ship. If this is done, the cockpit is more likely to get inundated by green seas. Also, the curve of the bilge will intrude on the cockpit floor space and some useful lockers will be lost.

The accommodation is unusual to illustrate a few ideas. The companion hatch is offset to starboard to provide easy access alongside the centre-plate casing. Where the settee berth fits behind the casing a folding chart table may be arranged high enough to allow a sleeping crew member's legs to fit underneath.

There is space for a fine galley to starboard, including a stool for the cook, and adequate hanging lockers. This shows what can be done when one does not have to overload a small craft with berths.

Two long settees beside the table allow six people to be seated. Root berths which roll up against the *ceiling* (the panelled sides of the boat) permit comfortable settees to be made and provide backrests.

A door leads to the fo'c'sle heads compartment, the fore hatch being joined to the coachroof fore coaming. An auxiliary engine can be fitted under the cockpit sole, driving a propeller on the quarter.

(5) *A 28 ft. (8.50 m.) Bermudan Cutter*

To sail well, most lifeboats need a bowsprit and here is a typical example. The mainsail measures 308 sq. ft. (29 m^2); the forestay-sail, 107 sq. ft. (10 m^2); the jib 102 sq. ft. (9·5 m^2). The mainmast

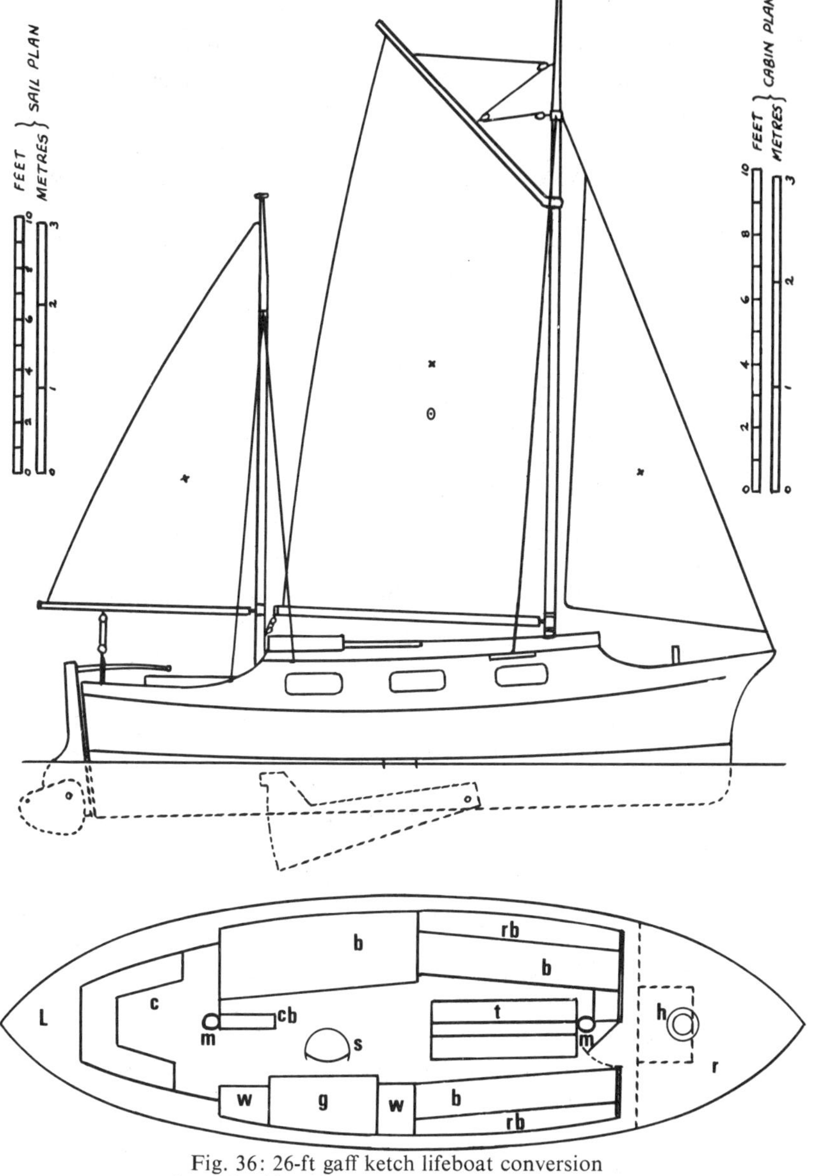

Fig. 36: 26-ft gaff ketch lifeboat conversion

b — *fixed berths*
c — *cockpit*
cb — *centre plate case*
g — *galley*
h — *heads*
L — *locker*
m — *masts*
r — *racks*
rb — *root berths*
s — *seat*
t — *table*
w — *hanging locker*

(stepped on the keelson) should be built of spruce in the following rectangular dimensions. From heel to forestay band, 6 in. (150 mm.) fore-and-aft with 1¾ in. (43 mm.) walls by 4½ in. (112 mm.) athwartships with 1 in. (25 mm.) walls, tapering to 4 in. (100 mm.) fore-and-aft with 1 in. (25 mm.) walls by 2½ in. (62 mm.) athwartships with ¾ in. (18 mm.) walls above the forestay band.

Backstays and topmast forestay are of 5 mm. diameter 1 × 19 galvanized wire rope. The lower forestay is to be 8 mm. while the two pairs of shrouds are 6 mm. The running backstays are set up on track or spans along the side decks but Highfield levers could optionally be used. The bowsprit heel is fixed to the bitts and has a $\frac{5}{16}$ in. (8 mm.) chain bobstay.

The external keel weighs 3400 lbs. (1540 kg.) with only a small amount of inside trimming ballast. The rudder is hung on a new false sternpost to create a large propeller aperture. The drop rudder is ideal for sailing, but its tricing line would have to be led forward to the centre cockpit. Wheel steering is essential, connected by wires to a yoke or quadrant on the rudder head.

There is good space for the engine and tanks under the centre cockpit, but a fairly long propeller shaft is needed leading beneath the after cabin sole. An aft cabin is ideal for family use with two children on board, though the one shown is suitable for adult use with a dressing table between the settee berths and plenty of locker space. Compare the motor/sailer design (Fig. 3) described in Chapter 2.

The saloon contains one settee berth and one root berth, the latter folding down over a settee close to the table. Note that the table is conveniently mounted to surround the masts, its after section in the form of a hinged flap which can be used by the cook or folded down to improve saloon access. This is not a good table to spread charts on, but a chart table can be hinged to the oilskin locker bulkhead to fold down over the navigator's berth.

A roomy toilet compartment is shown with separate hand basin. By shifting the heads to the starboard side (with a folding basin above) space could be made for a shower with standing headroom under the coachroof on the centreline.

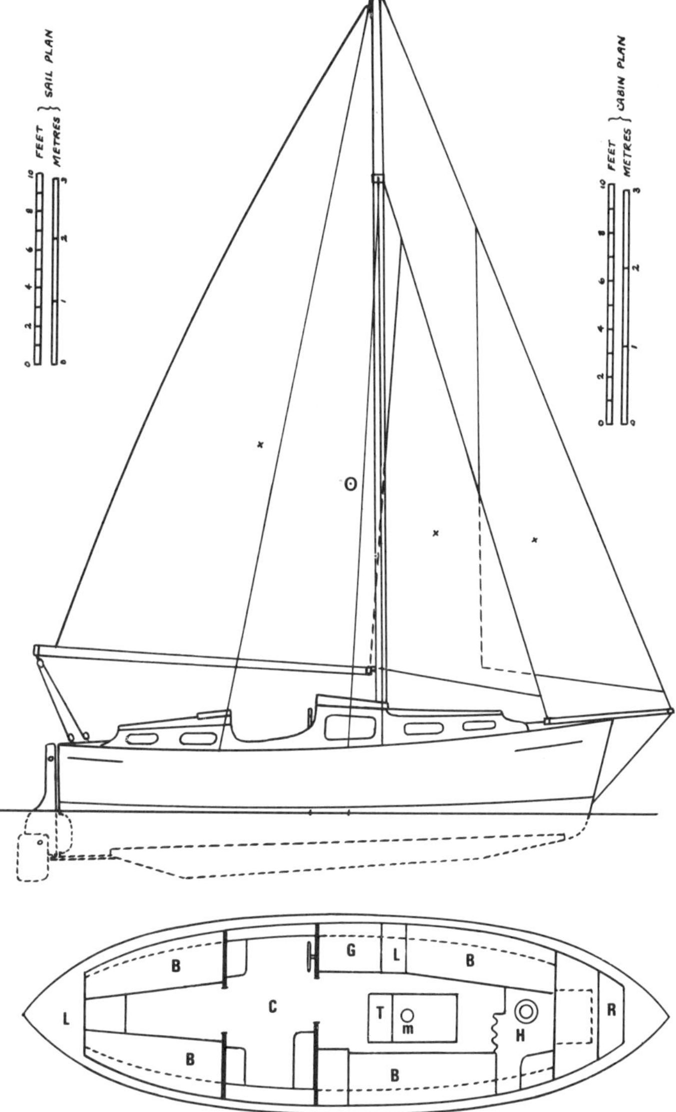

Fig. 37: 28-ft bermuda cutter lifeboat conversion

B — *fixed berths*	L — *lockers*
C — *cockpit*	m — *mast*
G — *galley*	R — *racks*
H — *heads*	T — *table*

(6) *A 30 ft. (9.15 m.) Bermuda Yawl*

Perhaps this boat should be called a ketch, but having the mizzen mast stepped at the after cockpit bulkhead with a long bumkin to take the mizzen sheet, she has a yawl-like appearance.

The total working sail area measures 410 sq. ft. (39 m^2), with 232 sq. ft. (22 m^2) in the mainsail; 106 sq. ft. (10 m^2) in the foresail and 72 sq. ft. (7 m^2) in the mizzen.

The coachroof is taken right out to the full width of the hull. There is no forehatch, giving a clear foredeck. The mainmast steps on the keelson, built rectangular to the following dimensions.

From keel to forestay band 6½ in. (164 mm.) fore-and-aft with 1⅛ in. (28 mm.) walls by 4½ in. (114 mm.) athwartships with ¾ in. (18 mm.) walls. Above forestay band tapering to 2½ in. (62 mm.) fore-and-aft with ¾ in. (18 mm.) walls by 2 in. (50 mm.) athwartships with ⅝ in. (15 mm.) walls at the truck.

If a solid mainmast must be used it should be 6¼ in. (158 mm.) diameter, tapering to 3½ in. (88 mm.) above the band. The mizzen mast is best made solid of 3 in. (75 mm.) diameter tapering to 2 in. (50 mm.) above the shroud band.

The aftermost pair of main shrouds may be of 8 mm. diameter 1 × 19 galvanized wire, the other pair of 7 mm., the forestay of 8 mm., and all mizzen shrouds of 6 mm.

The bumkin can be attached as shown in Fig. 38 with two stays of 6 mm. diameter 7 × 19 stainless steel wire rope to eyebolts through the topsides just above the waterline. As the mizzen mast would foul a normal tiller, one of the contrivances shown in Fig. 39 should be adopted. The enlarged rudder pivots on the skeg extension from the 3800 lb. (1730 kg.) external ballast keel.

A full-size dinette/double berth appears in the saloon. To create a wide passage through the saloon a root berth is shown opposite, with a relatively narrow settee for daytime use.

The toilet compartment door is so arranged that when open it closes against the saloon but when closed the passage-way between the fo'c'sle and saloon is open. Spacious accommodation has been achieved with this open-plan layout, using the minimum number of doors. Although situated with restricted headroom over most of its length, the fo'c'sle berth shown is a full-size one.

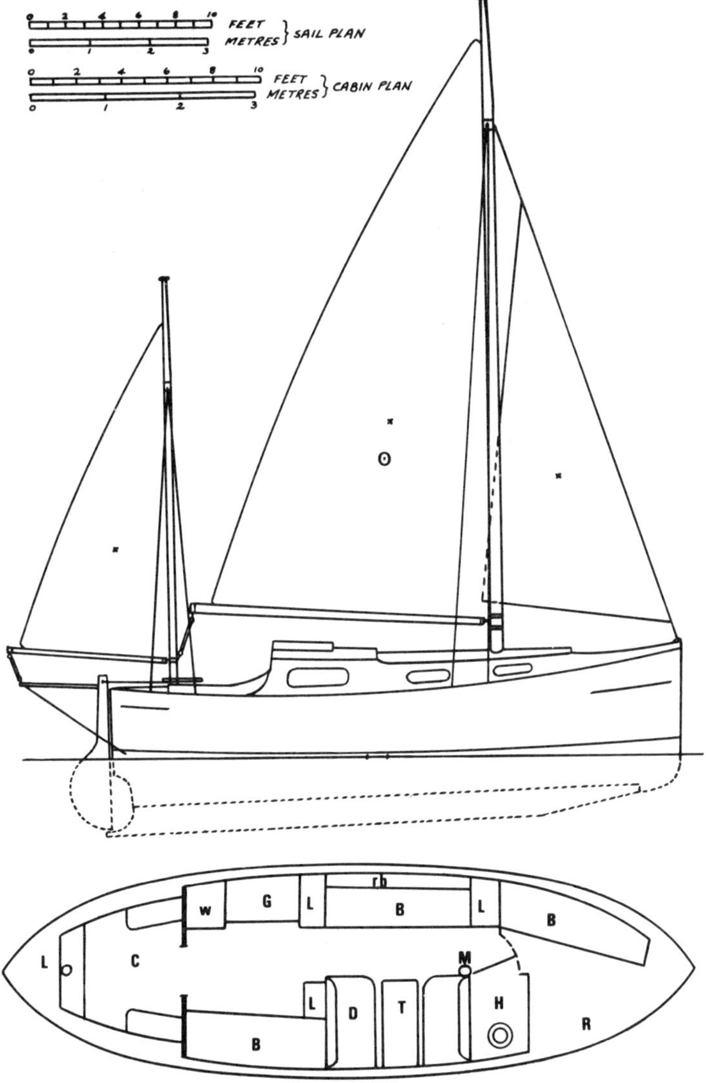

Fig. 38: 30-ft bermuda yawl lifeboat conversion

B — *berths*
C — *cockpit*
D — *dinette/double berth*
G — *galley*
H — *heads*
L — *lockers*
M — *mast*
R — *racks*
rb — *root berth*
T — *table*
W — *oilskin locker*

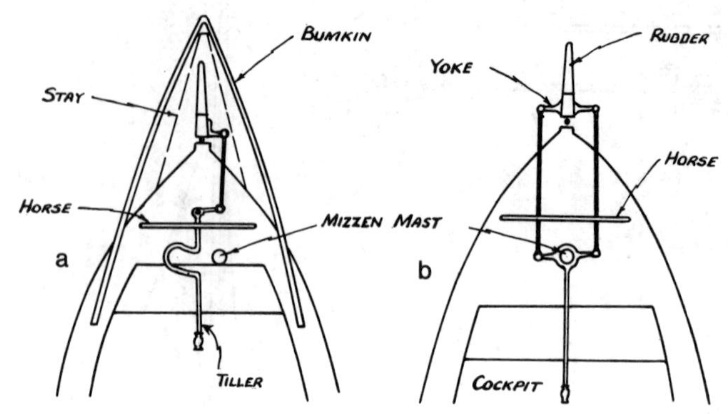

Fig. 39: Steering linkages to avoid the mizzen mast

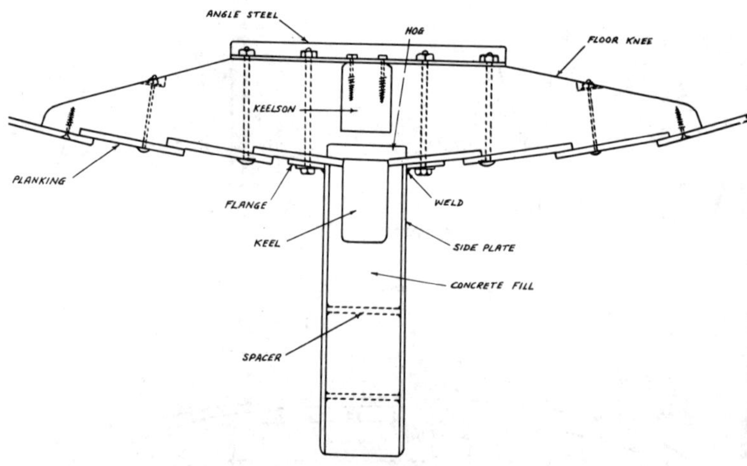

Fig. 40: Plan for composite ballast keel

BALLAST KEELS

Although a conventional cast iron or lead keel may be added to a lifeboat conversion, one is normally striving for a fin to give lateral resistance, so concrete is quite suitable and much cheaper. Details of constructing keels in lead and concrete are given in Chapter 8.

The outside keels shown in Designs 2, 3, 5 and 6 are intended to be constructed as in Fig. 40 with permanent mild steel side plates. The space between the side plates is intended to be filled with a dense concrete plus a high proportion of small scrap metal such as chunks of steel bar or hole punchings.

With the hull turned keel uppermost, hardboard templates can be shaped to allow the steel side plates to be profile cut to order, using $\frac{1}{4}$ in. (6 mm.) for Designs 2 and 3 and $\frac{3}{8}$ in. (9 mm.) for Nos. 5 and 6.

Make the flanges of the same thickness standard steel flats. Where the angle between the garboard planks and the keel becomes too steep at each end of the hull to fit the through-bolts and new floors shown, the flanges can normally be terminated. The inside distance between side plates should be 5 in. (125 mm.) for Designs 2 and 3 and 7 in. (175 mm.) for Nos. 5 and 6.

If an arc welding set can be borrowed, spot weld the flanges to the side plates *in situ*, together with the $\frac{5}{8}$ in. (15 mm.) spacer bars between the plates.

Trim the inner flange edges if necessary to butt to the side plates and bore the bolt holes before starting to weld. Having tack welded, lift the assembly off and complete the continuous welding. End plates, rudder skeg, and other attachments should then be welded on and all exposed edges rounded off. After this, the assembly can be sent away for zinc spraying on all surfaces except those to be covered by concrete.

On a steel lifeboat hull, plates of half the above thickness should be used if they are to be welded direct to the hull skin. The floor bolts can then be made with hooked ends cast into the concrete. A different method of casting a concrete keel direct on to a steel lifeboat hull is described in *Lifeboat into Yacht*.

A concrete keel can be fixed to a hull which cannot be turned over by welding up a complete trough with bottom plating and partially filling this before bolting to the hull. However, the inverted hull method is superior as the concrete forms a complete seal between the keel and the garboards.

ADDITIONAL FLOORS

Ship's lifeboats have a deep keelson on top of the hog (see Fig. 41) to take the stress of hoisting on davits when loaded. This keelson is a nuisance when converting, and some enthusiastic conversionists take it right out to enable proper wooden floor timbers to be fitted. These are essential when a ballast keel is added and if they are run over the top of the keelson they become too deep to bolt through properly, and the cabin sole may also have to be raised needlessly.

An alternative idea is to fit separate floors each side of the keelson, joined across the top by galvanized steel angle bearers as detailed in Fig. 40. A similar idea must be used where a centreboard case is added. In this instance specially fabricated angle plates are fitted to secure the half-floors to the case members, as seen in Fig. 41. Angle plates are also used with engine bearers as described in Chapter 9.

Additional floors are nearly always necessary for a motor cruiser conversion as well as to resist sailing loads. Without these, if a boat is grounded on a sand bar with seas running, as the keel crashes down, the garboard planks may break away from the keel, or the engine bearers may break every timber beneath them, causing the adjacent plank seams to burst open.

Solid floors of oak or other hardwoods are the easiest and quickest to make, but they do sometimes warp or crack after fitting unless carefully chosen, well seasoned, and cut out roughly a good while before final fitting. Laminated, metal, or g.r.p. floors (as described in Chapter 4) can be used instead. They are stable, but more costly in time and material than solid floors.

Floors should fit close to the planking between two timbers, fastened through the planking with screws, bolts, or clenches. Shaping therefore entails accurate joggling over the planking lands. Marking out can be done by spiling (see Chapter 3) while the roughly cut floor is held in place. Sometimes it proves easier to first shape an offcut of hardboard in this way, then scribe the floor from this pattern. If the roves of land nails foul a floor, depressions can be cut into the timber with a big drill to house them. This is better than removing the fastenings.

For Designs 1, 2 and 3, oak half-floors should be sided $1\frac{1}{2}$ in. (37 mm.), strapped across the keelson with $1\frac{1}{2}$ in. × $1\frac{1}{2}$ in. × $\frac{5}{16}$ in. (37 mm. × 37 mm. × 7 mm.) steel angle at 36 in. (900 mm.) intervals. Without a keelson through-floors would be sided $1\frac{3}{4}$ in. (44 mm.) and $2\frac{1}{2}$ in. (62 mm.) respectively. Where screw fastenings are used through the planking, these should be bronze, $2\frac{1}{2}$ in. (62 mm.) × No. 16 and 3 in. (75 mm.) × No. 18 respectively.

All floor intervals can be varied to coincide with the keel bolts and to come between two timbers. In vessels with sawn frames the floors may be side-bolted to adjacent frames in addition to the usual plank fastenings.

INSTALLING A CENTREBOARD

A lifeboat keel is not wide enough to permit cutting a centreboard slot through it safely and many fastenings get in the way. A better way is to cut the slot alongside the hog and through one garboard plank, the casing being installed as shown in section in Fig. 41.

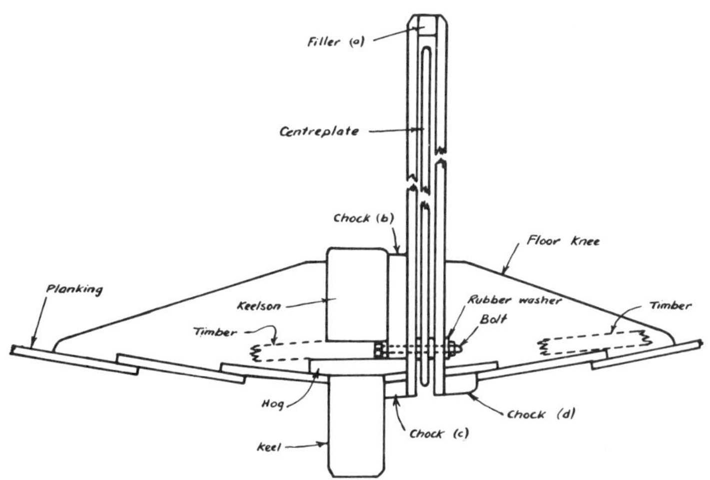

Fig. 41: Installing a centreboard

In way of a centreboard case the floors should be closer than suggested above and as deep as possible. At each end of the case a through-floor attached by knees is a great advantage. If such a floor comes above cabin sole level, it may be possible to incorporate a step there.

Cruising boat centreboard cases are always boxed in at the top and may be below the waterline except for the tube or trunk at the after end which takes the chain for raising and lowering the board. If this end can be extended upwards to a deck beam, great strength is added.

Although a steel case can be welded into a steel lifeboat hull, or a plastics case into a g.r.p. hull, timber is the best choice for a traditional wooden lifeboat.

Solid iroko or afrormosia is ideal for the sides, $1\frac{1}{2}$ in. (38 mm.) thick for Design No. 1, and 2 in. (50 mm.) for No. 4. Planks about 6 in. (150 mm.) wide are ideal, with *splined* joints glued together with resorcinol glue and no fastenings. To make a joint, plane the board edges to a good fit (and dead square); cut a groove into the centre of each edge just wide enough to house a spline of $\frac{3}{8}$ in. (9 mm.) marine plywood. Cut out the spline and make sure it does not foul the bottom of the grooves when offering up the joint dry, then glue every part and cramp.

It may prove very difficult to buy marine plywood thick enough for centreboard case sides, as $1\frac{1}{4}$ in. (32 mm.) and $1\frac{3}{4}$ in. (44 mm.) would be needed for the above instances. Several sheets can be glued together to build up the thickness, but this method proves costly and difficult to cramp.

Permali resin impregnated laminated board is ideal and may be ordered in any thickness direct from Permali Ltd., Gloucester, England. For the above jobs, 1 in. (25 mm.) and $1\frac{1}{4}$ in. (32 mm.) would do.

A case as drawn in Fig. 41 should be built up *in situ* piece by piece after having first assembled everything dry and then taken it apart again. Bolt the inner case side firmly to keelson and keel using sealer everywhere that leakage could occur past the garboard. Glue and screw the end and top framing to this side, then add the other side.

CENTRE-PLATES

Galvanized mild steel is the most practical material for the centre-plate of a lifeboat conversion, $\frac{1}{2}$ in. (12 mm.) suiting Design No. 1 and $\frac{5}{8}$ in. (15 mm.) for No. 4. Permali can be used, $\frac{3}{4}$ in. (18 mm.) for No. 1 and 1 in. (25 mm.) for No. 4, but ordinary marine plywood is not really suitable. Solid hardwood can be built up as for the case sides, using $1\frac{1}{4}$ in. (32 mm.) and $1\frac{1}{2}$ in. (38 mm.) thicknesses, weighted with galvanized steel or lead blanks and shoed with a suitable metal band.

On all wooden boards a bush is necessary to take the wear of the pivot pin, with spacer washers at each side. *Tufnol* bushes and washers with a large stainless steel bolt make an ideal combination.

The type of plate shown on the designs should be equipped with a step on the after end, engaging with a bolt through the case when the plate is fully lowered to prevent damage should the hoisting gear fail. This is also a wise precaution on a wooden board.

LEEBOARDS

As the fitting of a centreboard into a lifeboat hull is difficult, many conversionists prefer to use leeboards, see Plate 6. These do the same job as a centreboard, though not so conveniently. They are pivoted at the gunwale amidships each side, the leeward one being lowered under way while the windward one is raised by means of a chain (or wire rope) operated by a small winch. A terylene rope tackle can sometimes be utilized.

If sufficient inside ballast is used, any of the designs described can have leeboards. The boards are normally made of solid wood in preference to steel or plywood and therefore require weighting to ensure proper submersion when being pulled rapidly through the water.

The best type of weight for wooden leeboards and centreboards is generally a galvanized mild steel blank (with attachment lugs welded on) fitted across the bottom edge. This serves as protection against damage and a normal keel band can extend from the weight along the leading edge to well above the waterline. Alternatively, large holes can be trepanned through the board, chamfered in both directions, and filled with molten lead. Cool this rapidly with water and soak the wood to prevent scorching.

Permali sinks in water but needs some weighting. Solid oak or iroko boards each need ballast equal to the total weight of the wood.

Ideally, leeboards should be shaped like an airplane wing in cross section, the flat surface being outboard, the inner surface bowed from a round on the leading edge to a thickness of about one-quarter the maximum at the trailing edge. The bottom of the board can be left at a constant thickness to enable a suitable weight to be profile cut from standard thickness mild steel.

Leeboard dimensions for the suggested designs should be as follows:

(1) 5 ft. (1500 mm.) long, tapering from 1 ft. 8 in. (500 mm.) at the bottom to 9 in. (230 mm.) at the top. Solid hardwood $1\frac{1}{4}$ in. (32 mm.) thick, or Permali 1 in. (25 mm.).

(4) 6 ft. 6 in. (2000 mm.) × 2 ft. (600 mm.) × 10 in. (250 mm.), using $1\frac{3}{8}$ in. (35 mm.) hardwood.

Hardwood boards cannot be assembled with clench bolts driven edgeways as the bolts would be revealed when shaping the aerofoil. Resin-glued splined joints using planks 9 in. (230 mm.) or 10 in. (250 mm.) wide are ideal.

Although leeboards are best hung by means of special eyebolts permitting outwards as well as fore-and-aft movement, these are not always easy for the amateur to make neatly and three links of heavy galvanized chain do the job equally well. In any case, the bolt or bolts through the sheer plank must be tightened on to a substantial chock inside to augment the shelf.

Another bearer bolted to the outside of the planking just above the waterline should be arranged to keep each board vertical athwartships when the boat is sailing at a slight angle of heel. The chocks must be long enough to support the boards when they are triced up to allow sailing over a shoal or to adjust the *centre of lateral resistance* (C.L.R.) in relation to the *centre of effort* (C.E.) of the sails for best balance. The chocks should ideally give the boards a slight toe-in towards the stem when under full pressure but this may be difficult to arrange on some boats without making the chocks unduly thick aft.

Note that the horizontal locations of the C.L.R. and C.E. are shown as small marks on the waterline for each of the six lifeboat conversion designs. The for'ard mark in each case represents the C.E. and the after one the C.L.R. When adopting leeboards these should be centred slightly forward of the C.L.R. while bilge keels should coincide with the C.L.R.

Bilge keels (Plate 23) can be added to Designs 2, 3, 5 and 6 to improve windward sailing ability and enable the boats to sit upright. These keels would vary between 15 in. (380 mm.) and 24 in. (610 mm.) deep and between 3 ft. (915 mm.) and 5 ft. (1520 mm.) in length. They are most easily made of timber, the smaller keels 3 in. (76 mm.) thick tapered towards the ends, the bigger ones $3\frac{1}{2}$ in. (88 mm.) thick. Bilge keels should be through-bolted to stringers inside, $3\frac{1}{2}$ in. × $1\frac{1}{2}$ in. (88 mm. × 38 mm.) Tanalized fir about 10 ft. (3 m.) long being ideal.

Plate 23: Bilge keels on a lifeboat conversion

Bilge keels should be bedded on to one clinker plank and approximately at right angles to it, either parallel to the main keel or with a slight toe-in for'ard. The keels should splay outwards from the vertical and be set as far from the main keel as possible provided they do not stick out beyond the boat's topsides.

BUILDING HER UP

Before much interior work can be started on a lifeboat conversion, all thwarts and side benches must be stripped out, but temporary beams between the gunwales must be fitted beforehand. Then, with plenty of room to work inside the hull, the centre-plate or external keel can be added, the engine installation can be lined up temporarily and all the extra floors detailed above can be fastened in place.

As mentioned in Chapters 1 and 2 it proves best to raise the lifeboat's topsides by adding two or three extra strakes of clinker planking to merge exactly into the appearance of the original hull. Where a carvel-built or steel hull is concerned, it will be wisest to leave the original gunwale as an obvious fore-and-aft band and to raise the topsides with ordinary carvel planking to the required height, in the same way as shown in Plate 4. Whatever method is adopted, it will first be necessary to scarf an extra piece of oak onto the tops of the stem and sternpost, leaving these pieces amply long to be sawn off later.

Next, a number of dwarf frames should be fashioned and glued and screwed to the inside of the planking as detailed in Fig. 42. These frames should also be left amply long so that temporary beams can be tacked between them to ensure rigidity while the planks are sprung into position.

THE CABIN TOP

When adding extra strakes of clinker planking, the original sheer strake and rubber should be removed, but when it has been decided to add carvel planking, it proves neatest to leave the gunwale as shown in Fig. 42.

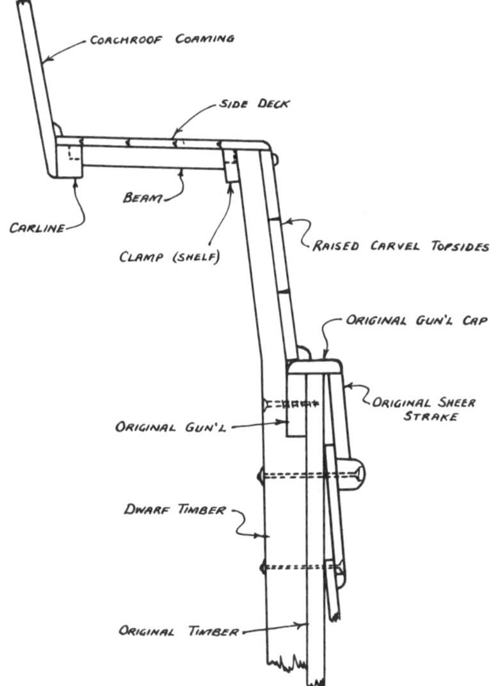

Fig. 42: Raised carvel topsides wih tumble-home

A far more attractive appearance is obtained if the dwarf frames are given a considerable tumble-home as indicated in Fig. 42. This need not be too exaggerated, however, and a slope of approximately one in eight proves ideal.

Having erected the new frames, a batten of springy timber should be clamped from stem to stern to represent the new sheer. This batten can be adjusted by eye for the most pleasing position, and the strakes of planking to be added should be marked out evenly between the old and the new sheers.

The same procedure may be adopted where the coachroof coamings are taken right to the outside, the same dwarf frames serving to support the extra planking and the coachroof coamings, the latter usually of varnished hardwood, containing portholes or other forms of window as seen in Plate 7.

Most of the permanent deck beams and carlines must be fitted before all the temporary beams can be removed to allow access for continuing with the interior work. The beams should be half-dovetailed into the clamp, (as described in *Complete Amateur Boat Building*) and the carlines are used to support the cabin-top coamings, where fitted. The cabin-top deck beams are dovetailed similarly and are mentioned again in Chapter 12. Lodging and hanging knees should be fixed to the majority of the deck beams, especially in way of the masts. It often proves convenient to make the side-deck beams into *hanging knees* (making a neater job as well as a much stronger one for the weight) instead of attaching separate knees to these short beams.

Where the mast can be stepped directly on top of the coachroof, it is best to reinforce the beams beneath the mast by adding a double framework of welded angle steel in the form shown in Fig. 43. This frame need not be accurately shaped so as to touch the topsides and coamings at every point, but the legs of the frames should be securely bolted through the original lifeboat's planking fairly low down the hull. Where there are inaccuracies in the shape of the steel framing, chocks of oak can be fashioned to fit between the angle steel and the planking.

The steelwork must be hot-galvanized or zinc-metallized after fabrication, and then painted. Note that paint does not adhere well to new galvanizing. If this cannot be left to weather for a month or two, it should be treated with A.C.P. Lithoform (I.C.I. Ltd.), and a self-etching primer used.

Hefty blocks of oak should be bolted between the two steel frames above and below the coachroof deck, to receive the heel of the mast. To allow a little fore-and-aft adjustment of the mast position, the steel frames should be approximately 18 in. (450 mm.) apart. Most garages or small engineering works will weld up these frames to correspond with drawings or rough timber templates. For Design No. 2 $1\frac{1}{2}$ in. $\times$ $1\frac{1}{2}$ in. $\times$ $\frac{1}{4}$ in. (37 mm. $\times$ 37 mm. $\times$ 6 mm.) steel should be used, and 2 in. $\times$ 2 in. $\times$ $\frac{5}{16}$ in. (50 mm. $\times$ 50 mm. $\times$ 7 mm.) for bigger lifeboats.

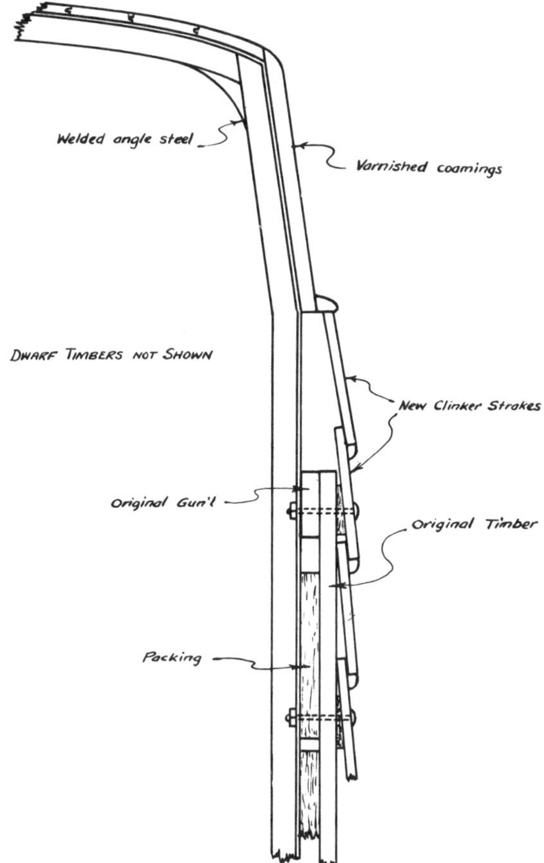

Fig. 43: Welded angle steel mast frame

Timber deck beams for Design Nos. 1 and 2 should be of $1\frac{1}{2}$ in. (38 mm.) thick oak or high-grade softwood with a depth of 3 in. (76 mm.) for the longest through-beams. For Designs Nos. 3 and 4 these dimensions should be increased to $1\frac{3}{4}$ in. × 3 in. (44 mm. × 76 mm.) and for Designs Nos. 5 and 6, 2 in. × 3 in. (50 mm. × 76 mm.). There should be one of these beams on either side of the mast (unless angle steel frames are used) with stout oak *partners* connecting them around the mast. The beams for cabin-tops with side decks can be much lighter and the corresponding sizes would be about $\frac{3}{4}$ in. × 2 in. (18 mm. × 50 mm.) $\frac{7}{8}$ in. × $2\frac{1}{2}$ in. (22 mm × 63 mm.) and 1 in. × $3\frac{1}{4}$ in. (23 mm. × 82 mm.), spaced at 12 in. (305 mm.) 15 in. (380 mm.) and 18 in. (460 mm.). For main deck beams the spacing should be 18 in. (460 mm.), 24 in. (610 mm.) and 30 in. (760 mm.) respectively. Note that for the full-width coach-roofs of Designs 2 and 4 the cabin-top beams are actually main-deck beams. The cabin-top coamings should be of the following thicknesses: 1 in. (25 mm.) for Design No. 1, $1\frac{1}{4}$ in. (32 mm.) for No. 2, 1 in. (25 mm.) for No. 3, $1\frac{1}{2}$ in. (38 mm.) for No. 4, $1\frac{1}{4}$ in. (32 mm.) for No. 5 and 6. Further details of cabin-tops are given in Chapter 11.

7

Rigs and Rigging

There are four items to tackle when re-rigging an old yacht or completing a conversion with a sail plan.

(1) A design showing the basic details of sail areas, mast heights, positions of stays, mast fittings, sheet leads and winches.

(2) A schedule of standing and running rigging, including length and diameter of all wire ropes and cordage, the type of eye or terminal at each rope's end, the number and size of each rigging screw or other tensioning device required, plus a list of shackles and other special connectors.

(3) The making of all masts and spars (in wood, alloy, or other material) and the making or ordering of sails.

(4) Fabrication (or ordering) and installation of all fittings such as tracks, bands, chain plates, tangs, tabernacles and stemhead fitting.

SAIL PLAN DESIGN

A good basic sail plan is the first essential for the conversionist, on the lines given in Chapters 2 and 6 for various ship's lifeboats and an M.F.V. When deviating from recommended plans or perhaps changing the sail plan completely on an existing yacht, the amateur is advised to submit his preliminary drawings to a yacht designer to be vetted or redrawn.

While doing this, the designer should also complete the next stage by including mast and spar dimensions and thicknesses plus standard rigging sizes. The choice of fittings is then simplified for when stock items are ordered the makers can advise one regarding the correct sizes to match the breaking stresses of the chosen wire ropes. If mast fittings and chain plates are to be home made the designer can check the material strength and proposed method of fastening these.

Many naval architects advertise in the yachting journals and it should not take many telephone calls to find one willing to undertake this kind of work. His fee may vary between £20 and £100 ($100 and $500) according to the amount of work involved, and the urgency of the job. This cost is usually worth while, giving the amateur confidence and ensuring that the finished job is satisfactory and safe.

It may seem a good idea to copy exactly the rigging details of a similar craft of known performance, or to fit the complete outfit of sails, spars and rigging mass-produced for one of the popular cruising or racing classes.

However, this method is not necessarily safe as the hull design should enter into the calculations. For instance, a multi-hulled craft may require a stronger mast for a given sail area as the hull cannot heel readily to relieve the rig of high stress in a sudden blow. At the same time, the shrouds on a catamaran may be well spread due to the great beam and can therefore be of comparatively thin wire. Similarly, a modern light displacement high performance yacht may have a rig which is unsuitable for all-weather cruising in a heavy displacement conversion.

A light-weight mast is a boon to good sailing performance but safety comes first and suitable dimensions for wooden masts for conversions are given in Chapters 2 and 6. Any maker of aluminium alloy spars will advise one concerning the correct section to use for a certain job and on the best system of standing rigging. Metal spars have many advantages if their cost is not prohibitive but wooden spars often look more suitable on a conversion. Alloy spars invariably have stainless steel fittings nowadays and these are costly. However, correctly made well-galvanized steel fittings are quite suitable for wooden masts and details of how to fabricate these cheaply are given in Chapter 8.

CHOICE OF RIG

The conversionist is often a heretic who prefers gaff rig to Bermuda and with so many modern sailing craft having rigs of identical appearance it may be just as well that a few people are keen to add some character to the yachting scene.

Gaff rig is more efficient than Bermuda off the wind and as many conversions do not sail easily to windward without the help of an auxiliary motor, this type of rig suits such craft admirably. With shorter masts, no sail tracks, no halyard winches and galvanized rigging, the cost of such a rig can be half that of a modern type.

Wishbone rig (which is similar to gaff but highly efficient) can also be created by the handy-man. Spritsail rig, as perfected on the famous Thames Barges, has its own advantages, one especially being the fitting of brails which enable the sail to be triced up to the mast in rapid time to reduce sail area in an emergency or when manoeuvring.

On large craft, picturesque rigs can be devised by having permanent yards aloft from which square sails can be set. Modernized versions of such rigs can have all sail handling carried out at deck level and an infinite number of combinations can be created by the enthusiast.

Modernized junk rigs, with fully battened sails, have been used for trans-ocean cruising and are surprisingly efficient even without headsails. The staysail schooner rig is attractive and easy to handle with a small crew. Well-equipped Bermuda ketches have a mizzen staysail in the locker and there is no reason why this sail should not be used in conjunction with a gaff mainsail if the mizzen mast is tall enough to make it worth while.

Every basic rig can have variations, and the enthusiast should inspect other craft to note any useful ideas which may be incorporated in his own boat.

With correct deck construction, a mainmast can be stepped on deck with certain advantages. This means a shorter mast to build, less interruption to accommodation and the doubtful advantage that if the rigging should fail there is a possibility that the mast may go overboard without breaking. Most deck-stepped masts are mounted in tabernacles to facilitate raising and lowering at fitting-out and laying-up times and to enable a yacht to shoot bridges on inland waterways. The type of mast which can fall overboard without damage is normally stepped into a shallow square cup on deck, the square preventing the mast from twisting due to the thrust of the gooseneck. Such a mast acts as a true strut without even the support given by a tabernacle and additional stiffness in the form of a larger cross section is normally necessary.

There are many other important details to be observed in sail plans of apparently similar types. Mainsails may be laced to the boom (or on a track) for roller reefing, while with points reefing the sail can be loose-footed or even boomless. A loose-footed mainsail may be more efficient than one fixed to a boom and if a wave breaks into the belly of such a sail it can readily spill away.

Roller reefing is a boon to the single-handed sailor, but sails with reef points set better when reefed and avoid the drooping boom problem.

Without roller gear, a boom can be rectangular in section (which is easier to make) and with this are coupled the advantages of a mainsheet attachment inboard from the boom end without needing a claw ring, simple attachment of a *boom vang* (kicking strap), while a topping lift tackle and clue outhaul tackle may be fitted along the side of the boom.

Each type of rig can have quite different standing rigging arrangements. The Bermudan sloop may have masthead rig in which the forestay leads from masthead to stemhead, counteracted by a permanent backstay from the masthead to the boat's stern. This rig enables a useful masthead genoa jib to be set on the forestay. However, such a mast needs to be of very large section (with no taper at the top) unless a lower forestay opposed by running backstays can also be fitted. If a headboard lock can be fitted, enabling the main halyard to be left slack when sailing, the compression on the mast from this source is halved.

Gaff-rigged boats generally have to manage without the benefits of permanent backstays but observation may show that a correctly designed gaff rig of conventional cruising area does not need runners if the shrouds are set well aft, Pilot Cutter fashion. Note that a permanent backstay may be impracticable on the mizzen mast of a ketch or yawl, even when Bermuda rigged, so the mizzen shrouds are set well aft, especially when a *triatic stay* is fitted from the mainmast head to the mizzen masthead. Such a stay can rarely be fitted to a gaff ketch but is customary on most types of schooner.

The amateur may find many kinds of standing rigging materials in use. The high specification racing craft may have streamlined stainless steel rod rigging for minimum weight and windage. An expensive cruising boat may have stainless steel wire rope rigging with swaged terminals connected to stainless steel rigging screws (*turn-buckles* or *bottle screws*), plus stainless steel chain plates and mast tangs.

Single strand 'piano' wire may be used on a racing dinghy. One popular class of auxiliary sloop might have galvanized steel rigging with *Talurit* eye splices at the ends, while another similar class boat might have plastics-coated rigging wire with *Norseman* (*Mate*) terminals.

A gaff-rigged boat does not need to have hand-spliced rigging, parcelled and served from top to bottom with deadeyes and lanyards, though this may suit the old-fashioned type of hull best. If the shrouds and forestay (and perhaps the running backstays) are made with a soft eye at the top to slip over the mast onto a stop, bolster, or thumb cleats, this makes the cheapest form of mast and rigging for the do-it-yourself man.

The shrouds on a gaff boat do not need to be strained bar tight with rigging screws, and the lanyards of Italian hemp (which are rove through the deadeyes) give the rig elasticity to prevent things breaking under difficult conditions. One can sometimes insert a rigging screw below (or above) each set of deadeyes to facilitate adjusting the tension in the shrouds during the season. Numerous hints on standing and running rigging and on the different sorts of wire rope and cordage used for them are given in *Boat Maintenance*, together with instructions on canvaswork and sail repairs. Sail making is covered in the book *Make Your Own Sails* by R. M. Bowker and S. A. Budd (Macmillan).

The enthusiast may learn more from observation and reading than from conversations at the club bar, but most sources of information have some value. Discussions with experienced yachtsmen often help to clear up small problems which may be difficult to find in print. For instance, you may wish to fit your forestaysail on a boom to facilitate tacking when single-handed, but you may find yourself in an embarrassing situation the first time the sail is used as it may prove impossible to hoist it without first removing the boom! This is because the foot of the sail is nearly always longer than the shortest distance from clew to luff.

Of the numerous ingenious devices in use for overcoming this difficulty, the following are often considered the best.

(1) Attach the clew of the sail to the end of a *club*, this being a spar considerably shorter than a conventional boom and not laced to the sail: the forward end of the boom must be attached to a swivel on deck and this may be mounted on a length of stout track to enable the club to slide forward when hoisting or lowering sail.

By experimenting with the position of the swivel (and the length of the club) it may be possible to improve the efficiency of the sail, for the tension on the foot is automatically slackened as the sheet is let out. Too short a club lowers the efficiency off the wind, but if the distance from swivel to clew can be made equal to the distance from swivel to tack, the club can be hinged right over, facing forward, to enable the staysail to be given a harbour stow just like an ordinary boomless jib.

(2) If the staysail is made to special order, it can have an extra strong wire luff rope incorporated to enable it to be set flying from the tack to a point well above the girt position, the remainder of the luff being hanked to the stay in normal fashion. To prevent over-straining a weak luff rope, a wire jack-rope can be rove as in Fig. 44, to allow hanks all the way. Normally, the jack-rope can be left belayed so that it tightens automatically on hoisting sail. For reefing, the jack-rope must be tensioned afterwards and re-belayed.

A simpler device might seem to be a clew outhaul which can be freed or tensioned as required, but in practice, if the sail is loose-footed the boom crashes to the deck (and the sail starts to flog) as the outhaul is released, while foot lacings will rarely slide along a boom smoothly when required.

When investigating the intricacies of boomed staysails, the amateur is bound to encounter the many sheet alternatives. As the intention is to aid single-handed tacking, a horse across the deck is

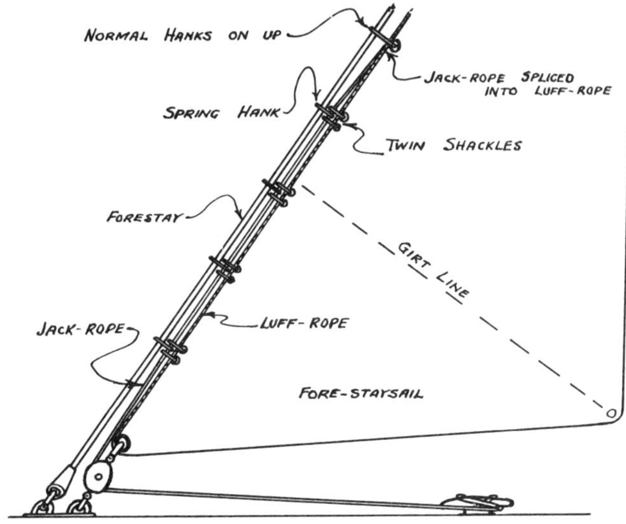

Fig 44: Wire jack-rope to reinforce weak luff rope

normally essential and the fall of the sheet must lead aft. To keep the sheet adjustment constant as the sail slides across, a single fall should lead from the top sheet block to a single block near the boom swivel before leading aft. This also enables the clew to be bowsed down tightly when closehauled.

To eliminate the need for a horse, the simple system shown in Fig. 45 can be used, the falls leading to sheet winches or tackles. This does not pull the clew down as tightly as the former method will but it allows automatic tacking and the endless sheet is less likely to wear in the blocks. Many other systems can be seen in use and some liberties can be taken because the pull on the sheet of a boomed staysail is very much less than that with an ordinary jib of equal area.

Headsails with reef points are rarities nowadays but for single-handed cruising reefing is sometimes simpler than changing sail. Twin forestays (side by side and not too close together) are a big

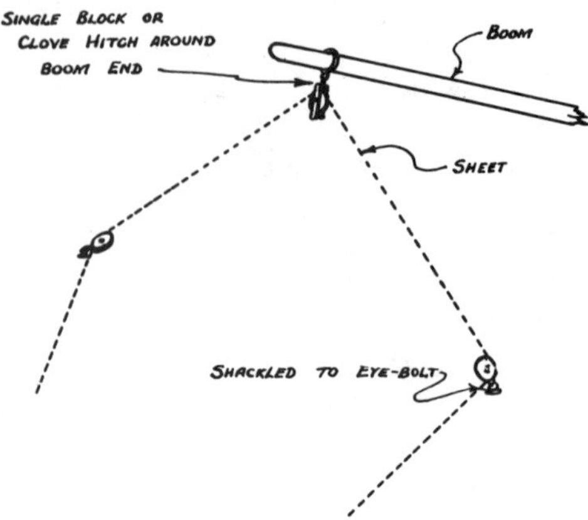

Fig. 45: Sheeting a boomed staysail

advantage in this connexion as two sails can be hanked on ready to hoist at the same time.

Jib roller furling gear works well on racing dinghies but unless special arrangements are made on bigger craft, the top of the luff rope will not always wind in unison with the drum at the bottom. Enthusiasts have tried many methods to master this problem, from spring-loaded swivels at the head to a length of twisted small chain sewn along the luff.

Observe how expensive halyard winches can be dispensed with by fitting simple tack tensioners. Note that halyard falls are traditionally cleated to the starboard side of the mast to facilitate reefing and sail changing on the right-of-way tack. Both peak and throat halyards on a gaff boat should be equipped with the same ratio purchase so that the falls can be pulled in unison.

Much has been written about the rigging of twin running staysails and the deep water cruising enthusiast is advised to study this subject carefully before equipping his boat.

Even the humble topping lift is worthy of careful thought. On a ketch the main boom topping lift block can sometimes be fixed to the mizzen mast. In other cases twin topping lifts are ideal and the blocks may be hung beneath the cross trees (instead of being close to the mast) to avoid chafe. When a single topping lift must be used, its block should be situated at the masthead for a Bermudan sail and above the topmost peak halyard block with gaff rig, to avoid snarl-ups when hoisting sail.

You may observe other methods. With points reefing, the topping lift tackle can be along the under side of the boom, helping to keep the base of the mast free from clutter. On small cruisers the topping lift can be a simple pendant attached to the backstay, clipped to the boom end by means of a carbine hook when required.

Other interesting fields for observation concern such items as boom gallows (scissors, crutches etc.); mainsheets; anti-chafe devices; deck fittings for running backstays (Highfield levers, tracks, wire rope spans etc.); adjustable jib sheet fairleads; inner forestay release mechanisms and all halyards.

SPAR MAKING

Given the correct sort of timber, there is no reason why the average handyman should not make perfectly good masts and spars. With modern glues, a warm shed, and dry wood, there can be no fear that a hollow mast will fall apart when it gets wet.

A solid grown stick is a rarity nowadays (even on the gaff rigged fishing boat type of yacht) but a spruce pole with the heart running straight up its centre is cheap when it can be found. Such a mast can be made for one-sixth the cost of a built spar of clear timber. After removal of the bark, the surface is usually pimpled with tiny knots, making outside shaping rather troublesome when using a drawknife and plane.

A glued mast is superior to a solid grown one for several other reasons. It is not prone to warping and to surface cracking; it will not rot secretly in the heart, and it can be made hollow, the lighter weight being an advantage at laying-up time as well as improving performance under sail.

Hollow wooden masts are generally built up in the sections detailed in Fig. 46. The sailing dinghy and light displacement cruiser may adopt a luff groove as in Fig. 46a, but this is generally unsuitable for big craft as there is too much friction and the sail is not self-stowing when lowered rapidly. The section in Fig. 47a can

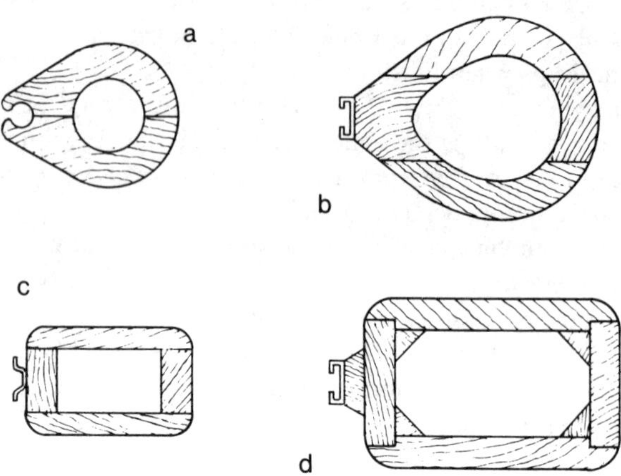

Fig. 46: Luff attachments for hollow masts

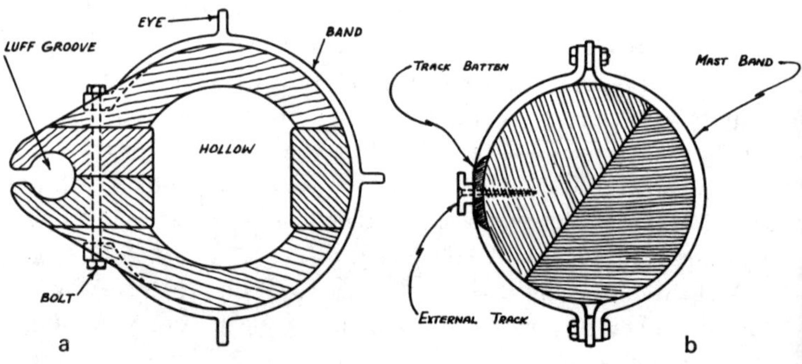

Fig. 47: Fitting mast bands with luff groove or track

be used for big masts with luff grooves, but internal track, (46b), is more popular. Dinghies can also have rectangular masts with a light external track, (46c), while big craft can use the stronger rectangular construction shown in (46d).

Booms are usually solid, glued up from two pieces, either round or rectangular. A foot-rope groove or track can be incorporated. For cruisers where the mainsail is left stowed under a sail coat, the foot is often secured by lacing, and then a semi-circular cove is cut along the top of the boom to align the foot rope. This is done mainly on round booms designed for roller reefing. Gaffs and gunter yards are best made hollow for minimum weight aloft.

Round and pear-shaped masts are ideal from the strength/weight viewpoint, but rectangular hollow masts are easier to make as hollowing is eliminated. Scarfing is permissible as long as no two scarfs are closer together than about 4 ft. (1200 mm.) with glue faces at a 1 in 10 angle.

Silver spruce (Sitka spruce) is almost universally specified for hollow spars. It should be *clear* (free from knots) and is best ordered from a timber firm specializing in boat timbers, or from a boatyard. The amateur may be given hemlock in lieu of spruce at some sawmills, and this is a stringy, heavier timber, though with similar grain. Where weight is not critical, clear B.C. pine (Douglas fir) may be used for rectangular spars, and this is considerably cheaper than spruce. Parana pine is readily available clear and is quite cheap, but it looks terrible when varnished and is not so resilient as spruce.

GLUING THE JOINTS

The only problem likely to arise in gluing up a mast is in getting it cramped up quickly enough owing to the great number of cramps required. Hollow masts were jointed with casein glue successfully for over twenty years, so results should be ideal nowadays when resin glue with its considerable gap-filling properties is used.

Most spar makers prefer a two-part glue such as Aerolite, as no hardening occurs until the pieces are brought together just prior to cramping. *Cascamite* one-shot glue is suitable, but in warm weather it pays to get a few helpers to assist in spreading the glue rapidly.

Smooth planed surfaces are far from ideal for good bonding, so a flat rub with extremely coarse garnet paper is advisable, taking care not to round off the edges.

Cramping the joint is quite simple once the equipment has been borrowed or fabricated. All timber should be left square outside until after gluing and a few temporary wire nails may be driven to align the parts perfectly before cramping. Such nails are essential in a mast of type (c) as you then have four joints to glue in unison and the parts can slip out of alignment rather easily. For a type (d) mast, the four corner fillets would be glued and brass pinned to the big pieces prior to final assembly.

One can rarely borrow enough G-cramps, as these should be set at about 5 in. (130 mm.) intervals for a dinghy mast and at 9 in. (230 mm.) for a big 40 ft. (12 m.) spar. The intervals should be slightly closer for a rectangular job, as the side pieces are not so stiff as in a round section. Improvised cramps can be made as in Fig. 48 from two strips of softwood with two carriage bolts, pref-

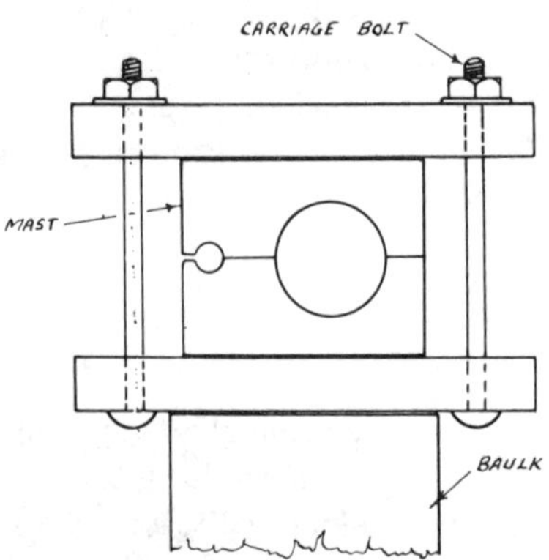

Fig. 48: Improvised cramps for making hollow mast

erably having wing nuts and washers. One of the top strip holes can be cut out to a slot to facilitate rapid assembly.

Take care to get the bolts of exactly the right length to avoid the use of packing pieces, though these may be needed on the tapering top part of a mast. For a dinghy mast, strips of 2 in. × 1 in. (50 mm. × 25 mm.) deal with $\frac{1}{4}$ in. (6 mm.) carriage bolts will do. For a cruiser mast 2 in. (50 mm.) square deal or $1\frac{1}{2}$ in. (38 mm.) square hardwood with $\frac{5}{16}$ in. (8 mm.) bolts would be suitable.

If cramps cannot be made or borrowed, pairs of oak wedges may be used instead by laying the assembly on a truly flat floor with chocks of wood nailed at intervals each side of the mast.

Surplus glue should be wiped from the outside after cramping using dry rags, though a better way is perhaps to scrape this off with an old chisel when the glue has gelled but before it hardens.

It may seem a waste of time, but a trial run of fitting and tightening the cramps is advisable before any glue is spread. The time taken should be noted, and checked with the glue makers' data sheet at the room temperature concerned to see whether the allowable manipulating period has been exceeded. If it has, arrange for more assistance to be available, or tighten every other cramp only initially.

Unless a flat floor or a full length spar bench is available the job should be set up on baulks of timber cleated together end-to-end and planed true with a jointer plane. A few vertical soldiers nailed to the sides of the baulk will prevent the cramped assembly from rolling off.

Instead of continuous baulks one can use cross trestles or chocks at 2 ft. (600 mm.) intervals for a dinghy mast or 4 ft. (1200 mm.) for a big spar. Another alternative is to fix brackets out from a wall. Both these methods have the advantage of a better working height than baulks lying on the floor. Furthermore when working in a heated shed in winter, the air temperature will be about 10° F (6° C) warmer at 3 ft. (1 m.) above floor level. Brackets or trestles can be set in line by sighting along them carefully from one end. Any packing used must be pinned firmly in place.

PRELIMINARIES TO SHAPING

Whether standard fittings are to be bought, or whether the amateur intends to make these himself, it often pays to have them before spar making begins. If a band happens to be slightly larger than intended, a swelling can be left in the timber to obviate the use of packing, and in any case a snug fit can be ensured before the final external shaping is done.

The rigging fittings for rectangular and pear-shaped masts are usually in the form of tangs mounted on plates which are secured with a pattern of woodscrews, sometimes with additional small through-bolts.

For round cruiser masts, standard forged mast bands with eyes make the cheapest fittings. Remember that they have to be tapped down to their correct place from the top of the mast, so shape the outside accordingly, leaving shallow shoulders where possible. Without a shoulder many boat builders fit wooden thumb cleats under a band to prevent it from pulling downwards, see Chapter 8.

It may be possible to eliminate the necessity for a complicated masthead fitting with tangs by gluing a hardwood truck staff into the top of a round mast (see Fig. 49) to form a bolster. All the

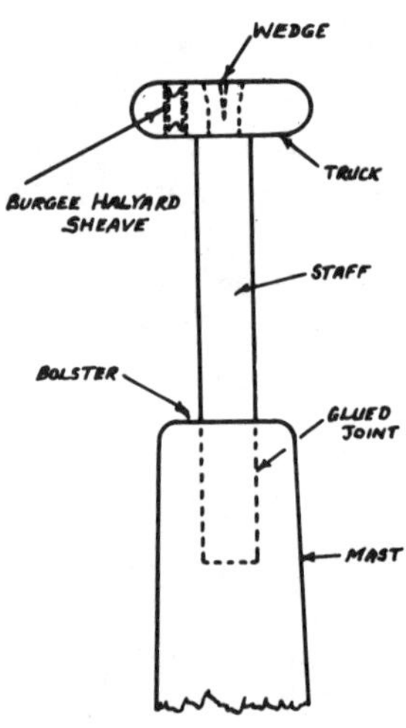

Fig. 49: Hardwood truck and bolster at masthead

masthead rigging wires are then made with soft spliced eyes to slip over this post before the truck is wedged on. The strops for main, spinnaker, and masthead jib halyards may also be incorporated.

Gooseneck bands are normally split with bolts to pull them up tightly. Sometimes a strip of sail cloth is used to parcel the mast underneath them. Where ordinary mast bands are fitted, the sail track must be mounted on a batten as in Fig. 46c to allow the bands to pass under the track. Give the wood under all fittings a couple of coats of varnish, and if tang plates do not fit perfectly, set them in bedding compound to prevent water getting beneath. The same procedure as above applies to boom fittings.

Order the timber about $\frac{1}{8}$ in. (3 mm.) oversize to allow for finishing and any necessary swellings, but get it planed (specifying the finished sizes after planing) as you will then be able to mark it more easily, and to see any defects which should be turned to the inside.

Examine the timber for twist and bend, and arrange to glue it up so that these tend to oppose each other. If possible, oppose the end grain in adjacent pieces as seen in Fig. 46a. If the timber is a bad shape do not despair. Cramp the pieces together as intended with G-cramps at 18 in. (450 mm.) intervals, and sight along. If the athwartships faces are not dead straight, this can be rectified when the spar is glued by forcing it in the opposite direction.

Remember to impart this set while the cramps are slack. Check the correct amount of set by trial-and-error. Strut the spar approximately, then tighten the cramps and take the struts away. If the amount of set has been correct, the spar should spring back dead straight.

If cramping on a baulk, chocks can be fitted to provide the set, augmented by struts from the roof or cramps through holes in the baulk. When cramping on wall brackets or trestles, struts can be rigged from both floor and roof, or from higher wall brackets if there is no roof.

INTERIOR SHAPING

Hollowing the inside of a spar, whether composed of two or four pieces, cannot be called a difficult job, though it takes some time. Luckily, the timber used is always an easy cutting variety.

Construction drawings for spars usually show a vertical section appearing somewhat as shown in Fig. 50. The longitudinal dimensions are marked on while the widths and wall thicknesses are drawn to an exaggerated scale such as half full-size, so that any dimension can be scaled off readily with a rule. The length and

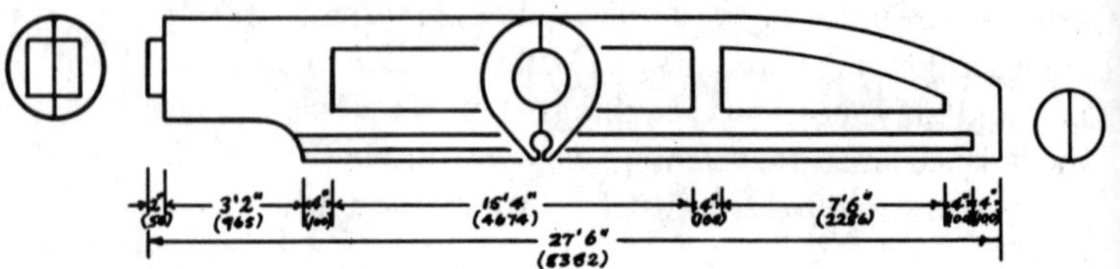

Fig. 50: Designer's drawing for a hollow mast

position of all solid cores is given on the longitudinal dimensions. The luff face of a mast is normally kept dead straight.

Note that if one requires to fit internal halyards in a mast designed with solid cores at the rigging fittings, this can be done by leaving holes with funnelled ends through the cores, but if a halyard ever breaks it will be difficult to draw in a new wire.

The wall thickness normally remains constant throughout, including the tapered top section, so these lines can be scribed on to the timber with an ordinary carpenter's gauge. Lay the pieces of timber side by side so that the positions of cores can be marked straight across to correspond exactly. This is especially important where sheaves have to be boxed in.

Before hollowing starts, separate templates should be made from thin metal for the centre hollowing and for a luff groove, appearing as in Fig. 51. The hollows must not be cut deeper than the template shapes, nor should there be any humps or unevenness.

Hollowing can be accomplished entirely with gouges, and a mallet is not essential for spruce. A good finish can be effected by using a round moulding plane of smaller radius than the hollow, but a gouge finish is satisfactory. For the luff groove, a moulding plane should be used all the way (accuracy being ensured by means of a guide batten tacked to the timber) completing a length of about 10 ft. (3 m.) at a time. Do not plane down the outer lip of the luff slot until the groove has been hollowed completely, and sanded dead smooth.

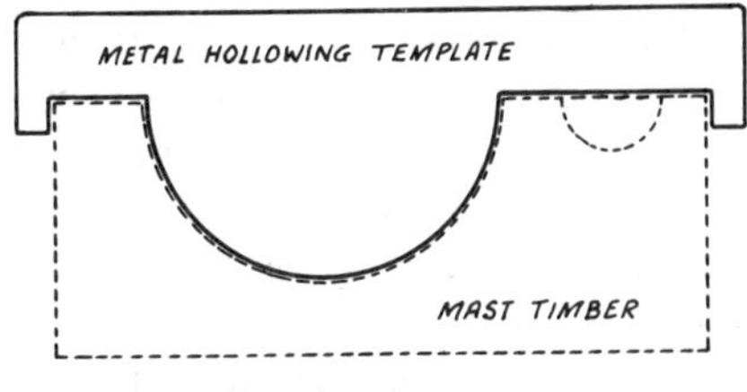

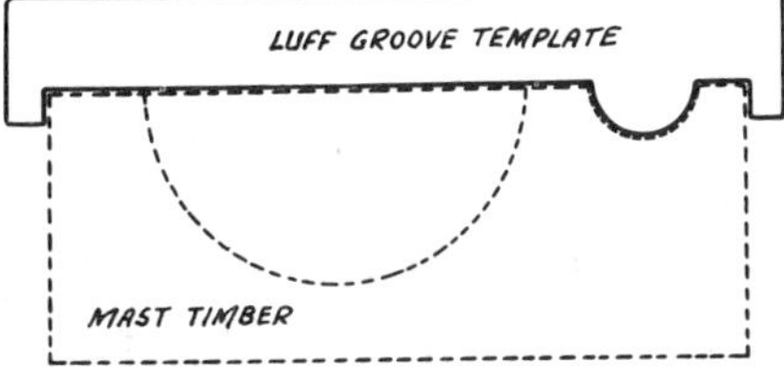

Fig. 51: Templates for mast hollow and luff groove

To speed up the centre hollowing, a portable electric saw can be used to rout it with a series of closely spaced cuts, appearing in section as in Fig. 52. Get a trial piece of timber correctly marked

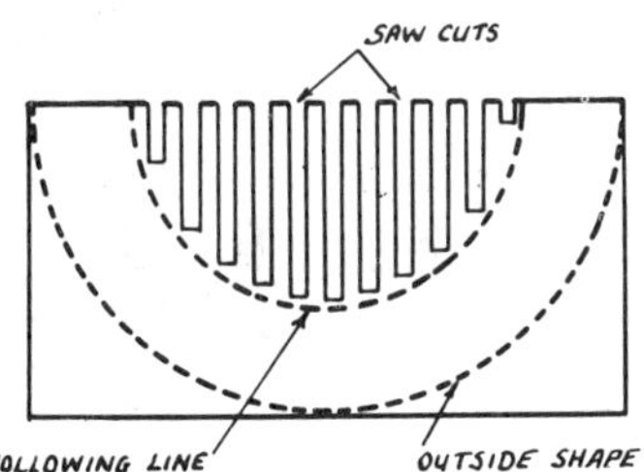

Fig. 52: Cutting out the mast hollow

out on the end grain and test the adjustment of the fence and depth gauge on this before each mast cut is made. Breaking out the remaining bits is then simple, and little gouge work is necessary, though some hand cutting will be required up close to the solid cores. If preferred, the cores can be made as separate filler blocks to be glued into the continuous hollow.

If internal halyards are specified, the sheaves should be bought (or made) housed in cages, and these must be available when the notches are made. Before gluing up, the hollows and notches should be given two coats of varnish. If water can get into the mast via sheave openings, the wood can get wet and increase the weight of the mast. This is especially important in racing dinghies, as a capsize could mean impregnation with salt water, and the salt will attract moisture continuously.

EXTERNAL SHAPING

After varnishing the inside, a jointer plane set fine can be used for final surfacing of the gluing joints. Cords should be laid inside the hollow to pull in any inside halyards. Smear the cords with vaseline to prevent accidental adhesion by surplus glue squeezed from the joints on cramping.

As soon as all the cramps are stripped off, outside shaping can commence. A round mast is first planed into an octagon, then into a sixteen-sided section, before final rounding and sanding. A pear-shaped mast is similar, but the octagon is then a distorted one, as shown in Fig. 53.

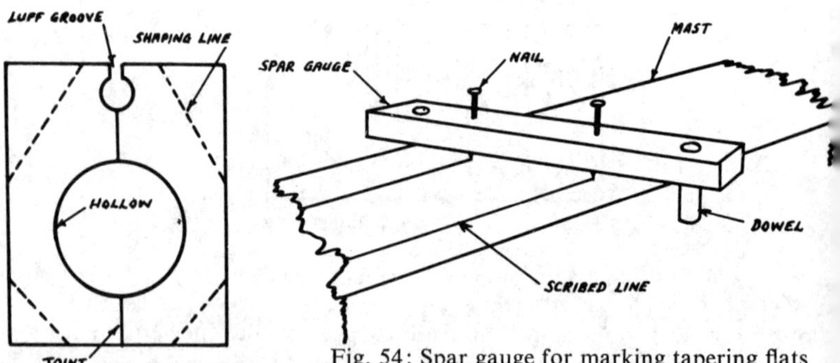

Fig. 54: Spar gauge for marking tapering flats

Fig. 53: Marking out a pear-section mast

To mark out the planing flats, a *spar gauge* (sketched in Fig. 54) is useful. It marks two lines in unison. The sharpened nails act as scribers, and as long as the pegs are kept in contact with the sides of the mast, it proportions the scribed lines automatically when drawn along a tapering spar. This is especially useful for tapered sweeps, yards, booms, gaffs and bowsprits. The nails should not be pressed too deeply into the wood and stubs of pencil may be preferred.

A drawknife or spokeshave handles rounding work rapidly, but these tools do tend to produce a wavy surface, and a smoothing plane is really the best thing to use. The first octagon cuts can be roughed off with a circular saw to speed up the work, then finished down to the marks with the plane.

Sandpaper should never be wrapped around the normal cork block for fear of creating flats. Instead, make a hollowed softwood chock of the correct radius to fit the spar. If a scraper has been used, only very fine sandpaper should be necessary, and as with all softwood varnishing, a thorough but fine sandpapering is needed after the priming coat to remove any minute hairs of wood that stick up.

ALLOY SPARS

Aluminium alloy masts and spars have almost superseded wood for all production craft nowadays and although the amateur can work in this material, it generally proves considerably more expensive than wood, and unless extrusions of known strength are obtained from a metal mast maker there may be some doubt about the load capacity of an amateur effort.

Many different specifications of aluminium alloys are available in tube form and the designer who vets the sail plan should be asked to approve the type of tube to be used for spars before this is ordered. For a cheap job, cadmium plated steel fittings can be attached to the alloy tube, but stainless steel fittings are superior. It may be possible to utilize some standard fittings (especially for a dinghy mast) but otherwise all fittings may have to be fabricated as described in the next chapter.

For a cruiser mast, standard aluminium or stainless steel internal track with side flanges or intermittent side brackets for fastening (as made for fitting to round wooden masts) may be attached to alloy tube. For a dinghy (or similar small craft mast or boom) where a luff rope or foot rope groove is required, the groove may be formed by cutting a slit along the full length of a piece of thick walled alloy tube of appropriate diameter and bonding this to the mast with epoxy resin. The edges of the slit must be well rounded to prevent damage to the sail and the tube may be given a long taper at the lower end to form a neat entry. Instead of metal tubing, a similar luff groove can be formed in exactly the same way by using glass-fibre tube.

All metal mast fittings can be attached by means of aluminium pop rivets, but the usual $\frac{1}{8}$ in. (3 mm.) rivets and gun sold by hardware stores should be used only for the smallest dinghy mast. For increasing sizes, $\frac{3}{16}$ in. (4 mm.) and $\frac{1}{4}$ in. (6 mm.) rivets are necessary and although the much stronger monel metal rivets are readily available, aluminium ones are less likely to create corrosion and are strong enough if correctly spaced.

When standard fittings for wooden masts are utilized, these may already have fixing holes bored through them for wood screws which will undoubtedly be too large for pop rivets. Additional holes will in any case be necessary to take the rivets and the original holes can be ignored.

Extra security can be given to highly stressed tangs by using stainless steel bolts in addition to the rivets. To put these in, solder a long length of thin copper wire to the tip of each bolt to enable it to be drawn from the base of the mast into its hole. To prevent the head turning while tightening the nut, the excess length of bolt can be held with grips prior to cutting it off and riveting over.

Plugs for each end of a spar can be turned on a lathe from *Tufnol* to be secured in position by means of stainless steel self-tapping screws. Alternatively, the ends may be plugged with discs of wood, sealed with g.r.p. putty.

ADDING MORE HEADSAIL

The majority of modern cruising sloops have stemhead rigs with tubby hulls for maximum accommodation. Consequently, many are under-canvased and hard-headed in strong winds. Great improvements to both sail area and balance can often be effected by adding a short bowsprit, shifting the forestay from the stemhead to the tip of the bowsprit in preference to adding a second stay.

The job must be done in a workmanlike manner to ensure safety and the following notes are intended to show a few of the possible methods, one of which is often more applicable to one class of boat than any of the others.

When no information can be obtained from the owner of a similar craft who may have experimented with a bowsprit, it usually pays to jury rig one to enable the performance improvement to be checked before getting to work with saw and drill. A secure bobstay is almost essential for this and to get a good anchorage near the waterline at the cutwater fix a strop of thin flexible steel wire rope from the stern alongside the keel to the stem, if necessary with one or two strops passing underneath the keel to prevent the wire rope from shifting when under stress. Any bulldog grips used for making connexions and thimbled eyes should be carefully wrapped to prevent them from scoring the hull surface.

For a yacht built as in (a) in Fig. 55 a jury bowsprit of 3 in. × 3

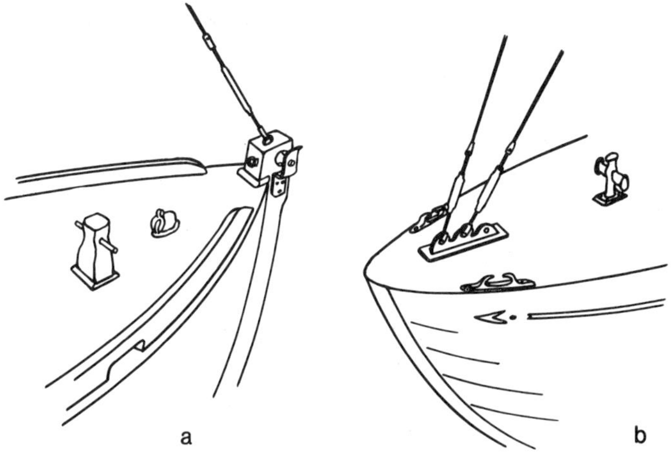

Fig. 55: Alternative stemhead structures

in. (75 mm. × 75 mm.) square timber might be suitable, lashed against the port side of the stemhead upstand (to counteract athwartships movement only) with its heel lashed firmly against the forward face of the samson post to resist the backward pull from the forestay and bobstay. The original forestay can be utilized quite easily by making up a short lizard, or by using additional rigging screws to lengthen it. Standard heavy duty eye bolts can be fitted to the end of the spar to take both forestay and bobstay.

Fitting a temporary bowsprit to the type of construction shown in (b) in Fig. 55 is not quite so simple and to ensure a secure stem-head lashing it may be necessary to take this down the topsides to the bobstay strop and under the keel.

TYPES OF BOWSPRIT

The flat plank bowsprit shown in Fig. 56a makes a neat job and variations of this type are widely used in America and New Zealand where they are sometimes referred to as 'Walk-out bow-sprits'. With an overhang of less than 18 in. (450 mm.) it may be possible to dispense with the need for a bobstay on small boats provided the plank is 1½ in. (38 mm.) thick oak, not less than 4 in. (1200 mm.) wide.

Before cutting off the stemhead of a type (a) deck leave a tenon in the middle of it to notch lightly into the underside of the bow-sprit. This takes the majority of the loading and a single ⅝ in. (15 mm.) bolt welded to the stem band (or a similar purpose-made fitting fastened to the face of the stem with coach screws) may prove sufficient. If the underside of the plank is shaped to fit snugly to the underside of the deck and laid in bedding compound at least one extra fastening should be fitted through the deck between the stemhead and the samson post to prevent the plank from flexing. Such deck bolts must be used entirely for a type (b) installation. When a bobstay is fitted, a resilient timber such as spruce, ash, or hickory proves best.

A bowsprit may look neater if given an upward steeve to follow the sheerline of the vessel and this can be achieved as in Fig. 56b

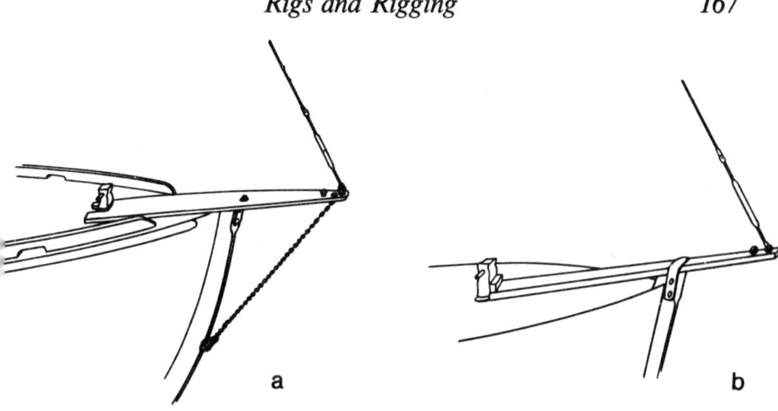

Fig. 56: Methods of fitting bowsprits

by cutting the stem off a short distance above deck level. The awkward space between the bowsprit and the deck can be filled by a tapered chock set in bedding compound. The gammon iron type of stemhead fitting illustrated can be used to secure a conventional round spar as well as a square or plank type. An eye can be incorporated to enable a jib to be set at the stemhead if ever required.

Flat plank bowsprits can have an anchor stowed underneath them with the cable roller towards the tip of the bowsprit. The anchor may be catted beneath the bowsprit to prevent it from swinging about and dragging in the water.

A conventional stemhead roller can be retained if the plank-on-edge type of bowsprit shown in Fig. 56c is adopted. A bobstay is rarely needed with this type and excellent fastenings through the stem and samson post are simple to arrange. However, if the plank is made too thin it could flex alarmingly athwartships unless bowsprit shrouds are fitted.

A rather superior design is the box girder or twin plank type illustrated in Fig. 56d. This requires neither bobstay nor shrouds for normal lengths and an anchor cable roller is simple to incorporate. Unfortunately the design often looks unsightly though this can be minimized by tapering in each direction from the stem but keeping the top edge straight as viewed from one side.

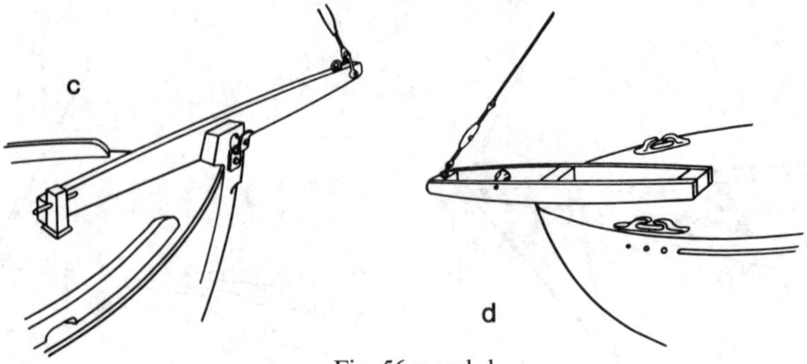

Fig. 56 c and d

For a 2 ft. (600 mm.) overhang on a 23 ft. (7 m.) sloop, the planks would need to be of 1⅛ in. (28 mm.) spruce, 4 in. (100 mm.) deep at the stemhead. For a 4 ft. (1200 mm.) overhang on a 33 ft. (10 m.) boat, the thickness should be 1¼ in. (32 mm.) and the stemhead depth 6 in. (150 mm.). When a roller fairlead is incorporated, the sides of the timber can be protected with copper sheeting. Should the bitts or samson post be set a long way from the stem the heel of the bowsprit can be held to the deck by a chock as shown in Fig. 56d.

The type pictured in Fig. 56e can be made of attractive appearance if well proportioned. For a cutter with permanent inner forestay, the heels can be hinged to enable the bowsprit to be swung inboard when at moorings. This necessitates the slackening of the outer forestay rigging screw and the removal of a slip-hook on the bobstay.

The planks should be laminated from 5 or 6 strips of oak or spruce bonded with phenolic glue, the minimum width being about 2½ in. (64 mm.) and minimum thickness 1⅛ in. (28 mm.). As the main thrust is along the planks the chocks at the heels must be well secured with stout brass backflap hinges at each side when the bowsprit is to be hinged.

The use of a pulpit naturally leads to the fabrication of a complete assembly of steel tubing as sketched in Fig. 56f. Plumbers ½ in. (12 mm.) steel barrel pipe is suitable for very small assemblies, but ¾ in. (18 mm.) is best for craft between 26 ft. (8 m.) and 35 ft. (11 m.) in length, the outside diameter of this being just over 1 in.

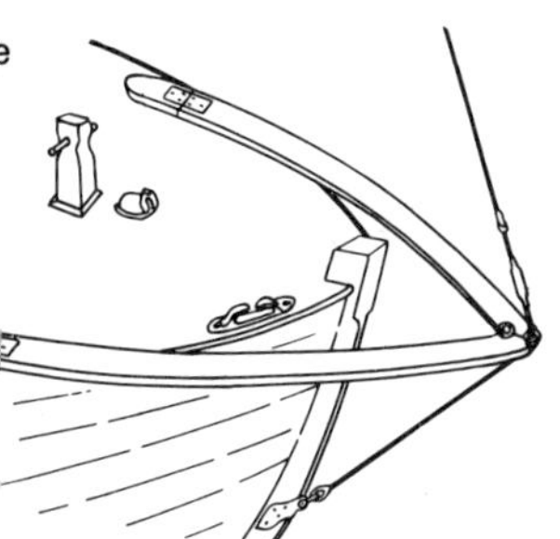

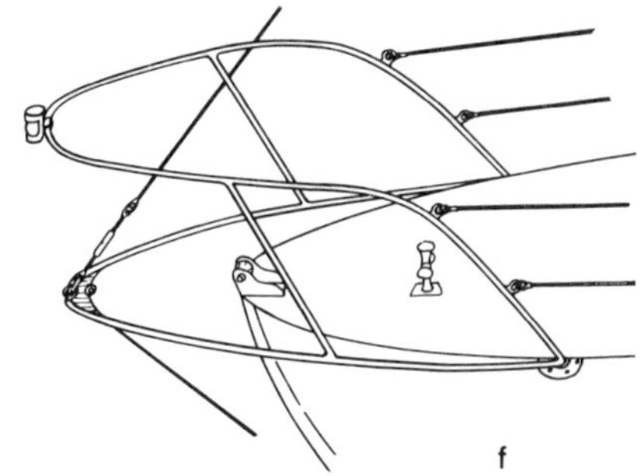

Fig. 56 e and f

(25 mm.). Any blacksmith or boatyard machine shop will bend and weld the tubing prior to galvanizing or zinc spraying.

One great advantage of this sort of bowsprit is that the heels can be bolted to the topsides just below the deck so that no part encroaches upon the deck space.

The bobstay stem bolt can be a single galvanized eyebolt (see Fig 56a) on very small boats and for almost any size of craft built in plastics. For large wooden craft the hole might be too long for a standard eye bolt and prove difficult to bore, so a special bracket may have to be fabricated as described in the next chapter. Alternatively, it may be possible to utilize two standard stainless steel or galvanized shroud plates fitted on either side of the stem with a bolt connecting them together through the eyes.

For a rough job, a long-jawed shackle can be opened at the mouth and fitted by means of a long bolt passing through an athwartships hole well inboard from the face of the stem.

A bobstay of tested galvanized chain is generally better than one of wire rope due to possible anchor cable chafe. Most bowsprits permit a small amount of give and if the bobstay is made to the exact length it may be set up taut automatically as soon as the forestay rigging screw is tightened.

8

Fabricating Fittings and Keels

Although the average do-it-yourself yachtsman may not possess extensive workshop facilities for carrying out metal work, the price of boat fittings is often so high nowadays that the amateur may be tempted to fabricate a good number of the parts needed for a new boat or a conversion and thus gain much pleasure and useful experience.

TOOLS

Curiously enough, a set of basic hand tools for working metal costs less than a similar carpentry outfit. The only expensive item, which is almost impossible to manage without, is a vertical drilling machine. One of the old hand-operated types will do, but a proper drill press (belt driven from an attached electric motor) may be bought secondhand quite cheaply.

A complete set of twist drills from $\frac{1}{16}$ in. to $\frac{1}{2}$ in. (1.5 mm. to 12 mm.) with stand is ideal. Carbon drills are cheaper than High Speed Steel, especially in the bigger sizes, and carbon steel is suitable for most amateur work. A hand bench grinder is essential for sharpening drills, while a small machine vice to hold work for drilling is a valuable safety asset.

The remaining hand tools are not expensive. Marking-out tools should include a scriber, dividers, centre punch, small steel rule, and try-square. Most handymen possess a steel bench vice and a hacksaw, but your files must be in good shape, complete with handles. A minimum set of files should include one of each of the following: 8 in. (200 mm.) flat smooth; 12 in. (300 mm.) flat second cut; 4 in. (100 mm.) half-round smooth; 8 in. (200 mm.) half-round smooth; 12 in. (300 mm.) half-round second cut; 6 in. (150 mm.) round smooth; 10 in. (250 mm.) round second cut;

8 in. (200 mm.) square smooth; 4 in. (100 mm.) triangular smooth and a set of Swiss needle files.

This may seem an imposing list of files, but they are not costly. Nearly all hand shaping and finishing is done with files and workmanship equal to machining can be attained with practice. A 12 oz. (340 g.) ball pein hammer is useful for riveting. For cutting where a hacksaw cannot get one needs a few cold chisels, preferably one 4 in. (100 mm.) with $\frac{1}{4}$ in. (6 mm.) tip; one 6 in. (150 mm.) with $\frac{3}{8}$ in. (9 mm.) tip; one 8 in. (200 mm.) with $\frac{5}{8}$ in. (15 mm.) tip. Various items such as screwdrivers, spanners, pliers, etc., are normally available in one's engine tool kit, but extra small tools like tinman's snips, countersink bit, calipers, copper-faced hammer, and wire brushes always come in useful.

An improvised anvil and a few blocks of hardwood are required for hammering and marking metal parts. A block of cast steel (such as an old diesel engine crankshaft balance weight) can usually be scrounged from a garage, or perhaps a short piece of rail track.

The model engineer who has a $3\frac{1}{2}$ in. (88 mm.) lathe can fabricate wonderful things for a boat. He can turn the parts for sheet and halyard winches, make rigging screws, sheaves, and bullseyes, and by metal spinning he can produce fine ventilators, lamps, foghorn or copper tundish.

HEAVY PARTS

Generally speaking, one cannot save quite so much money when fabricating heavy parts such as bilge keels, centre-plate, or rudder, as for the intricate fittings like mast bands, tabernacle, or rope blocks. If the facilities are available, sheet winches can be made for about one-quarter the shop price, mast fittings about one-third, runner levers, stemhead and shroud plates, pulpit, blocks, and cleats, less than one-half.

If hardboard templates are made for bilge keels matched correctly to the hull surface, the plates may be cut out by an engineering firm having an oxy-acetylene cutter. Bending the flange plate to suit is then quite a simple matter of cramping but the bolt holes must be bored before the flange is welded on. The top edge of each bilge keel should be filed to a 'V' as seen in Fig. 57, so that the fillets of weld meet each other.

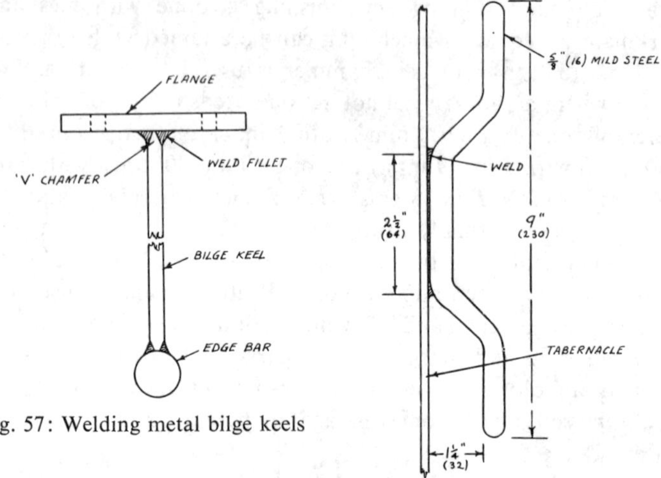

Fig. 57: Welding metal bilge keels

Fig. 58: Metal cleat for steel tabernacle

Some bilge keels are intended to have a length of round bar welded to the outer edges to make a neat finish (or a length of flat steel to prevent sinking into the mud) but a filed cutwater edge is likely to reduce water resistance more. On completion, the keels should be sent away for galvanizing through a boatyard. Alternatively they may be metal sprayed with ·010 in. (250 microns) of zinc.

When making a steel tabernacle the process is much the same but make your halyard and topping lift cleats from $\frac{1}{2}$ in. (12 mm.) or $\frac{5}{8}$ in. (15 mm.) bar (as in Fig. 58) and weld these on during fabrication. Tabernacles supplied by chandlers rarely have cleats, but this is a better place than on the gooseneck band, where those ghastly T-shaped bollard cleats are used. Cleats welded at an angle of about 15° are generally more convenient than vertical ones.

Rudders are frequently galvanized, though bronze is better where a propeller is adjacent. Bronze rudders are best cast from a wooden pattern (see later) though they can be built up from plate, the stock being slit to fit over the plate (for a balanced rudder) and riveted or brazed in place.

Most plate rudders require two or more pairs of web plates brazed to the sides for additional stiffness, so it often pays to adopt a cast rudder. Castings can be smoothed over quite easily using a high speed abrasive disc. Some machining will be needed, for the stock has either to be riveted into a socket (Fig. 59a) as used for

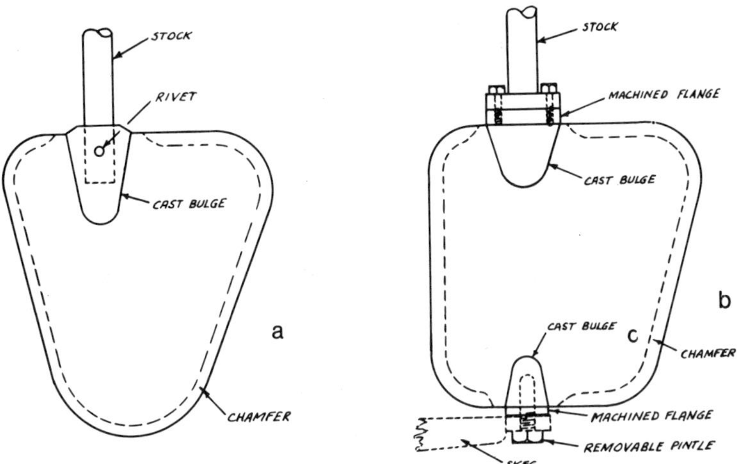

Fig. 59: Attaching a cast rudder to its stock

runabouts, or attached with a flange joint top and bottom (Fig. 59b) as for some motor cruisers.

MAST FITTINGS

Although expensive and hard to work, stainless steel is the best material for many small boat fittings, including pulpits and guard-rail stanchions. Any welding can be farmed out to specialists – similarly polishing, which is best done electrolytically. Aluminium alloy fittings are fine for metal masts and easy to fabricate if pop-riveted. Galvanized mild steel is ideal for big boat fittings. Brass is easy to shape, bore and rivet. It can be brazed or silver soldered if necessary. However, any heating tends to anneal brass and the best results are obtained if the initial hardness of the material is retained.

The typical masthead fitting shown in Fig. 60 might be fabri-

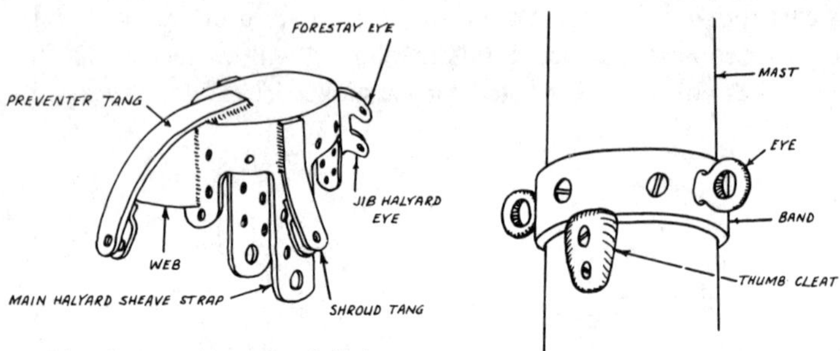

Fig 60: Metal masthead fitting

Fig. 61: Mast band with thumb cleat

cated in any of the above materials. One can obtain rivets from model engineer's suppliers, who also keep stocks of all standard brass sheets, flats, rounds, and angles. Masthead fittings can be attached with brass or gunmetal wood screws, as these fastenings do not take high stress.

Where a cylindrical mast band with eyes is used, perhaps to take a lower forestay, shrouds, or runners, one should always glue and screw adequate wooden thumb cleats to the underside, as in Fig. 61 (as a precaution against downward slipping) if no shoulder is provided.

Unless tubular with sockets welded to a mast fitting, spreaders are best made from hickory or oak and strapped to the mast as in Fig. 62. The aft strap should be recessed under a mainsail track, but must be made in two parts if there is a luff groove.

All curved sheets and straps required for mast fittings should be bent cold around a block of hardwood cut to the correct shape, or a little smaller. Hammering can be used where necessary. All holes should be bored after bending, otherwise kinks are bound to form at the weakened points. For tangs of sheet metal, where thumb cleats could not be fitted, it often pays to put a thin bolt right through the mast instead of relying upon a network of woodscrews. Remember that when using aluminium alloy, all rivets, bolts, screws and clevis pins, should be of the same material, or of stainless steel.

On small craft there is no need to make a full gooseneck band, whereas for any craft over about 36 ft. (11 m.) the best job consists of two full bands (see Fig. 63) with the gooseneck swivelling on a

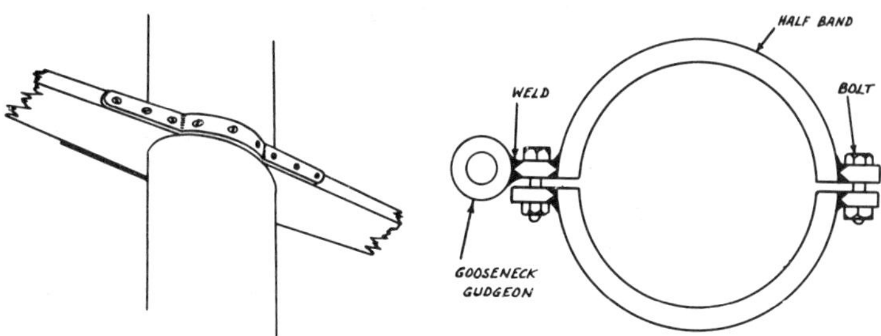

Fig. 62: Attaching wooden mast spreaders

Fig. 63: Gooseneck gudgeon on mast band

bar between them. To make the bands one may be able to scrounge from a waterworks a short offcut of mild steel pipe (not spun iron) which is about the right diameter. This can then be cut to form the band shown in Fig. 63 with appropriate welding and judicious hammering to get the diameter just right for the mast.

Dinghy goosenecks can be fabricated from sheet and bar, the parts being brazed where needed. The boom end fittings are equally simple, the loading never being as great as on a cruising boat. The man with a few taps and dies can make one of those

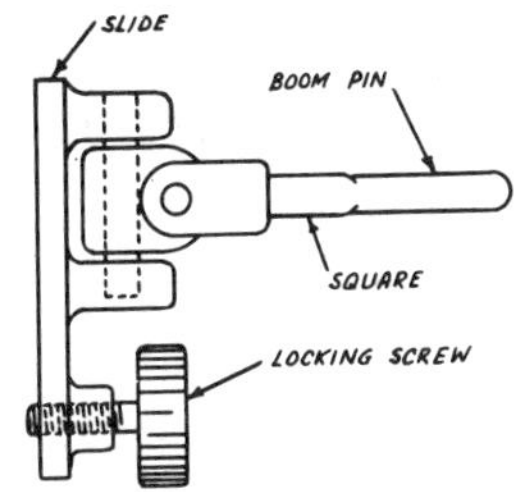

Fig. 64: Boom end fitting for dinghy

goosenecks that run on a length of mast track (Fig. 64) quite readily. Items such as mainsheet attachments and boom vang (kicking strap) fittings are all simple sheet metal work plus a little brazing.

BRAZING

Soft solder is useless for boat fittings, and a higher temperature metal of equal strength to the parent brass is necessary. The best source of heat is a propane hand torch having a range of nozzle sizes. The simplest spelter to use is *Easiflo* silver solder, available from toolshops, together with its correct flux. This runs beautifully as soon as the correct heat is obtained. It does not make a very big fillet as shown for welding in Fig. 57, so one should not cut a 'V' chamfer on the edge of a plate joining at right angles, but leave it flat for the solder to run underneath.

The parts should be cleaned up with emery cloth and then coated with liquid flux before cramping or wiring into position for brazing. On completion the parts may be quenched in water when still quite hot, as this helps to clean off the flux and avoid future corrosion.

Various brass brazing rods are available with higher melting points than Easiflo. These are also slightly tougher and will build into a bigger fillet. On complex jobs one sometimes has to braze one joint before attaching another part and brazing that. To avoid melting the first joint while tackling the second one, a spelter of lower melting point may be used in the final stage.

Work on large fittings is simplified by making up a tray containing tablets of firebrick on which to place the job, thereby avoiding excessive waste of heat.

RUNNING GEAR

Internally bound ash blocks with roller (patent) sheaves can be home-made, but modern blocks of laminated plastics (*Tufnol*) and stainless steel or brass are more popular. If you have no lathe,

the sheaves may have to be purchased from a chandler, but the rest is simple to make.

Blocks are narrower with special large diameter sheaves for wire rope, but for cordage the usual sheave sizes in millimetres are 28 × 7 for 6 mm. diameter rope, 34 × 9 for 8 mm. rope, 44 × 12 for 10 mm. rope and 56 × 14 for 12 mm. rope. The Tufnol side cheeks for these can be 3, 4, 6 and 7 mm. thick respectively. A

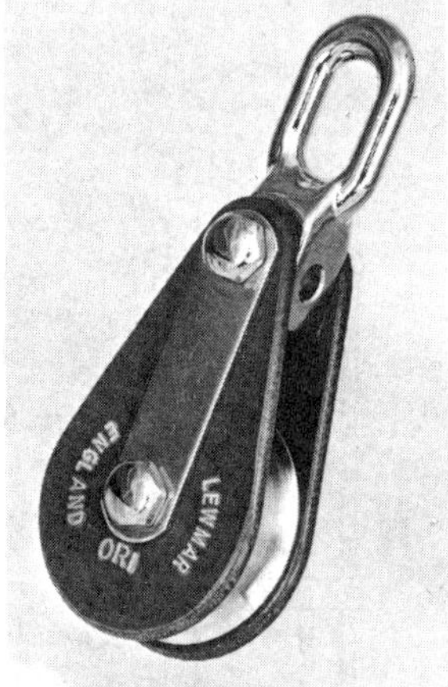

Plate 24: Lewmar single block with aluminium sheave

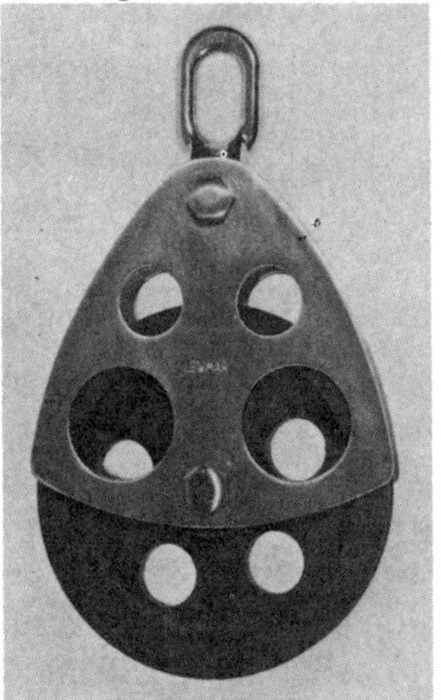

Plate 25: Crusader ocean racing block by Lewmar

small single block by Lewmar with swivel eye and no becket is shown in Plate 24 and a heavy duty block in Plate 25. There must be a brass binding plate on the outside to take the rivets (or screw heads) on all except the very light-duty blocks.

Do not try to rivet over the sheave pin and becket pin at each end, as these axles must be much larger than the rivet should be and they would thus have to be turned on a lathe or fitted as in Fig. 65.

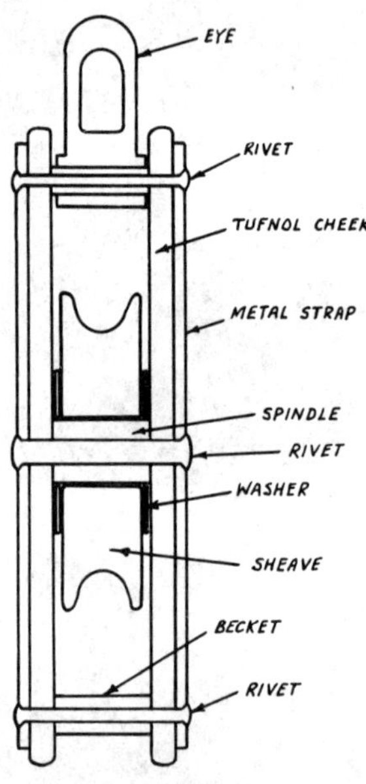

Fig. 65: Construction of a Tufnol block

Tufnol is easy to shape with normal metal-working tools, and all edges should be carefully rounded off. Make the cheeks in pairs (or threes for a double block) by boring the holes first, and then fixing them together with a couple of bolts prior to cutting out and shaping. The eyes are a straightforward filing job from pieces of square section metal. The washer at each side of a sheave must be quite thin to avoid any possibility of the rope jamming when the sheave has worn a bit.

Runner levers present an interesting fabrication problem for the keen amateur metal-worker, using Tufnol, brass, alloy, or steel. Several ingenious patterns of runner lever are marketed and it pays to look at those on other boats before designing one's own. Some measurement may be needed to find out whether a normal swing-over lever will supply enough slack, or whether a sliding sleeve must be incorporated to get extra slack. A fixed runner block is shown in Plate 26, together with an adjustable jib sheet fairlead assembly.

Plate 26. Lewmar adjustable genoa fairlead. Note also running backstay sheave on left

DECK FITTINGS

A stemhead fitting is very important and except on a dinghy, should have one or two roller fairleads built in. Galvanized steel rollers in many widths and diameters can be ordered through chandlery stores. On any boat longer than about 23 ft (7 m.) it pays to fit a Claud Worth pawl (see Fig. 66) to help check the load

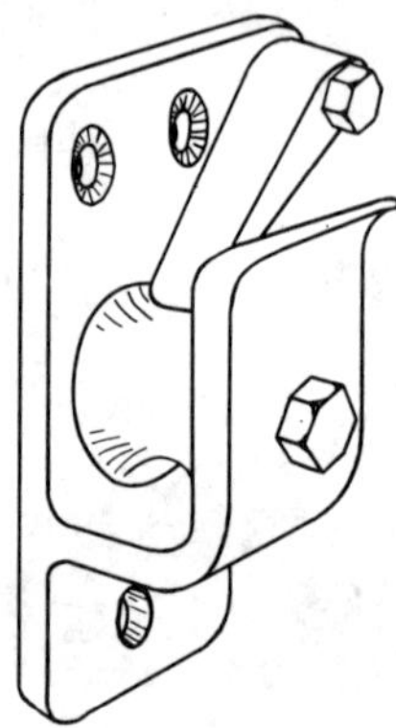

Fig. 66: Fairlead with Claud Worth pawl

on the chain while weighing anchor. All bolts should pass right through the stem.

Items like rope fairleads, mast track, hanks, and slides are not worth making, except in remote parts of the globe, but pulpits, stanchions, ventilators, deckhouse window frames, chain plates, and even an ensign socket, can save the handyman much money.

Pulpits and stanchions are usually welded up from heavy gauge black water pipe, the deck mountings being standard screwed plumbing flanges or welded plates. The pulpit bends (seen in Plate 27) are best carried out by two strong men choosing trees of various girth as formers, and working to a template bent from $\frac{1}{4}$ in. (6 mm.) bar. Galvanizing after fabrication is essential. If stainless steel tube is used, specialist welding is advisable before final polishing.

Small sheet horses are usually bent from $\frac{5}{8}$ in. (16 mm.) steel bar and threaded each end for nuts. Before welding on the deck flanges one should slip two collars onto the bar for welding close to each bend, as these prevent the sheet block from sliding beyond the bends and capsizing.

Deck flanges for fuel and water tanks are really lathe work, but very neat flag sockets can be made by brazing and hand finishing.

A useful bit of sheet metal practice may be gained by making a radar reflector from aluminium alloy.

Not many people like to maintain polished brass fittings these days, though nothing looks better. Brass mast fittings can be satin chromed to give them an appearance similar to stainless

Plate 27: A formed and welded pulpit

steel, but bright chrome looks terrible on most sailing craft. Otherwise a painted finish may be best, in which case the surface should be roughened with coarse emery paper or on an electric wire brush wheel. For polishing brass plate use very fine dry emery cloth as a final preparation before polishing with *Brasso* or on an electric buffing wheel.

CAST FITTINGS

Heavy rudder gudgeon brackets and straps should generally be bronze or gunmetal castings of very generous size and thickness with bronze pintles, preferably made floating in both parts, secured either with nuts locked with split cotter pins or collars and split pins.

Cruiser rudders often have a peg at the base pivoting in a cast heel fitting. To reduce friction and wear it may be wise to insert a bronze or stainless steel ball to take the thrust, or a Tufnol pad.

Castings can also be used for many other purposes including a bobstay stem fitting, chain plates, floors, stemhead fitting, hawsepipe, fairleads and bollards. However, all these parts can be made more cheaply in galvanized welded mild steel if their appearance suits the particular boat.

When a single eyebolt through the stem is not suitable for a bobstay (see Chapter 7) a fabrication as in Fig. 67a can be adapted,

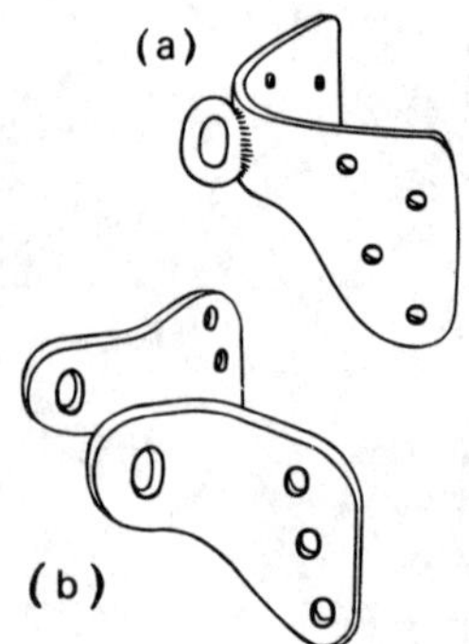

Fig. 67: Bobstay attachments for stem

either as a casting or in welded steel, attached with heavy gauge screws, preferably augmented by through clenches. The repair sheath shown in Plate 14 and described in Chapter 4 is very similar. Alternatively, twin handed plates can be used (see Fig. 67b) the eyes being connected by a bolt.

Before making such brackets one should take templates from the hull to ensure that a minimum of adjustment is necessary when the fabrication is ready to offer up. As well as making a replica of the finished part in thin sheet steel it may be necessary to shape cardboard templates of the cutwater at top and bottom of the fitting. Having made female templates, male ones can be cut to fit these which will be far more useful when shaping the actual bracket.

Remember, if the bracket is to be recessed flush with the hull (rudder gudgeons should correctly be mounted this way) the templates must be made to correspond with the sunken surface.

Flat chainplates of galvanized or stainless steel are a simple exercise in hacksawing, drilling and filing. Heavy gauge ones should be rolled to match any marked curvature of the topsides before galvanizing and the eyes above deck should be angled at the same time to align exactly with the slope of the rigging.

Heavy bronze chain plates are usually cast, but they can be cut from solid drawn flats. In both cases any curvature should be applied cold. If hammered when hot this metal fractures very easily. Floors and lodging and hanging knees can be made as castings or as welded fabrications.

MAKING PATTERNS

Before any part is cast by a foundry, a wooden pattern must be made and it usually pays to discuss this with the foundry foreman beforehand to make sure that the correct allowances are made for shrinkage and even to be certain that the proposed design can be cast at all.

For instance, a competent foundry can make perfect rudder gudgeon castings from patterns similar to the finish product, as pictured in Plate 28, while some foundries may demand patterns

Plate 28: Foundry patterns for gudgeon castings

in the form of solid blocks representing the outside shape, plus core boxes shaped to the inside.

Any fine-grained timber which is immune from warping will do for amateur pattern-making and plywood can be utilized to great advantage. All corners and angles should be generously rounded and resin putty (or decorator's cellulose filler) can be used to add various shapes to the wood and to provide fillets to internal corners. All final surfaces must be sanded smooth and given two coats of shellac varnish (knotting) or paint. Aerosol cans of car touch-up paint are handy for coating small patterns.

When making a pattern always remember that the moulder has to withdraw this from the sand he has packed around it before the metal can be poured. Therefore, the vertical surfaces must have a slight taper. To know which way the tapers run one must imagine just how the pattern will be used.

Wide or complex parts may have to be cast in two mould boxes joined together and a pencil line may be drawn on the pattern where the two boxes will meet so that the tapers can run each way from this thickest point. When a large number of identical small parts are to be cast, the foundry charge will be much lower if duplicate patterns are made, perhaps connected together with spacers of wire, enabling several parts to be cast in one pouring.

The largest pattern likely to be made by the conversionist is for a ballast keel. The pattern can be hollow (see Fig. 68) but the

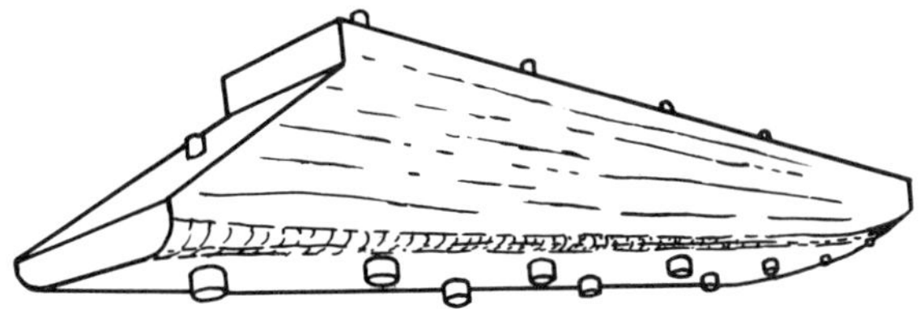

Fig. 68 : Pattern for a ballast keel

sides must be fairly strong to avoid buckling when the moulding sand is packed tightly around it. Deal boarding about 1 in. (25 mm.) thick is normally used for the top, bottom, ends and internal baffles, with $\frac{1}{4}$ in. (6 mm.) cheap plywood for the sides. Whether the keel is to be cast in iron or lead, the pattern must be made oversize by about $\frac{1}{8}$ in. per ft. (10 mm. per metre) to allow for the shrinkage of the metal on cooling. If a similar keel is to be cast in concrete, no allowance is necessary. The shrinkage allowance for brass and gunmetal is approximately $\frac{3}{16}$ in. per foot (15 mm. per metre) but where the external dimensions of a casting are critical, one should consult the foundry concerning shrinkage allowances as some commonly used alloys have peculiar coefficients of expansion.

The only other operation in pattern-making which the amateur may find troublesome concerns the making of *core boxes*. These are necessary in many instances where a hole or recess has to be made in a casting. Small holes can be bored through the metal afterwards, but much time and money can be saved if all large and long holes are formed during the pouring.

Foundries stock core material in standard rounds for making bolt holes of all sizes so that all one needs to do when pattern-making is to leave a *core print* the same diameter as the hole protruding from the surface of the pattern (see Fig. 68 and Plate 28) at each end and in the exact location of each hole. These round nobs leave depressions in the sand when the pattern has been removed and the core material can then be cut to correct length to fit between these recesses when the mould box is clamped shut. Core prints should be tapered slightly to facilitate withdrawal from the sand and they should each be painted black.

When a cavity of unusual shape is to be left in a casting, the pattern-maker must provide a core box, inside which the foundry can mould one or more cores which can then be suspended inside the mould box before pouring.

Some castings have cavities inside them which are completely sealed. To hold a core inside such a cavity before pouring necessitates the provision of special holes through the casting with core prints at each of these. A well-known example of a sealed cavity is in the water jacket of an automobile engine. The unwanted holes are machined and finally sealed with spring steel discs known as *core plugs*. These can be seen along the sides and ends of most car engine cylinder blocks.

Core boxes must be made in two halves with stub dowels to align the two parts correctly. The core box in Fig. 69 represents

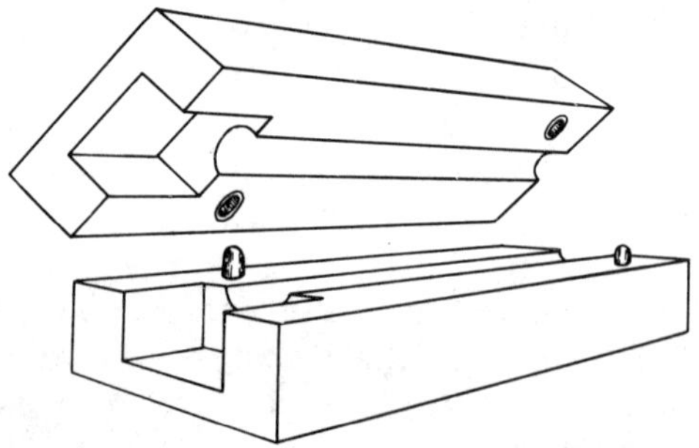

Fig. 69: Core box for keel bolt core

the internal shape required for making keel bolt cores, the bolts having square recessed heads. Where such bolts are of varying lengths, one only needs to make a core box for the longest one as the round shank can be cut to length after making the cores.

Note that the core box length must be equal to the length of the longest proposed bolt hole plus the length of the two core prints. In this instance, the core print at one end of each hole position on the pattern will be circular while the one at the opposite end must be square. The ends of the core box must be left open as shown to enable the special cement core material to be packed inside. It may be necessary to insert a reinforcing rod through the centre of the core to give it strength.

CASTING A KEEL

As lead melts at only 620° F (330° C) the amateur can cast his own lead keel by working out of doors using an improvised mould box, crucible, and furnace. This job can be quite dangerous and for safety reasons the whole assembly should be surrounded by a dwarf wall (timber stakes and boarding backed up with sand or soil will do) to prevent anyone from being spattered by molten metal should the equipment collapse.

A composite keel – a welded steel trough with poured lead filling – eliminates the need for a mould. The steel trough must be strengthened with cross bars welded inside and should be galvanized or heavily zinc sprayed outside.

For a 100% lead keel, the amateur should pack his mould with stabilized sand instead of the tricky conventional foundry mixture. To make stabilized sand, mix dry builder's sand (not the sharp sand used for concrete) with portland cement in the ratio 15:1 by volume. After careful dry mixing, continue mixing with water until the consistency of moist earth is attained.

Be careful not to make the mixture too wet. Pack some of it around a piece of smooth board, checking that the slot left when the board is removed remains stable for at least 10 minutes.

A mould box can be nailed up using secondhand 9 in. × 3 in. (230 mm. × 75 mm.) timber banked around outside with earth. The dimensions of the mould box should be arranged so that a 4 in. (100 mm.) minimum thickness of stabilized sand surrounds the pattern for a small keel and about 8 in. (200 mm.) for a large keel.

The amateur will not normally object to a certain amount of fettling with adze and Surform plane on the top of the completed lead keel so there is no need to have a top to the mould box. Instead, lay some pieces of thick steel plate across the top of the mould leaving narrow spaces between these to vent the air and steam during pouring with a space for the molten lead to run in. These plates can have holes bored through them to support the bolt hole cores and when these have been accurately aligned by measurement the plates should be weighted down with pigs of ballast or concrete blocks. With this system, the wooden keel pattern does not need upper core prints and it can even be made as an open topped box.

When casting a lead keel, some boatyards cast graphited steel bars into the lead to serve as bolt hole cores and when the lead has solidified these are driven out with a sledge hammer plus a steel bar drift of slightly smaller diameter. However, the amateur is not advised to use this method as proper cores can be made quite easily by filling cardboard tubes with 1:6 cement mortar having a piece of thin steel reinforcement rod running through the centre. This mortar is easy to break out eventually.

The cardboard tubes must be of the correct internal diameter. It should be possible to obtain suitable lengths from a builder's merchant, as cardboard tubes are frequently used for forming holes in concrete work. The thinner walled cardboard tubes sometimes available from drawing office suppliers (they are used inside rolls of drawing paper) are even better if of suitable diameter as the cardboard can be peeled away easily once the mortar has hardened. To form countersinks for the keel bolt heads on completion of casting, the lead can be carved out with an old wood chisel and mallet.

Some ballast keels have a scarf tongue at one end as in Fig. 68 to notch into the deadwood. To cast this tongue one must fabricate a plate of ¼ in. (6 mm.) mild steel and tamp the sand against this. To hold this plate into a mould box a number of lugs or staples can be welded on to it to receive steel bars which are inserted through holes in the mould box sides. The pattern can be replaced into the hardened sand temporarily to check that this plate is fixed in the correct position.

When packing the stabilized sand around the pattern in the

mould box, the material should be carefully tamped in 3 in. (75 mm.) layers and after tapping the pattern to free it, withdraw it gently, leaving the stabilized sand for about three days to harden and dry out before the metal is poured. Any repairs to the surfaces caused by incorrect packing (or slight slips when removing the pattern) should be made good after one or two days by trowelling on some mortar mixed with one part cement to five parts of fine sand.

THE MELTING POT

To melt lead successfully one needs a crucible firmly fixed above a furnace to permit the molten lead to run into the mould by gravity, a typical rig appearing in Fig. 70.

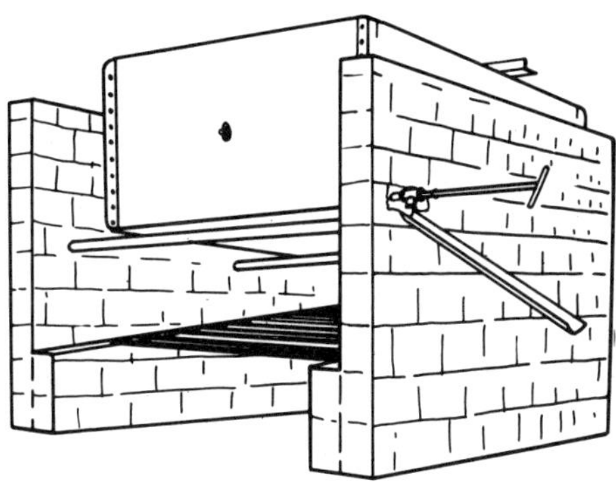

Fig. 70: Crucible from domestic cistern

A sealed, galvanized steel, domestic hot water cistern with additional stays through it makes a good crucible. A 20 gal. (90 litre) tank will hold one ton of lead and a 40 gal. (180 litre) tank will hold 2 tons.

A similar domestic header tank with open top is useless, having thinner gauge sides and doubtless being weak with rust if secondhand. Having obtained a sound hot water tank remove the inspection port and check for any serious internal rusting which might prove dangerous.

If only the original bottom of the tank has rusted, cut a large aperture through this and make it the *top* of the crucible.

Plug any unwanted holes by fitting a steel plate either side with a bolt through the centre and fit a stay of $\frac{1}{2}$ in. (12 mm.) diameter mild steel from about the middle of each tank panel across to the other side, secured with a nut and washer outside the tank at each end of the rod. To secure the bottom panel stay, make this fast to a length of angle steel resting across the top of the tank.

Readily available gate valves are normally made from cheap brass, and an all-steel outlet control device as shown in Fig. 71

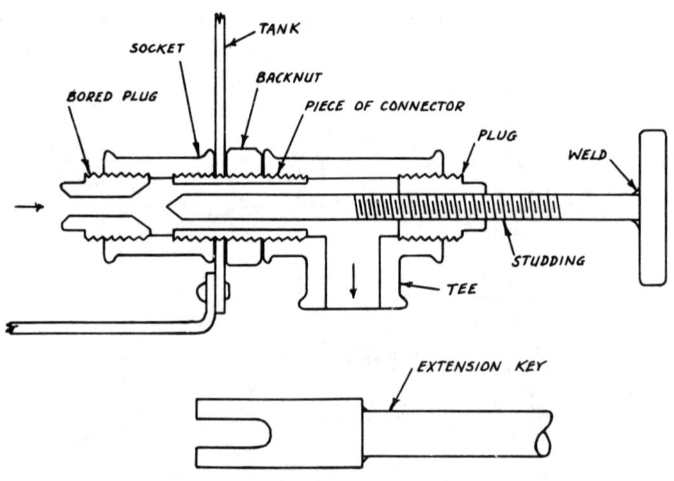

Fig. 71: All-steel crucible outlet control

is necessary. Most of this can be made quite safely at home and it will come to no harm if heated with a propane torch prior to pouring the lead to ensure that this runs freely. A short length of wide iron roof guttering will make a good chute from the outlet to the mould.

Build two brick (or precast concrete block walls) with strong girders let in to support the tank as in Fig. 70, tilted to ensure that most of the lead will run out. Place the walls 8 in. (200 mm.)

further apart than the width of the tank so the fire can heat the sides as well as the bottom of the crucible.

By making the walls thicker at the bottom, a ridge can be left as shown for the grate to rest on. Pieces of secondhand angle steel can form the firebars laid across with apex uppermost and air spaces of ½ in. (12 mm.) between each.

To make a more efficient furnace construct a back wall with chimney and a front wall with ash and stoking apertures. Rest metal plates on top of the walls abutting the crucible. Place a sheet of thin steel over the top of the tank to conserve heat but keep a thin layer of scum and litharge on the molten lead surface to prevent further oxidation.

Strong planks above the crucible help keep the operator clear of danger while the stoker should use long-handled tools and stand well clear. The control knob can be turned by means of an improvised extension bar.

A mixture of coal and dry wood makes the hottest fire although kerosene burners consuming about 4 gal. (18 litres) of oil per hour would be suitable. Have about 250 lbs. (112 kg.) of good quality coal ready for melting 1 ton of lead plus a couple of bushels of small dry ash or oak logs.

It pays to have a surplus of scrap lead ready as the keel must be completed in one pour. Any metal not used can be returned to the scrap dealer and it may be a good idea to have some moulds ready for casting internal trimming ballasts. However, remember that the keel will shrink as it cools and in normal practice extra lead is run into the mould just before solidification.

The metal may take several days to cool completely though stripping the mould box can start before this. When chipping away the stabilized sand the keel could topple over dangerously. If two bolt hole cores can be cleared out to allow steel bars to be inserted, guy ropes can be attached to these.

The external surface can be smoothed where necessary with a surform plane and any blow-holes can be filled with plastic metal or resin putty.

CONCRETE BALLAST

When the additional bulk of a concrete keel can be tolerated, this material has certain advantages for amateur work. Its very low intrinsic cost is especially attractive.

If pure concrete is used, the bulk is about three times greater than for iron but this disadvantage can be improved by using steel aggregate (as mentioned in Chapter 6) or by making the keel hollow and filling the void entirely with small scrap steel sealed in with mortar.

In places where welding is not possible, the spacer bars between the side plates (Fig. 40) can be in the form of hooks or screw eyes as shown in Fig. 72. With separate spacer bars placed inside, loops of wire can be wound between each set of hooks and windlassed up tight using a short piece of bar, or a 6 in. (150 mm.) wire nail in the centre. Where the wooden keel is wider than on a lifeboat, the keel bolts can be fitted through the keel and wired to the eyes or hooks somewhat as illustrated in Fig. 72.

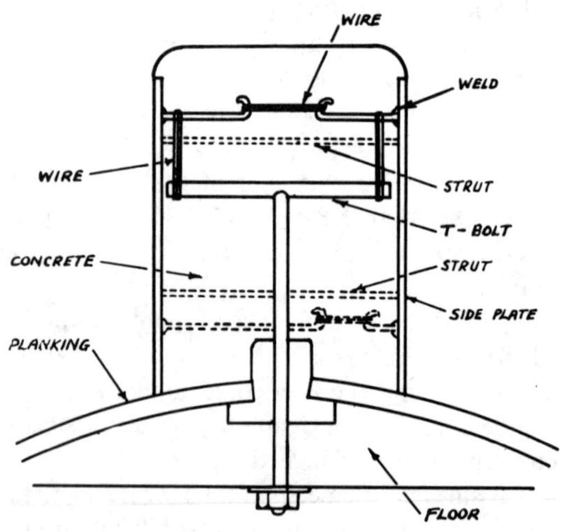

Fig. 72: Attachment for a wide concrete keel

A PRECAST KEEL

For casting a separate concrete keel (or pigs of ballast) a mould (shuttering or formwork) is required, fixed to a base board as shown in Fig. 73 so that the keel is inverted.

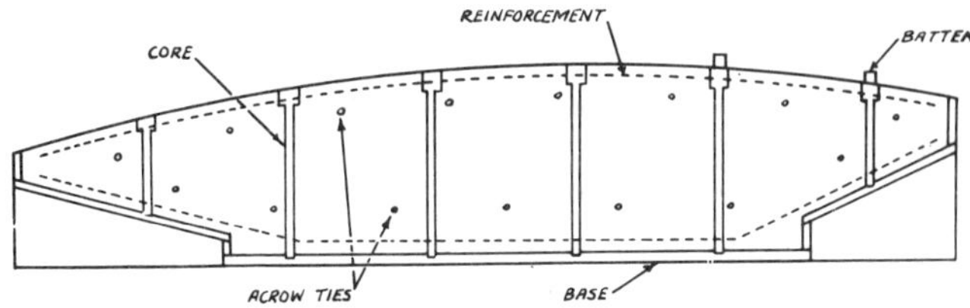

Fig. 73: Mould for casting concrete keel

The sides are best made from exterior grade plywood, ½ in. (12 mm.) thick up to 12 in. (300 mm.) in height and ¾ in. (18 mm.) up to 24 in. (600 mm.). If pine planks are used they must be nailed to *soldiers* of 3 in. × 2 in. (75 mm. × 50 mm.) timber at about 18 in. (450 mm.) centres with bolts top and bottom to hold the sides together as depicted in Fig. 74. Planking of 1½ in. (38 mm.)

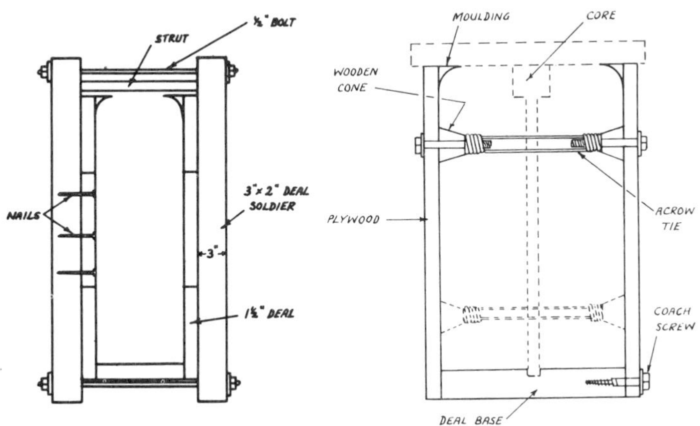

Fig. 74: Cross-section of wooden keel mould

Fig. 75: Acrow tie bolts for keel moulds

thickness is usual, but thinner timber is suitable with the soldiers closer together.

To withstand the pressure of the concrete where plywood shuttering is used the special tie bolts shown in Fig. 75 are available from builder's merchants. When the concrete has hardened, the coach screws are withdrawn to strike the shuttering, the cones are prised out and the spaces they leave are filled with mortar.

All radiused edges must be created by nailing coved mouldings (available from a joinery works) to the shutter, as grinding the concrete surface after hardening is a difficult operation. Special mould oil is available to serve as a parting agent on the formwork surfaces, but superior results can be obtained if two coats of shellac varnish (knotting) are applied to the wood beforehand.

When the keel is to have scarfed ends to notch into the deadwood, the baseboard must be raised accordingly as in Fig. 73. To leave holes for the keel bolts you must insert cores as when casting in metal. Thick-walled cardboard contractor's tubes are suitable and square or round wooden plugs can be attached to one end of these to form countersinks. Standard beech dowelling can be used for cores but these are liable to warp when moistened. Mould oil is not necessary on cardboard or wooden cores as they have to be drilled out (or burnt out) eventually.

Cores are easily fixed to the baseboard but will need cross battens to hold them at the top of the formwork. Plastics tubing or galvanized waterpipe can be used similarly and left in the concrete to form the bolt holes.

If the correct amount of water has been added to the concrete mix, a rockered keel (see Fig. 73) can normally be cast with an open topped shutter without the concrete slumping towards the ends. With a severe slope, cover plates of plywood may have to be nailed on top of the mould.

Note that some keels have curved sides when viewed in plan and to obtain ties to fit accurately between the formwork sides it may be necessary to cut and reweld standard length cages.

STEEL REINFORCEMENT

Although a chunky keel will not crack with no reinforcement it always pays to insert plenty of steel bars or welded mesh.

Especially for a long narrow keel, reinforcement bars should be placed all around as shown in Fig. 76. A typical keel 9 in. × 9 in.

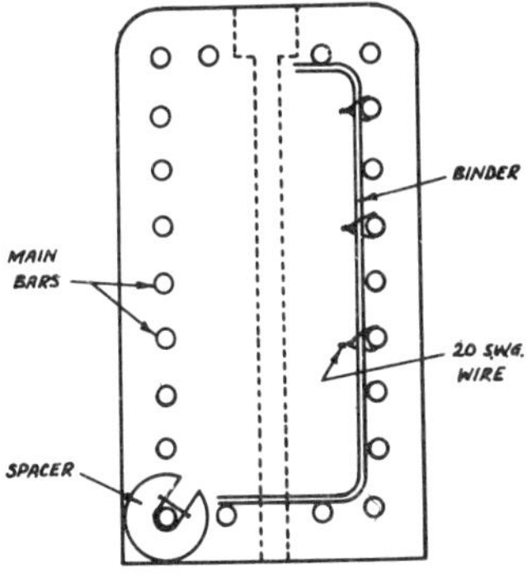

Fig. 76: Steel reinforcement for concrete keel

(230 mm. × 230 mm.) in section and 6 ft. (2 m.) long will use about twelve $\frac{1}{2}$ in. (12 mm.) bars held in position by vertical $\frac{1}{4}$ in. (6 mm.) bars (stirrups or binders) wired on at 12 in. (300 mm.) intervals.

For a keel 12 in. × 9 in. (300 mm. × 230 mm.) and 9 ft. (3 m.) long $\frac{3}{4}$ in. (18 mm.) bars and $\frac{5}{16}$ in. (7 mm.) vertical stirrups might be used, while for a keel 15 in. × 12 in. (380 mm. × 300 mm.) and 12 ft. (4 m.) long one could use 1 in. (25 mm.) bars and $\frac{3}{8}$ in. (9 mm.) stirrups at 18 in. (450 mm.) centres.

The bars should not be closer than 1 in. (25 mm.) to the form-work and they can be kept accurately in this position by attaching to them the special mortar or plastics spacers supplied by builder's merchants. Small mortar blocks with a loop of wire cast into them (for attaching to the reinforcement) can be moulded at home if necessary. Circular spacers with a hole through the centre can be threaded onto the main bars and are especially useful along the corners.

Temporary blocks of wood can be inserted between the main bars to ensure that spacing is even, as the stirrups are wired up and much time will be saved if a wire-twisting tool is borrowed together with a bundle of wire ties having an eye formed at each end.

For maximum density (and especially on very deep keels) a reinforced concrete trough (see Fig. 77) can be cast first by having

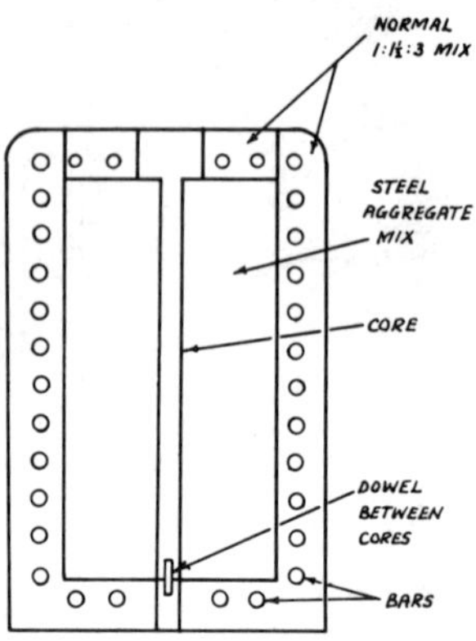

Fig. 77: Reinforced concrete trough keel

inside as well as outside formwork. The void can then be filled with scrap metal embedded in a minimum quantity of cement mortar.

Calculating the exact weight of a new concrete keel of any type using scrap metal is not always easy. Overweight is nearly always detrimental and to obviate this in a single pour keel (as in Fig. 76) it often proves wise to omit two of the top reinforcing bars running along the centre and insert wooden boxes before pouring to leave a series of narrow but deep slots. Forming a centreboard slot through the keel is done similarly.

Having taken the keel to a weighbridge to check its weight, these slots can then be filled with lead or scrap steel to make the final weight exactly right. A builder or engineering student will explain to the layman how to calculate the weight of reinforced concrete and various odd mixtures of metal.

When casting a hollow trough keel, remember to make the inside formwork easy to dismantle without hammering. The keel bolt hole cores will stretch only between the inside and outside formwork, but before the trough is filled, other cores will be necessary extending from the cast holes to the top of the mould. Once the correct weight of scrap metal has been embedded in the trough, it may be advisable to mould a row of reinforcing bars in the topmost layer.

THE CONCRETE MIX

An important reinforced concrete member to be submerged in sea water demands a high specification in materials and workmanship. Sulphate resistant cement should be mixed with sharp washed sand and $\frac{3}{16}$ in. (4 mm.) to $\frac{3}{8}$ in. (9 mm.) gap-graded crushed aggregate in the ratio 1 : 1½ : 3 by volume. With sand having the usual 6% of moisture by weight, only about 3½ gal. (16 litres) of water to 112 lb. (50 kg.) of cement should be added, or the very minimum of water to give a workable mix. Very little water should come to the surface as each layer is tamped in the mould.

A *poker vibrator* with the smallest-sized head available should, if possible, be hired to ensure thorough tamping and a perfect finished surface. If a poker vibrator is too large to get between the reinforcement bars, hand tamping using broom handles will be the next best thing.

Use proper *gauge boxes* (not shovelfuls) to measure the amount of material accurately. A mechanical concrete mixer makes a better job than hand mixing and is not so exhausting. Pouring must be carried out without pausing until the mould is filled. The ingredients must be thoroughly mixed dry as well as after the water is added.

When casting concrete between two steel side plates (as described for lifeboat conversions in Chapter 6) the concrete mix described above can be used when the metal added is in sizeable chunks. With small pieces (such as rivet hole punchings) these can take the place of the gap-graded aggregate and a 1 : 2 : 4 proportion by volume is then more suitable. For the best job, a 1 in. (25 mm.) layer of the 1 : 1½ : 3 mix should be used to top up with, to prevent the steel aggregate appearing at the surface with subsequent corrosion.

9

Engines, Steering and Anchors

Yachts are highly mechanized nowadays and the wise handyman owner will train himself thoroughly in the mechanical arts to ensure safety at sea, to obviate the need for employing professional services and to derive the maximum pleasure from his hobby.

POWER INSTALLATION

When fitting-out a bare hull or undertaking a conversion the installation of the power unit may cost more than the engine itself unless the amateur can do the work with his own hands. The cost of the installation includes buying materials for the sterngear, fuel, exhaust, cooling, electrical and control systems. The price of these materials can escalate to three or four times the cost of the basic essentials if one chooses to adopt flexible engine mountings, Vee-drive gearbox, hydraulic controls, closed circuit cooling, stainless steel propeller shaft with patent sterntube glands, or outdrive unit, and instrumentation to every part.

With simplicity the keynote one can often arrive at the most reliable as well as the cheapest installation. When costs must be pruned, try to leave room for adding improvements at a later date. For instance, hand-starting may be quite suitable at first. Similarly, if sufficient space is left, an effective layer of sound-deadening material could be fixed around the inside of the engine casing at some future time – see page 224.

Accessibility is most important. If you can only just squeeze the engine of your choice into the available space between surrounding fitments, get another boat or a different engine! Remember that although air-cooled engines seem attractively simple, the ducting required may be difficult to fit through the accommodation of certain yachts and water-cooled engines are usually less noisy.

Some enthusiasts are able to cut costs by converting vehicle engines for marine duties, while the ingenious amateur can adopt unusual types of drive such as multiple Vee-belts and hydraulic motors operated by oil pipes, enabling the main engines to be situated in any position, even athwartships. Water jet propulsion units (as made by Shipelle, Dowty, U.A.C. and others) may also be adopted to advantage on certain craft.

Where a conventional propeller is used for auxiliary propulsion it may be situated on the quarter (tucked under the bilge as in Plates 29 and 30) or on the centreline, either between the rudder and the sternpost (as in Fig. 78) or over the top of the rudder.

Except for those power craft with outboard motors or out-drives (inboard/outboard drives) mounted on a broad transom, twin engine installations normally have propellers on the quarters, invariably with twin rudders. A single propeller would be set into a nicely-fared opening in the deadwood (see Fig. 87) with the rudder well clear abaft it.

For conversions (either sailing craft hitherto without a motor or twin screw power installations) the side, or quarter, propeller arrangement is usually the simplest and cheapest. Small vessels rarely have enough timber in their sternposts to house a stern-tube, but although cheeks can be bolted to the sides of the stern-post to strengthen it, these in turn mask the flow of water to the propeller however streamlined they may be.

Sterntubes for lifeboat conversions are often placed alongside the sternpost, as shown in Plate 31, where there is a minimum loss of strength and few fastenings in the way.

The engine location needs early consideration though it need not influence the propeller position greatly. Engines are generally best situated well aft where noise, heat and smell are least trouble-some, while exhaust pipe runs, propeller shafts and control linkages are normally short. However, engines amidships or further for'ard can often be installed lower in the hull and to one side of the centreline if necessary, so that a compromise may be best. However, be cautious when fitting heavy twin outdrive

Plate 29: Fabricated A-bracket for quarter propeller

Plate 30: Sterntube blister with reversible propeller

Plate 31: Propeller shaft near centreline

units right aft as the hull should be designed to cope with this load.

An auxiliary engine driving a quarter propeller may be mounted on the centreline, but efficiency is increased slightly with the engine mounted on the same side of the hull as the propeller. By angling the shaft outwards a little it should be possible to eliminate the necessity to counteract the propeller thrust by means of the rudder at certain speeds. Engine makers will usually advise one on the best propeller specification, also on whether the engine rake can exceed the normal 12°.

PROPELLERS

The correct choice of propeller can have a vast effect upon the performance of a vessel. For conversions and auxiliary sailing craft it may be necessary to try several different propellers for optimum results for so many variable factors are involved that the experts have to rely upon empirical methods, as the lines of the hull, eventual displacement and anticipated speed through the water may not be known accurately.

Therefore, in some instances, it may be advisable to try to borrow a secondhand propeller of the likeliest diameter and

TABLE 1. TYPICAL POWER INSTALLATIONS

			Engines	
Type of Conversion	*Total B.H.P.*	*R.P.M.*	*Fuel*	*Total We* lb.
18 ft. (5.5 m.) Lifeboat	4	1500	Gasoline (Petrol)	190
24 ft. (7.3 m.) Lifeboat	10	1500	Diesel	508
27 ft. (8.2 m.) Whaler	8	2000	Gasoline (Petrol)	260
30 ft. (9.2 m.) Motor/Sailer	48	2500	Gasoline (Petrol)	612
36 ft. (11 m.) Launch	44	1700	Diesel	1680
40 ft. (12.2 m.) Trawler	30	800	Kerosene (T.V.O.)	1260
45 ft. (13.7 m.) Pinnace	75	1500	Diesel	2836
48 ft. (14.6 m.) Trawler	30	560	Kerosene (T.V.O.)	2420
55 ft. (16.7 m.) M.F.V.	44	750	Diesel	3170
65 ft. (19.8 m.) M.F.V.	88	560	Diesel	4350
72 ft. (21.8 m.) Navy M.L.	150	1500	Diesel	5672
83 ft. (25.2 m.) Barge	66	750	Diesel	3740
112 ft. (34.1 m.) Navy M.L.	450	2000	Diesel	8480

PROPELLER						Speed in Knots	Remarks
eter	*Pitch*			*Shaft Diam.*			
mm.	in.	mm.	*R.P.M.*	in.	mm.		
23	5½	140	1500	¾	18	5½	Auxiliary Single screw
280	6	150	1500	1	25	6	Auxiliary Single screw
200	5	126	2000	⅞	22	6½	Auxiliary Single screw
380	11	280	1250	1	25	8½	Full power Twin screw
560	16½	420	850	1¾	44	9½	Full power Single screw
530	12	300	800	1½	38	6	Auxiliary Single screw
710	17	430	750	2	50	8½	Full power Single screw
660	17	430	560	1¾	44	5½	Auxiliary Single screw
630	18	450	750	2	50	7½	Full power Single screw
860	17	430	560	2½	70	9	Full power Single screw
710	20	500	750	2	50	10	Full power Twin screw
740	12½	570	750	2¼	64	7	Full power Single screw
90	19	480	1300	2½	70	13	Full power Twin screw

pitch to see if this comes up to expectations before ordering a new one. If two additional ones can be tried out (one of slightly smaller pitch and one slightly larger) some very useful performance figures can be obtained. Reboring or sleeving a borrowed propeller is much cheaper than having to change to a brand new one.

Note that for most yachts (except high speed power boats) main or auxiliary diesel units are often matched to the propeller when turning at about 75% of peak engine revs to keep the noise level tolerable and to increase engine life. If the propeller is designed to transmit full engine power at maximum engine revs, this may add only ½-knot to the boat's speed.

The minimum information required by a propeller maker would be the hull's waterline length; beam and draft; engine type; b.h.p. and the intended maximum revs; details of any reduction gearing and maximum diameter of propeller that can be swung. Many further details can be added with advantage including estimated maximum speed of boat; hull displacement; shape of keel profile and midship section; shaft diameter and dimensions of propeller taper and keyway.

The most efficient propeller may not always be ideal, as weed cutting shapes are essential for some inland water craft, reversible

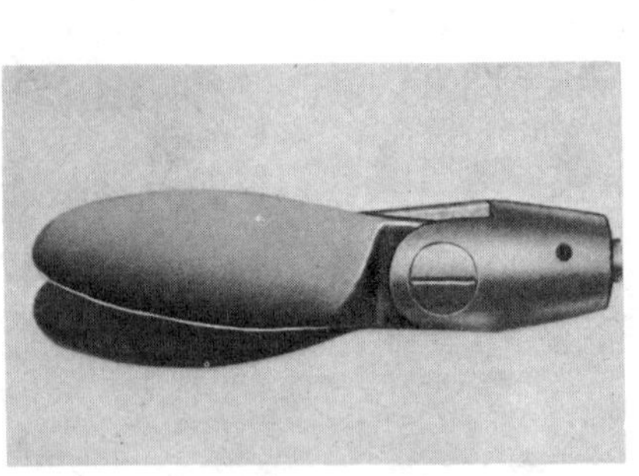

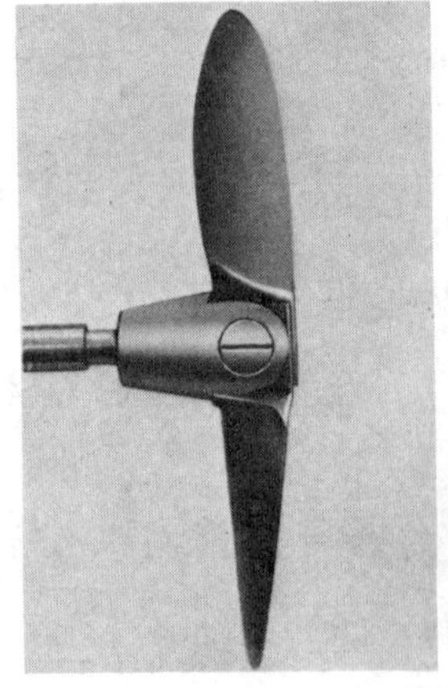

Plate 32: Folding propeller

propellers eliminate the need for gearboxes and are useful for fishing boats which need to troll at slow speed, while folding propellers (Plate 32) are ideal for some auxiliary sailing yachts, especially when positioned on the quarter or over the top of the rudder.

None of these propellers can be as efficient as solid ones with the correct blade area and shape, but their other properties outweigh the loss of efficiency. Note that when a reversible propeller (Plate 30) is used for auxiliary propulsion it should be of the type with blades that can be feathered in line with the water flow to minimize drag when sailing.

If a solid three-bladed propeller is fitted on the centreline or on the quarter a simple dog clutch on the shaft inboard will enable the propeller to spin freely when sailing to reduce drag. Alternatively, by adopting a two-bladed propeller on the centreline the shaft can be marked and equipped with a locking device to enable the blades to be fixed vertically in line with the stern-post when not in use.

Any good chandlery firm will advise on or obtain all the equipment necessary for unusual installations. Table 1 gives typical details and dimensions for propellers used on some of the conversions described in previous chapters. Interpolation from this table should enable one to get some idea of the size of power unit and propeller needed for many yachts except high speed power craft.

FITTING STERNTUBES

Once a decision has been reached regarding the engine model and propeller size a wooden mock-up of the engine should be made to ascertain the propeller shaft line. Although the engine bearers can be fitted at this stage, most amateurs prefer to bore the hole for the sterntube first. Then, if the hole proves inaccurate, it may be quite serviceable if the engine position is shifted slightly to bring it into line.

Do not order the sterntube until the boring has been completed and the hole length measured accurately. As soon as the propeller shaft diameter is known, the sterntube makers (or any good chandlery firm) will tell you the outside diameter of the sterntube to enable the hole to be bored slightly oversized.

Some sterngear and engine manufacturers will lend a suitable boring bar to the amateur, but the more nervous handyman may prefer to pay a boatyard to send over a man with the boring bar to help or explain how it should be done. Holes up to 1 ft. 6 in. (450 mm.) long are no problem at all but one over 3 ft. (900 mm.) is best tackled professionally.

Two methods are in general use for boring sterntube holes. For comparatively short holes a standard metal working twist drill is suitable and has the advantage that it will not be damaged if fastenings are encountered. Considerable pressure must be exerted on the drill, usually arranged by means of a long wooden lever at the far end which has a metal cup bearing attached to it.

The bar should be amply long enough to enable it to be aligned accurately on the proposed shaft angle and ideally there should be a keyway running the full length of the boring bar, the turning handle sliding along and having a registering key. The bar must run through a timber jig to keep it accurately on the shaft line at all times. Boring normally starts from inside the hull and a vertical face may need to be cut into the internal deadwood or stern knee at the start of the hole.

The position of the starting point is usually best obtained from a drawing of the boat, but failing this it may be expedient to bore a $\frac{3}{8}$ in. (9 mm.) test hole from inside or outside to check the position. If in error, shift the starting position accordingly, but first plug the small hole with a dowel to prevent the big drill from wandering into it.

The second type of boring bar is quite different. It consists of a long rod about $\frac{3}{4}$ in. (18 mm.) in diameter with a screw thread cut along the majority of its length and with a winding handle fitted to one end. A sharp steel cutter is held by a grub screw into a hole bored diametrically through the rod. A nut plate running on the screwed rod is attached to the deadwood (or to a temporary bearer) so that on turning the handle the cutter is propelled through the timber making a hole of any desired size. The cutting diameter can be adjusted by resetting the cutter with its grub screw and different length cutters can be fitted for exceptionally large or small holes.

Before the boring bar can be used, a pilot hole (about half as big again as the rod) must be bored using an extended twist drill or a bullnosed auger. This latter tool is similar to a conventional long shaft wood auger but without the lead screw at the tip. This prevents it from wandering, but necessitates the application of considerable pressure.

A smaller hole can be bored first to check the line and either reamed if correct or plugged and shifted if not true. The traditional way for rectifying an incorrect boring is to slide a red hot steel bar into the hole, but it pays to keep a fire extinguisher or a hose pipe at the ready!

Making the pilot hole larger than the threaded rod not only eases the work of the cutter but it also enables some inaccuracy to be ironed out by setting the boring bar exactly on the proposed propeller shaft line. Where the shaft extends to an A-bracket (see Plates 29 and 30) or a single strut P-bracket, it may be possible to fit the bracket first and use it as a bearing for the boring bar.

When the nut plate is to be attached to the deadwood the auger hole must be enlarged for a short distance (using an expanding bit or a gouge) to make room for the cutter. If the cutter should become damaged or prove too stiff to wind by hand it may be necessary to make two or three borings, the cutter being advanced an amount each time until the correct size hole is cut.

A screwed boring bar may take some time to set up, but it makes the most reliable job. Difficulties arise where fastenings are encountered. If these are visible it may be possible to extract them, or an extended twist drill can be used to break right through.

Large centre-line bolts through the deadwood are usually foreseen. If many of them need extracting they will have to be replaced with pairs of thinner bolts passing through each side of the sterntube. Because of this problem (or lack of timber thickness) sterntubes are sometimes placed at one side of the deadwood and sternpost (see Plate 31) with chocks bolted athwartships inside and out, well-sealed with bedding compound to prevent leakage.

The position of the sterntube in a fishing boat conversion is shown in Fig. 78. The original rudder has been replaced by a

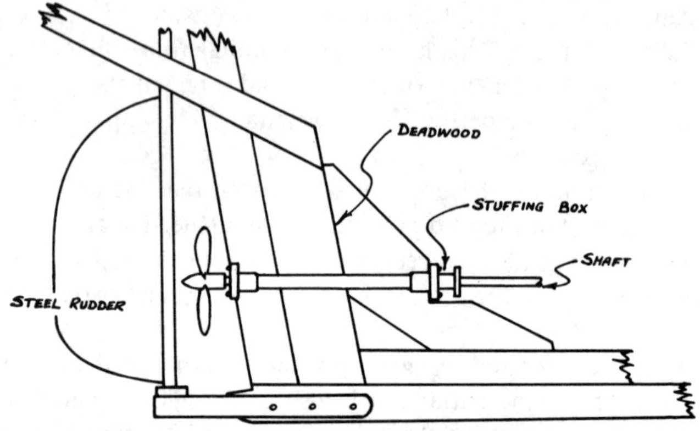

Fig. 78: Sterntube for fishing boat conversion

steel one set more vertically to leave space for the propeller between the sternpost and the rudder. The position of the sterntube for a quarter propeller installation in a similar craft is shown in Fig. 79. Old fastenings are much less likely to prove

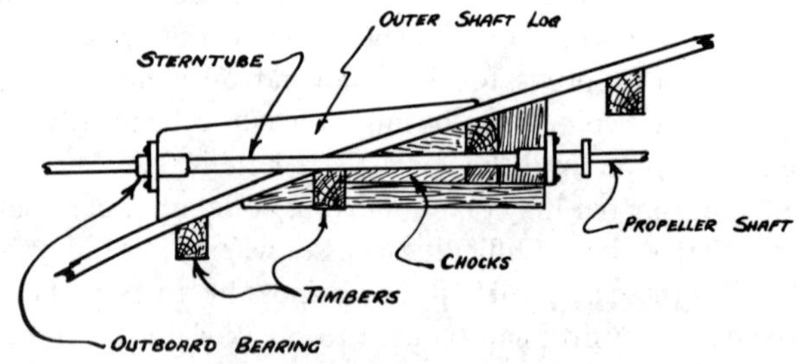

Fig. 79: Quarter propeller installation

troublesome in this position and the fitting of the chocks (or blisters) is easier.

To avoid the need to align three bearings, which is always a tricky operation, a quarter sterntube is often continued from the blister to the A-bracket. However, in most modern twin screw motor yachts it will be found that the propeller shafts are exposed all the way aft from the blisters. If a sterntube is used to cover an open length of shaft, this may afford some protection but when damage does occur the tube may get buckled as well as the shaft and repair work costs would then escalate. On an exposed shaft, the bracket usually has a cutless rubber bearing to eliminate the need for lubrication.

The shaft arrangement for runabouts (and also for some small auxiliary yachts) is somewhat different as no sterntube is required. An inboard gland and bearing is fitted to a chock of hardwood known as a *shaft log* which is bolted to the hog and the shaft runs exposed from the keel direct to a P-bracket having a single strut (or to an A-bracket with two splayed struts) below the transom. Modern runabouts use *flexible shaft logs* (see Fig. 80)

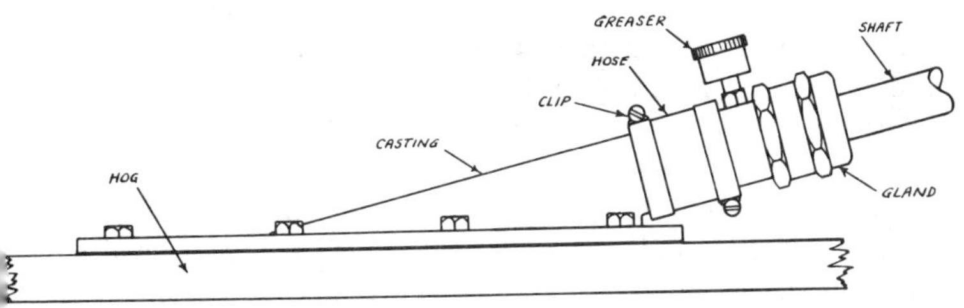

Fig. 80: Flexible shaft log for runabout

consisting of a bronze casting bolted direct to the hog with the gland and bearing attached by a swivel joint, sealed against leakage by a short piece of rubber hose attached with Jubilee clips. This device simplifies lining up considerably.

Sterntube bearings are normally screwed on to each end of the tube and it may be necessary to shave down the timber face at one or both ends to get the bearing flanges to lie in the correct position when screwed up fully. The special bronze coach screws securing the flanges are normally ordered with the sterntube.

The bored hole should be large enough to leave space for a thick smear of bedding compound to be placed around the tube, with more compound under the flanges. If the tube proves too tight for mastic, just soak the inside of the hole with thin paint or rot preservative. Note that where a sterntube has a cutless bearing small scoops protrude at each side to force water through the bearing when the boat is moving. These tubes must always be kept free from blockage.

With a new installation on the centreline, always ensure that the deadwood is fared off as much as possible for a clear water flow to the propeller. Keep adequate clearance between the propeller blade tip and the planking, skeg or other obstructions, about 1 in. (25 mm.) being the minimum.

Bronze, monel metal and stainless steel are used for propeller shafts, bronze being the most common. Stainless steel (of the correct formula) is the strongest material available and its use can reduce the size of the sterntube boring to a minimum.

When installation work is not desperately urgent it pays to order the propeller shaft after having seated the engine on the bearers. The shaft can then be ordered to exact length with the ends machined for coupling flange and propeller. For cheapness, it may be possible to buy a longer length of secondhand shaft which may be as good as new with the worn part cut off.

Almost any engineering works or large boatyard should be able to bore out the coupling flange supplied with the engine and mill the slot for the Woodruff key (which is normally used at the flange end of the shaft); turn the propeller taper at the other end; cut the thread for the propeller retaining nut and mill the keyway. For very long propeller shafts, common bright mild steel can be used for the intermediate shafting inboard and this can be kept free from corrosion by paint or a smear of underwater grease. Coupling flanges are invariably of mild steel and should be similarly protected.

Long shafts must have intermediate bearings (plummer blocks) at intervals of approximately 40 shaft diameters, to stop vibration and to prevent the shaft from getting buckled by accidental damage. Most modern marine gearboxes (or reduction gears) have a thrust bearing incorporated. This is essential as the entire thrust of the propeller is transmitted along the propeller shaft to the engine and thence to the bearers which, in effect, push the boat along. When an improvised car gear box is used (or perhaps multiple V-belt transmission) a separate thrust race must be incorporated along the propeller shaft. In some types of reversing propeller the control lever mechanism takes the thrust.

Plummer blocks need good stout bearers to keep them in alignment, but a thrust race needs even stronger support to take the additional fore-and-aft stress.

Note that a space (equal to at least one-half the shaft diameter) should be left between the propeller boss and the adjacent external bearing or gland to allow for forward movement and wear in the thrust race.

When a stray rope gets entangled with a spinning propeller this short length of shaft is the part most difficult to free. If a short sleeve of closely fitting tube (in the same material as the shaft) is slipped over this place before the propeller is fitted, a tangled rope can often be pulled away with comparative ease as the sleeve rotates.

FITTING BEARERS

To describe all the possible systems of bearer arrangement to suit various engines, propeller positions, hull shapes and hull materials would take two chapters. The following list covers most of the basic types.

(1) *Auxiliary yacht, deep or shoal draft.* A typical section appears in Fig 81. With the engine below the cockpit long bearers would

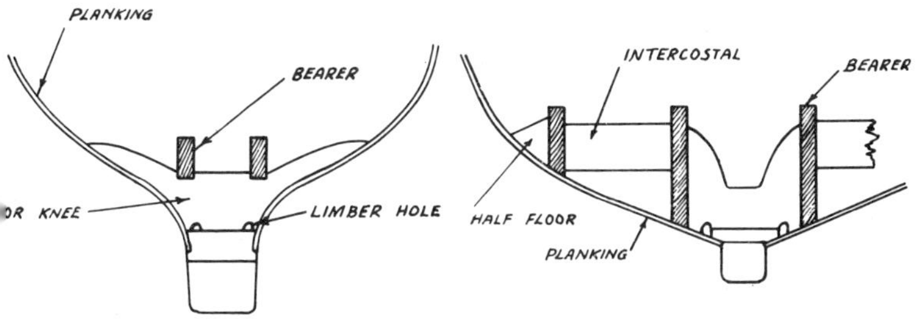

Fig. 81: Engine bearers in deep draught yacht

Fig. 82: Intercostals and bearers for motor cruiser

protrude into the cabin space. Therefore, short bearers are used, bolted to a minimum of three stout floors running athwartships.
(2) *Motor cruiser or motor/sailer.* With powerful heavy diesel engines the bearers must be long fore-and-aft with adequate floor knees and intercostals, the arrangement for a twin engine installation similar to Fig. 82. Where the boat's timbers are steam bent, each bearer should be *joggled* (notched) over each rib to be through-bolted snugly to the planking (see Plate 33).

Plate 33: Engine bearer joggled over ribs

Should the boat have thick sawn frames, it may be better to partially joggle at each frame, say, to a depth of $\frac{3}{4}$ in. (18 mm.) and fit separate chocks beneath to close the gap, not forgetting to leave *limber holes* alongside each frame for draining purposes.
(3) *Lightly-built open launch.* If there are no floor knees, fore-and-aft bearers could cause all the bent timbers to crack along the line of the plank seams nearest to the bearers, especially if a heavy engine is installed. One solution is illustrated in Plate 13: fitting welded steel frames across the hull with short fore-and-aft bearers secured only to these, as described in Chapter 4.
(4) *Plywood hard chine hull.* For the weight to be well distributed

with no stout floors or thick planking to fasten the bearers to, a honey-comb structure of plywood webs jointed together somewhat as in Fig. 83 is ideal. The whole assembly can be glued and screwed

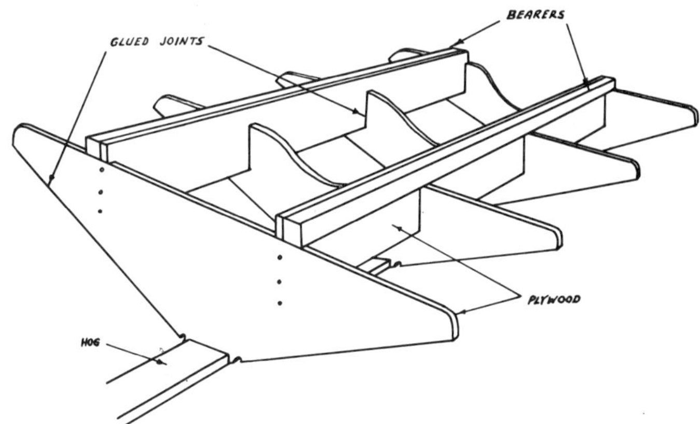

Fig. 83: Plywood engine bearer honeycomb

to the bottom skin. In flat floored craft, strength may be added by taking the athwartship members right across and fixing them to the chines.

(5) *Glass-fibre craft.* Some light frameless hulls may be too frail to take a powerful engine, but a timber grillage (as described in Method 4 above) may be used if properly bonded to the hull skin and also completely encased with a thick g.r.p. laminate. Motor cruiser hulls usually have stout reinforcement ribs and encased timber can again be used on the lines described in Method 2. Auxiliary craft with ballast keels have very thick hull sections and can be treated as in Method 1.

Such parts as engine bearers can be moulded as complete hollow g.r.p. assemblies and then bonded into the hull. Although the amateur may find timber quicker and easier to use, it should not be forgotten that the encasing and bonding with g.r.p. must be completely leakproof. If moisture gets in, rot could start and the timber could swell, causing a breakdown of the laminate. This means that nut plate apertures and engine mounting bolts should also be completely sealed.

ENGINE BOLTS

There are many ways of bolting an engine down, but the square *nut plate* method illustrated in Fig. 84a is the most common.

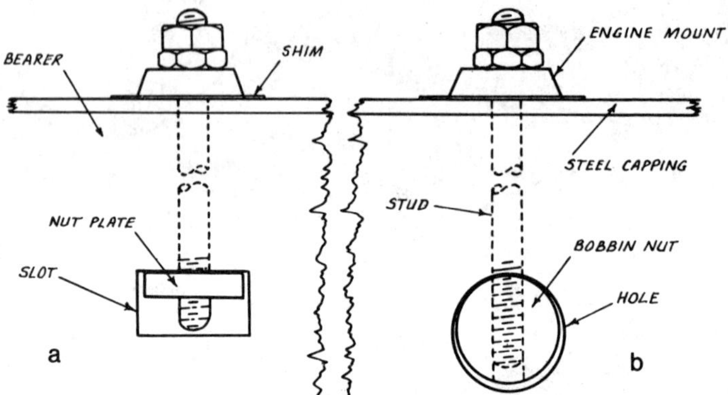

Fig. 84: Engine bearer bolts and nuts

One alternative is to make the nut from a piece of round brass bar which slides horizontally into a hole through the bearer, see Fig. 84b.

This recessed nut method can be used for the bearer to floor fastenings required in the Fig. 82 method. A common alternative is to fit galvanized steel angle plates into each corner, secured with through bolts or coach screws.

Timber bearers must always be capped with thick steel flat plates to prevent the mounting brackets from digging in, thus causing the bolts to loosen and the shaft alignment to be thrown out. Isolated washers at each foot are not normally sufficient, long lengths of plate being advisable to distribute the pressure. A thick g.r.p. capping is usually satisfactory. Sometimes it may be possible to bolt steel *angle* plates through the *sides* of the bearers. The engine mounting feet can then fit on the horizontal flanges and be bolted to them.

When a bearer is very deep, as in Fig. 82, it may have to be laminated by bolting several planks together, though a more rigid job may be possible by building up in the manner of Fig 85. All pairs of fore-and-aft bearers must be firmly tied together by

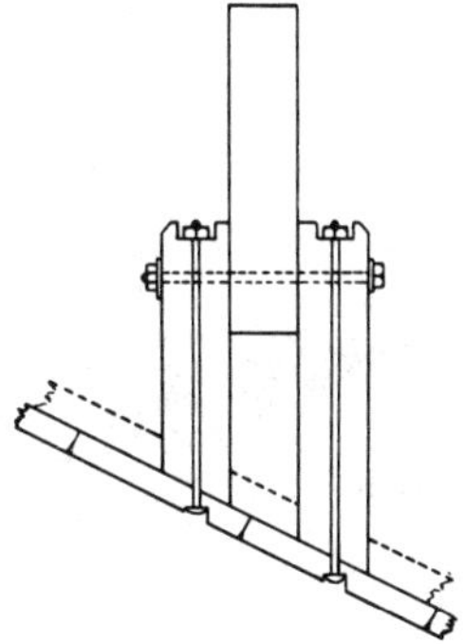

Fig. 85: Composite deep engine bearer

means of intercostal webs with half-floors on the outside as indicated in Fig. 82. Instead of using nut plates or angle brackets to secure these joints, neat fixings can be achieved by ploughing a groove at top and bottom of each intercostal, housing long bolts with nuts each end outside the bearer.

ALIGNING THE ENGINE

Many amateurs worry needlessly over the achievement of perfect alignment at the coupling flange, but this is usually a fairly simple, if tedious, operation involving the insertion of metal shims under the engine mounting feet while checking between the flanges with a feeler gauge to get the angular alignment correct within a tolerance of about 2 thou. (50 microns) and the axial alignment correct by ensuring that the spigot on one flange engages neatly with the socket on the other one.

The only way to avoid this chore is to fit a short intermediate shaft with a universal coupling at each end, but there may be insufficient space for this in an auxiliary engine installation. Having a flexibly mounted engine (see Plate 34) only eases the task of accurate alignment slightly and a rigid metal bobbin has to be used to obtain fairly accurate alignment before being replaced by the special flexible coupling.

Flexible mountings help to make a smooth silent installation,

Plate 34. Resilient engine mounting and coupling
Photograph by Silentbloc Ltd

but the components required can be expensive. Some flexible engine mountings have a height adjustment mechanism incorporated. Remember that the alignment changes slightly in some boats when they are taken into the water, so it pays to make a final check on the alignment before starting the engine after the laying-up period.

EXHAUST SYSTEMS

An exhaust pipe may lead from an engine in many ways to avoid obstacles and discharge in the best position, usually well aft to avoid the troubles which arise when spray and fumes are blown inboard from a topside exhaust outlet.

Whether a wet or dry exhaust is used, the pipe must be taken up to a point well above the possible waterline under the worst conditions of heel and loading, then sloping downwards to the outlet as indicated in Fig. 86. This is arranged with a wet system

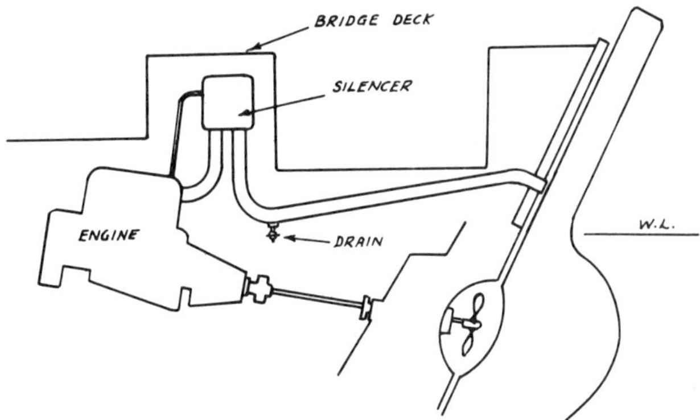

Fig. 86: Wet silencer exhaust system

by having the silencer (muffler) well above the engine (perhaps to one side in a cockpit locker), the cooling water being injected into the silencer and the mixture of exhaust and water then descending to the outlet. Although after leaving the silencer the exhaust pipe can be contorted in any manner, a short straight pipe with a fairly constant fall is the most satisfactory.

Although many outboard motors are designed to exhaust under water, for most inboard engines the exhaust outlet should never be submerged below water for more than a few seconds. For an auxiliary exhaust system with the outlet in the topsides it may be necessary to fit a two-way cock at a T-junction just after the silencer so that the exhaust can be directed through an alternative pipe to a duplicate outlet on the opposite side of the ship, in case the engine is required when the vessel is sailing at a considerable angle of heel.

With a dry system the cooling water is discharged separately overboard. If the pipe must fall below the waterline on leaving the engine (as in Fig. 87) a swan-neck bend should be made within the stern locker to prevent water from entering the pipe. When this cannot be done, a seacock must be fitted to the outlet, but this may cause trouble with inexperienced operators. Alternatively, it may be possible to arrange for a bung on a lanyard to be kept

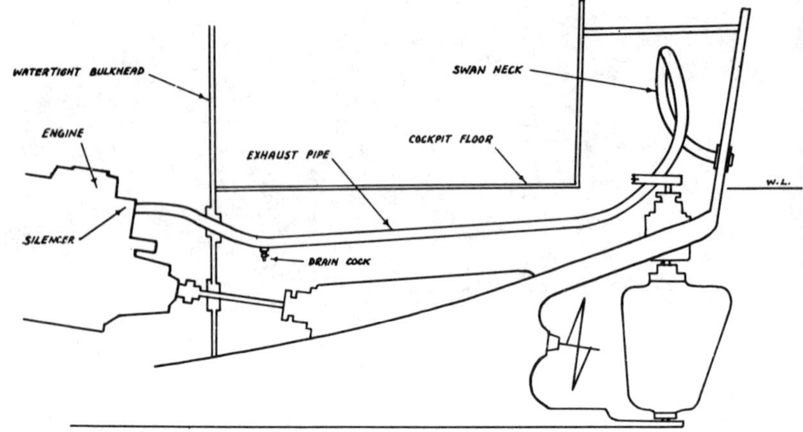

Fig. 87: Dry silencer with swan neck exhaust

firmly pressed into the outlet hole whenever the engine is out of use.

Dry exhaust lines are liable to become very hot. They should be kept well away from any woodwork and thickly lagged with asbestos tape, remote from fuel tanks and with the outlet skin fitting kept clear of a wooden transom by fitting thick asbestos gaskets.

In a large motor cruiser conversion a dry exhaust is best taken up through a funnel (see Fig. 88) but there must be a trap with drain cock to prevent rain or spray from getting to the engine. In some conversions it may be possible to direct the exhaust upwards through a lining tube inside the mizzen mast! A drain cock at the lowest point of any contorted inboard exhaust line is essential to prevent frost damage during laying-up.

Exhaust piping may be made from various materials. From a water injection silencer to the outlet special rubber hose may be used provided the instrument panel is equipped with a cooling water temperature gauge to obviate damage by circulation failure. The same precaution applies to *Elastomuffle*-type neoprene silencers fitted near to the outlet end of a wet system.

Copper piping is suitable for small petrol (gasoline) engine

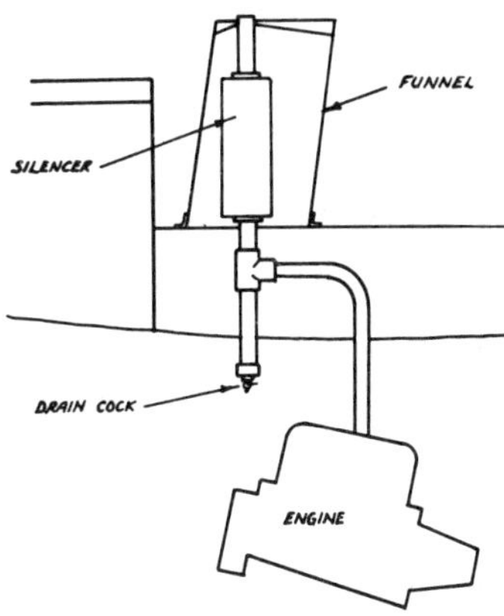

Fig. 88: Dry exhaust through funnel

exhausts, but standard heavy gauge steel water pipe is markedly cheaper in the larger sizes and for long runs. This pipe is often specified for wet or dry diesel exhaust systems. To facilitate renewal and inspection, *connectors* should be incorporated into screwed steel pipe joints where necessary, though generally it pays to weld circular flanges to the ends of each section, each pair of flanges having four stainless steel bolts with a gasket of thin graphited asbestos jointing material between the faces.

Contact the engine makers to determine the correct exhaust pipe diameter, stating the length involved. For a 30 h.p. diesel with dry exhaust, the pipe might be 2 in. (50 mm.) bore up to 15 ft. (5 m.) in length; $2\frac{1}{2}$ in. (63 mm.) thence up to 30 ft. (9 m.) and 3 in. (76 mm.) beyond that.

For an engine with resilient mountings, the exhaust system must have flexibility. If the water injection point is rigidly mounted on the engine, a length of the special rubber hose can be fitted from that point to the outlet or for a short distance leading to a metal pipe. Alternatively, or with a dry system, from the engine to the silencer a length of flexible steel pipe (with copper packing between the segments) is suitable.

COOLING ARRANGEMENTS

As mentioned previously, air cooled engines are delightfully simple, eliminating the need for water intakes, piping and pumps. However, the advantages of a water cooled exhaust system are normally lost and elaborate air ducting is required with any sort of enclosed or sound-proofed engine compartment. Square ducting for a 30 h.p. diesel would need to be about 10 in. × 10 in. (250 mm. × 250 mm.) in section. The hot air can be used for space heating on board craft which are used in cold weather while on certain motor cruisers it may be possible to direct both intake and outlet ducts up through an attractive-looking funnel, with adequate provision for rain and spray proofing.

Conventional sea water cooling presents no problems. The intake skin fitting must have a seacock, an external grid and a filter which can be cleared while the engine is running. There must be an adjustable by-pass or thermostat to enable the engine to run hot enough and preferably a 3-way cock with telltale pipe through the topsides to check readily that all is working correctly.

Piping is best made in copper with union joints. Good quality hose may be used for some parts, but if this is used from the intake to the pump it must be a special rigid-walled type which will not collapse under suction. Drain cocks may be fitted to obviate damage by frost during the lay-up period but it usually proves better to remove each section of pipe at this time.

Fresh water cooling is ideal though more complicated and the engine makers must be consulted when this method is used. One can either adopt a keel cooler with a small fresh water header tank, or use an inboard *heat exchanger*. If a wet exhaust is required, a separate pump is needed with the former method. A temperature gauge is almost essential as there is no tell-tale outlet and a thermostat or by-pass is also essential to ensure that the engine is kept at around 80° C. Anti-freeze solution can be added to the fresh water during winter, but the sea water side of a heat exchanger must be drained in severe weather.

TANKS AND FUEL PIPES

Much information on fuel and water storage tanks is given in *Boat Maintenance*, including how to make these in glass fibre. If fuel tanks are to be fabricated to special shapes the use of correct material for the type of fuel is important to safety and so is the correct provision of air venting, filtering, sludge drainage, cleaning and inspection panels and filler pipes. Try to avoid odd shapes and boxing-in tanks with joinery to make future removal difficult or impossible. Fit strong supports to take the great loads which may be imposed in a seaway and keep petrol (gasoline) and kerosene tanks a good distance from the engine or cooking stove.

Having two tanks with separate piping is a wonderful safety measure. Allow about 6 in. (150 mm.) minimum head for a gravity feed after allowing for heeling and try to lead the pipes to the engine on an even gradient. Two filters to each system are best, one at the tank and the other at the lowest point, or just before the engine. Wind a large radius two-turn coil in the pipe near the lower filter to absorb vibration and clip the piping securely at intervals of about 2 ft. (600 mm.) throughout its length. Only use plastics piping or hose when essential for a flexibly mounted engine as overheating could fracture these.

All unions at the end of fuel lines must be fixed with silver solder or by brazing unless the unions are of the compression type sealed with an annealed copper olive. Cooling water pipes should be treated similarly and no unions should be soft soldered.

When a vehicle engine is converted for marine use it should be remembered that safety precautions against fire hazards are much more important for the enclosed engine spaces on a boat than in a vehicle where the engine is exposed to the road and ventilated by a fan.

As well as a drip tray to keep oil out of the bilges, every petrol (gasoline) engine must have a fairly large drip tray beneath each carburettor and flame traps over the air intakes if not fitted with filters capable of doing this job. Fuel tanks and fuel lines must be kept remote from heat sources or adequately shielded and insulated where this is unavoidable. With gasoline aboard (and also with butane gas) a proper alarm system capable of detecting these fumes is always a wise precaution.

A tray between the bearers for the full length of the engine helps to keep a boat free from oily smells, keeping bilges clean and safe from fire. A removable tray is ideal where access permits this and sometimes removal is possible if the tray is made in two or three separate sections.

A fixed tray should have a sump at the lower end which can be kept filled with cotton waste to absorb any oil. In a small craft where copper nails come close to the drip tray, using a sheet copper or brass tray will avoid any trouble from galvanic action with the bilge water. Such a tray is simple to make from sheet by folding the sides upwards and brazing. For large craft, a welded steel tray, well galvanized may be suitable.

FRESH WATER TANKS

The type and size of each water tank for a big conversion needs careful consideration and depends largely upon whether drinking water only is to be carried, whether any fresh water is to be used for washing purposes and whether an evaporator is installed to enable sea water to be distilled in large quantities.

For small craft, pliable tanks made like buoyancy bags are available through yacht chandlers and have the advantage of easy removal for cleaning and renewal plus the convenience of stowage in cavities beneath berths or in the bilges.

Standard rectangular galvanized totally enclosed domestic hot water cisterns make a cheap source of new tanks for M.F.V.s and similar conversions. These are made in a good range of shapes and sizes. Remember, when using a hole cutter through a steel tank to attach the various inlet and outlet pipes, always remove the inspection cover to clear out any trace of metal swarf from inside the tank, as the presence of such particles can cause rapid internal rusting.

Water tanks are much simpler for the amateur to make than fuel tanks, as the safety aspect (and slight leakage) is less important. As well as by moulding in glass fibre, water tanks can be made to any shape from Permali resin-impregnated laminated wood, in the form of a box with resin-glued corners with strengthening fillets inside. When ordinary marine plywood is used similarly, the inside is best sealed with g.r.p. sheathing, but whenever drinking water is stored in glass fibre containers the taste may be affected for some considerable time.

The top of a water tank is sometimes inaccessible making it necessary to fit the inspection cover on one side or end. This makes construction more difficult as the cover must be firmly bolted to a rubber gasket to prevent leaks. For a g.r.p. tank, it may prove best to mould a cast brass ring into the panel, the ring having studs attached to it for securing the cover.

Although g.r.p. tanks can be built into a plastics boat using the hull skin as one wall, this is not viewed as good practice nowadays (due to the possibility of contamination or hidden leakage, while the rough hull surface is difficult to keep clean even when an inspection port is provided for this purpose) so removable tanks are generally best.

A g.r.p. tank can be made quite successfully at home, laying up the two halves over a polished male plug or mockup, giving a glossy interior surface to the tank with a rough exterior. Before bonding the two parts together it usually pays to fit one or more internal baffles, especially when a tank is longer than about 3 ft. (1 m.), to prevent the liquid from surging and shooting up the filler pipe or keeping one awake at night.

ENGINE CONTROLS

Although hydraulic gear-shift and steering controls are simple to install, the older mechanical linkages are still widely used and demand the use of some ingenuity, at the same time saving considerable sums of money on the outlay for equipment. The flexible steel cables running in an external sheathing frequently used for controlling the throttle can fail at sea if not given correct maintenance while solid linkages are generally foolproof. A satisfactory throttle linkage used on some small auxiliary engines consists of a thick brass wire running inside a length of small bore copper tube while a similar arrangement can be used for controlling the choke.

Morse, Teleflex, Armstrong and similar sophisticated remote controls for all purposes can be ordered through chandlers. Much fun can be derived by devising one's own gear-shift control system, perhaps using a bulkhead mounted hand wheel with chain drive, utilizing an old car steering box, or making up a lever system with linkages made from ¾ in. (18 mm.) water pipe, steel flats and angles, with the knuckle joints from old car steering parts welded on as necessary.

The cumbersome but everlasting slow-revving boat engine is almost a thing of the past. It required no electrics, remote controls, or instruments. Modern engines nearly always have an instrument panel and this should have a waterproof glass-fronted housing if exposed to the weather. A full panel generally has ammeter, oil pressure gauge, oil and water thermometers, tachometer and fuel gauge, plus low oil, charging and filter warning lights. Capillary tubes and wires from the panel need good protection against heat, chafe and crushing.

Sound insulation is almost essential with high speed diesels. This is most easily done under the sole by screwing pegboard under the bearers, packing all spaces with rock wool matting, then laying the sole. Inspection panels must be treated similarly, also all bulkheads and partitions around the engine space. Engine controls and connexions should pass through grommets or rubber tubing, with asbestos tape around the exhaust pipe.

Adequate ventilation is essential (see Chapter 12) and the batteries should not be positioned in a hot compartment. The special air ducting requirements of air cooled engines have already been mentioned.

Outboard motors are frequently housed in trunks set through the after bottom planking of both sailing craft and power boats. If such trunks are enclosed to minimize noise, it may be impossible for sufficient air to reach the engine. Even when ventilation holes are provided, the exhaust from the engine may get back and vitiate the power output.

STEERING GEARS

For a conversion, the new steering arrangements need careful thought, whether for an old ship's lifeboat or a large ex-fishing craft.

Tiller steering direct to the rudder is favoured by many yachtsmen for sailing craft smaller than about 35 ft. (11 m.) in length, providing the helmsman with a better feeling of the yacht's performance. For most power craft and sailing boats with centre cockpit, wheel steering is favoured. As well as its other well known advantages, wheel steering simplifies the fitting of an auto-pilot when required.

Provision should always be made for fitting an emergency tiller to the top of the rudder stock to guard against some unexpected failure. When converting ship's lifeboats, wheel steering is usually arranged by fitting yokes to the rudder head and leading flexible wire cables from these to a drum on the wheel shaft.

Well lubricated sheaves should be provided where each wire turns through an angle. The cables may be run on deck or below, one to each side of the hull or both on one side with rigging screws incorporated to enable the tension to be adjusted. When the cables are led through metal tubes or behind cabin fitments preventing routine inspection, it may be best to use stainless steel rope.

On craft where the rudder stock is a shaft passing through an inboard gland, a quadrant (similar to one-third of a wide pulley wheel) is fitted to the top of the shaft, held there by means of clamp bolts and a keyway, or by forming the top of the shaft into a square. As the quadrant turns, the cables keep a constant tension as they stretch around the periphery.

Proper yacht steering wheels complete with shaft, bearings, wire rope drum, or chain wheel drive, are expensive new and difficult to find secondhand. The impecunious lifeboat conversionist may have to adopt a tiller and when his boat has a mizzen mast one of the devices shown in Fig. 39 can be used to get the tiller around the obstacle of the mast. Many ingenious linkages can be devised to suit special circumstances, but the most important consideration is to build in adequate strength.

Some large old fishing trawlers have an oak rudder stock passing through a trunk in the counter. A crude but strong chain steering gear can be fabricated for this type of installation as sketched in Fig. 89. Instead of a built-up quadrant, a short tiller of steel bar

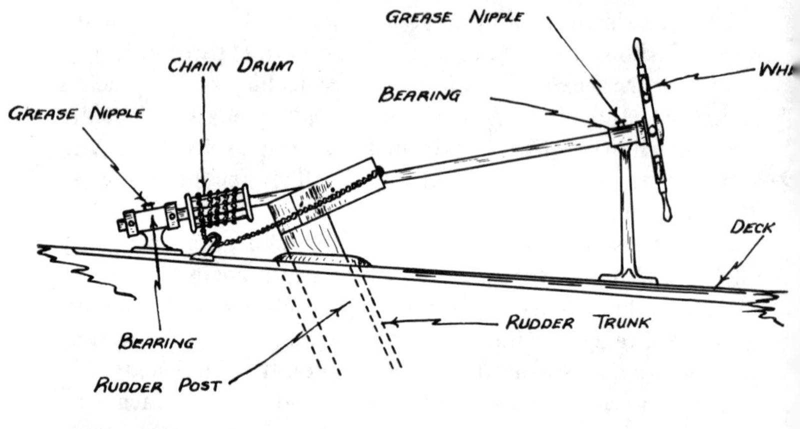

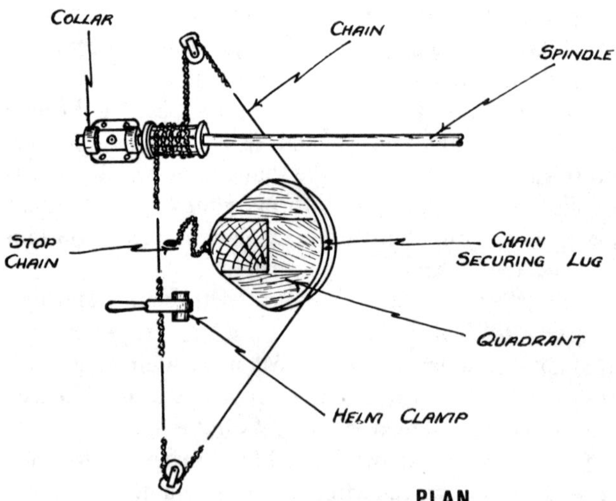

Fig. 89: Chain steering for fishing trawler

can be attached to the rudder head with the chains leading to a sleeve which is free to slide along the tiller. In practice, the sleeve should be pivoted between two steel straps, the chains being made off at each end of the pair of straps. This device prevents the sleeve from jamming when the tiller is well over.

When money is available, the above type of rudder can be controlled by fitting *Edson* steering gear to the top of the rudder stock. This American gear is marketed in England by Pascal Atkey Ltd., Cowes, and it operates on the same principle as the traditional Thames Barge gear, the steering shaft having short lengths of left-hand and right-hand two-start screw threads turned on it, connecting rods leading from yokes on the rudder head to a nut sliding on each thread.

On very big boats like M.F.V.s where the rudder shaft comes through a gland into the stern locker, *Mathway* steering gear is ideal. In this system a robust reduction gearbox transfers the rotations of the steering wheel to a short moving arm or direct to the rudder stock.

Other examples of these and similar gears can still be obtained secondhand from some ship's equipment dealers as they were used extensively on war-time power boats. The drive from the steering wheel to the gearbox is by means of rotating shafting equipped with enclosed bevel gear units, plummer blocks, and universal joints to permit the shafting to turn corners and through angles.

Hydraulic steering is another expensive mechanical system applicable to any type of rudder or steering position. The wheel unit is connected to the tiller ram by means of two small-bore tubes, the system being similar to the hydraulic controls used for tilting outboard motors and moving gearbox levers. All this equipment can be obtained through big chandlers or from firms advertising in the yachting magazines.

Many people do not care for hydraulic steering systems on small sailing craft as the 'feel' of the rudder is not transmitted to the wheel. Otherwise they are ideal: noiseless, with low friction losses, and convenient to lead any distance.

With chain and wire systems a strong spring buffer can be built

TA

Type of Conversion	BOWER ANCHOR						
	Fisherman Weight		*Plough Weight*		CHAIN		
					Length		*Siz*
	lb.	kg.	lb.	kg.	Fthms.	m.	in.
18 ft. (5.5 m.) Lifeboat	25	11	15	7	20	36	$\frac{1}{4}$
24 ft. (7.3 m.) Lifeboat	35	16	20	9	25	46	$\frac{5}{16}$
27 ft. (8.2 m.) Whaler	40	18	25	11	30	55	$\frac{5}{16}$
30 ft. (9.2 m.) Motor/Sailer	55	25	35	16	35	64	$\frac{3}{8}$
36 ft. (11 m.) Launch	55	25	40	18	40	74	$\frac{3}{8}$
40 ft. (12.2 m.) Trawler	70	32	55	25	50	92	$\frac{7}{16}$
45 ft. (13.7 m.) Pinnace	90	40	55	25	50	92	$\frac{7}{16}$
48 ft. (14.6 m.) Trawler	90	40	75	34	60	110	$\frac{1}{2}$
55 ft. (16.7 m.) M.F.V.	110	50	105	48	60	110	$\frac{1}{2}$
65 ft. (19.8 m.) M.F.V.	140	64	120	54	70	128	$\frac{5}{8}$
72 ft. (21.8 m.) Navy M.L.	120	54	105	48	90	164	$\frac{1}{2}$
83 ft. (25.2 m.) Barge	200	90	150	68	90	164	$\frac{3}{4}$
112 ft. (34.1 m.) Navy M.L.	200	90	150	68	120	220	$\frac{3}{4}$

ND TACKLE

SECOND BOWER							KEDGE ANCHOR							
man ght	*Plough Weight*		CHAIN				*Fisherman Weight*		*Plough Weight*		NYLON ROPE			
			Length		*Size*						*Length*		*Diam.*	
kg.	lb.	kg.	Fthms.	m.	in.	mm.	lb.	kg.	lb.	kg.	Fthms.	m.	in.	mm.
—	—	—	—	—	—	—	15	7	10	5	20	36	½	12
—	—	—	—	—	—	—	20	9	15	7	30	55	½	12
—	—	—	—	—	—	—	25	11	15	7	30	55	½	12
18	25	11	25	46	⅜	9	25	11	15	7	40	74	⅝	16
18	25	11	30	55	⅜	9	35	16	20	9	40	74	⅝	16
25	40	18	35	64	7/16	11	40	18	25	11	50	92	¾	18
25	40	18	35	64	7/16	11	40	18	25	11	40	74	¾	18
32	55	25	40	74	½	12	55	25	35	16	50	92	¾	18
40	75	34	40	74	½	12	55	25	35	16	50	92	¾	18
50	105	48	50	92	⅝	16	55	25	40	18	60	110	1	25
40	75	34	60	110	½	12	70	32	55	25	90	164	1	25
50	75	34	60	110	¾	19	70	32	75	34	90	164	1	25
64	105	48	60	110	¾	19	90	40	75	34	120	220	1¼	32

in to prevent shock loads on the rudder from carrying away some part of the steering gear. This cannot be done as effectively on screw or hydraulic arrangements. The simple drum and wire systems used for steering outboard motors and small inboard runabouts and launches are usually kept in stock by the larger chandlery stores.

GROUND TACKLE

Unless any type of yacht larger than about 30 ft. (9 m.) in length has a power windlass, weighing anchor may become the one operation which keeps the boat in harbour due to inadequate crew strength.

Many a gin palace which cruises only from marina to marina never uses an anchor, but one day an engine fault may demand either good ground tackle or a rescue operation.

Table 2 lists the sizes of anchors and chain cable commonly used for a wide range of craft including various converted working vessels. *Plough* and *Danforth* type anchors are the most suitable for modern yachts though on certain types of weed-covered bed they refuse to hold, while an equivalent Fisherman anchor with its greater weight and longer arms may hold well.

Stockless anchors are generally only suitable for very large power craft with power windlasses. Their great weight is then not detrimental and being housed directly in the hawsepipe (like an ocean liner) they do not need to be lifted on board.

Tested galvanized chain still makes the best anchor cable for yachts over about 30 ft. (9 m.) in length, its weight being a great advantage for springiness, while its life is long and it will stow itself neatly into a cable locker on weighing anchor.

For smaller craft, a stout nylon warp with a 2 fathom (4 m.) length of chain at the anchor end may suffice. For very deep anchorages, a long length of flexible wire rope reeled on to a specially made drum winch above or below decks can save a lot of weight and hard labour. Heavy vessels longer than about 45 ft. (14 m.) must have two completely separate sets of main anchors and cables. To be successful, this means separate cable lockers, windlass gypsies (wildcats) and stemhead rollers (or hawsepipes). In addition, cruising boats of all sizes need a kedge anchor with ample nylon warp. For convenience, two or three coils of warp can be stowed aboard, to be joined together for emergencies.

On craft with no windlass (or with an inefficient one) there should be a chain pawl on top of the stemhead fairlead to prevent the chain from slipping back when weighing anchor. Every effort should be made to make the cable self-stowing from the deck into the cable locker below. A straight *navel pipe* through the deck (instead of a curved neck type) assists in this direction and as the cable locker should be situated to keep the cable weight low and away from the bows, a chute can often be arranged from the navel pipe down to the locker.

A pear-shaped cable locker which will ensure that chain is laid down neatly and without tangling as it feeds in, is a luxury rarely to be found on even large yachts. With a conventional timber-lined square box in the bilges, there should be easy access to the top of this locker and the chute should have an open top. Yachts cruising in British coastal waters normally lead the main bower anchor through the port side stemhead fairlead. The reason for this is that storm winds tend to veer on increasing in these waters and with the port anchor down first, when a second anchor is required at some later time, an open hawse cable arrangement is more likely to result when the wind is at its severest strength. However, it should not be forgotten that on small boats (where the cable is taken in by hand) for a right-handed person weighing proves easier with the cable lying on the starboard side of the fore deck.

To avoid damage to the topsides when weighing anchor, a craft with anchors heavier than about 60 lbs. (27 kg.) requires a *cat davit* at the stemhead to enable the anchors to be lifted clear of the rail and swung inboard. Such a davit can be made to serve two bower anchors if positioned correctly.

The hook on the cat tackle (which ships into a gravity ring on the anchor shank) should have a line attached to its back so that as the anchor is lowered to the water surface this line tightens and capsizes the hook, thus freeing the anchor. In all craft smaller than about 40 ft. (12 m.) in length it is possible to do without a cat davit and to use the spinnaker halyard as a burton. See Chapter 7 for details of anchor stowage under a bowsprit.

WINDLASSES

For small craft a double-acting ratchet windlass operated by means of a long vertical handle is generally more convenient to use than a toy-like handle-operated windlass which can only be turned from a stooping or kneeling position. Small electric and hydraulic winches are made and they help an elderly yachtsman to sail single-handed.

For big craft, a power windlass is almost essential unless a strong crew is always available. Under the right conditions a hand windlass is generally more powerful than a motorized one and is more flexible with regard to the speeds at which cable may be handled.

The rope warping drums on any type of anchor winch are valuable for dealing with heavy loads, such as hauling the craft off a mud bank by means of the kedge anchor and warp or when shifting moorings against a strong tide.

When an old trading ketch is converted into a yacht she may have one of the antique pump handle windlasses which were traditional on these vessels. In spite of their crude appearance these contraptions were quite efficient, though slow in action. It may seem a pity to scrap one of these, but they prove difficult to motorize and if a new power winch is to be fitted it cannot normally be done with the old windlass still in position.

Such a wide choice of equipment to do with windlass and anchors is available that it pays to study the pages of the British and American chandlery catalogues before placing an order.

10

Plumbing and Wiring

The importance of water supply and electrical installations on board a modern conversion necessitates considerable advance planning to ensure that internal fixtures do not obstruct the fitting of tanks, piping, etc. It may be expedient to install the plumbing at an early stage, but alternatively, certain joinery may have to be removable.

In similar fashion, certain hatches or skylights may need to be of a special size to enable cumbersome objects such as engines, tanks and stoves, to be taken below or removed at some future time. Very rarely is it possible to place all such objects into position before decking is completed and it might be advisable to decide whether one requires a piano in the saloon before work proceeds too far!

WATER SUPPLY

Small craft possess little in the way of water supply, but many larger conversions have complex plumbing arrangements which are essential for the efficient running of the ship and the enjoyment of all on board.

The cost of installing a complex water supply system can vary. It can either be done quite cheaply in do-it-yourself fashion with hand pumps, or it can include automatic electric supply pumps with an evaporator to produce fresh water in large quantities.

Running water can be supplied by gravity; by a hand pump at each outlet; an electric pump on the main supply pipe, or compressed air applied to sealed tanks.

The type of feed to be adopted depends upon the number and kind of supplies and outlets contained in the system and whether the vessel is for long distance cruising or for coastwise jaunts.

For the deep sea vessel without an evaporator, sea water may have to be used for all duties except the galley supply. On the coastwise vessel fresh water can be used for a shower bath and hand basins also. The complexity increases if provision is made for feeding basins and showers with fresh water when in harbour (or when supplies are adequate) with a change-over device to enable sea water to be used as an alternative.

A gravity tank is usually quite small and situated on deck or concealed in the base of a dummy funnel. This arrangement has the advantage that, with fresh water especially, any leakage at the outlet can only drain the small header tank without causing serious wastage. The pressure on a gravity supply is normally low and this may help to conserve water.

One disadvantage of the header tank system is that this must be filled at regular intervals and it may run dry at an awkward moment. Filling may be carried out by hand or power pump, according to the cheapness of the installation. Gravity supply can sometimes be arranged direct from the main water tanks, but if these are situated low down in the hull (which is normally best for stability), water may have to be drawn off into buckets and transferred to the galley or other location. A header tank can sometimes be fitted below the deckhead, but it may fail to operate when the vessel is heeling.

Many attractive types of lever-action hand pumps are available for supplying fresh water from a tank set low down in the boat to hand basins and sinks. This is the most widely used system for small craft and has the advantage that wastage is almost impossible. As a certain amount of effort and time is needed to produce water from the outlet, people not accustomed to the ways of the sea are less likely to waste fresh water than they might be with an automatic pressurized supply.

Perusal of the chandlery catalogues will reveal many of the different makes of automatic supply units available. In the 'BEE' system an electrical contact is built into each tap (faucet) operating the electric pump simultaneously with the opening of the valve. In most of the other systems (such as the *Godwin*, *Stuart Turner*, and *Raritan*) the power unit is brought into action by the pressure drop created as soon as a tap is opened. This is the system most commonly used for bath or shower supply, especially when hot water is also involved. If both sea water and fresh water supplies are required it would be necessary to fit two completely separate electric supply units.

To do a similar job cheaply the amateur can fit up any number of centrifugal pumps connected to small electric motors (or one larger motor driving several pumps) to supply fresh, salt, and hot water for various duties, as well as bilge-emptying and deck-wash purposes.

Separate motors and pumps are generally better, as there is no power loss when the pump is not delivering and should one unit fail, it may be possible to operate a supply in an emergency capacity by changing over the pump connexions.

Centrifugal pumps are not harmed when run with the outlet closed and the power loss involved is not usually critical for the intermittent periods likely to be involved. A single pump dealing with sea water can be made to serve two or three purposes by fitting multiple valve manifolds, with the controls duly labelled at inlet and outlet sides of the pump.

To ensure that centrifugal pumps will always prime instantly, it may be advantageous to fit them below the intake water level. When this is not practicable (as for bilge pumping) a foot valve can be fitted to the strumbox end of the intake pipe. One other way to keep water inside the pump is to loop the inlet pipe up above the level of the pump. Electrical *submersible* pumps are available for bilge pumping.

The method of water supply using a pressurized tank is rarely used but it enables the amateur handyman to install a fully automatic pressurized hot and cold water system quite cheaply. Several different arrangements can be adopted. In the simplest, with one outlet only, the air pump to pressurize the tank can be situated near the outlet and just given a few pumps when water is required if the pressure in the tank happens to have faded since last being used. When several outlets are required, a hand air pump can be situated near the tank (or in any other suitable position) and a pressure gauge added to ensure that the pressure stays at the requisite level at all times.

In the most complicated arrangements, a small air compressor is fitted to the engine to enable a *receiver* (a small high pressure air tank) to be kept fully charged when underway. Air from the receiver is fed to the water tanks through a reducing valve so that the tanks are permanently charged with air at about 5 lbs. per sq. in. (120 gr. per cm^2.). With the usual amount of cruising, if the air is shut off when the vessel is unattended, there should always be an adequate supply of air when in harbour.

This method of supply has advantages besides its cheapness. The speed at which water emerges from the outlets can be controlled by varying the air pressure and the piping required can be of smaller bore than would be necessary for gravity or centrifugal pump systems. A safety valve on the tank is a useful precaution against failure of the reducing valve.

Sea water is rarely used on small craft and is collected direct by bucket and lanyard when required. On larger vessels, running sea water supplies have many uses and can help to economize in the use of fresh water. If special sea water soap is used, one can wash quite successfully with sea water though it pays to rinse off with a small quantity of fresh water whenever possible.

Sea water can be supplied hot for baths and showers, but to prevent the water heater from fouling up with salt, keep the water temperature below 120° F (50° C).

A sea water deck wash hose is almost essential on big craft cruising in tropical climates. Its pump may be driven from the main engine, electrically, or by means of a small auxiliary engine. Remember that a deck wash hose is also valuable for cleaning mud from the anchor and cable when it comes aboard.

WATER AND SPACE HEATING

When cruising early and late in the season in cold and temperate climates some form of cabin heating is essential according to modern ideas of comfort. In small craft a coal or charcoal heater may suffice while on larger vessels hot air supplied through ducts from an oil-fired heater is an ideal solution, but by no means a cheap one. By piping the main engine cooling water through one or more large storage tanks, sufficient hot water can be retained for a whole day's use, while engine cooling water can also be circulated through radiators in the cabins for space heating while underway. In order to continue such heating while in harbour, an auxiliary oil-fired water heater would need to be brought into use.

This whole sphere contains great potential for the individual yachtsman or conversionist and some extremely successful installations have been completed very cheaply. Many people still prefer the cosy dry warmth of a coal-fired cabin stove or cooking range and many of these units are available with back boilers to produce hot water without incurring additional fuel charges.

Good stoves of this type can be kept burning all night, but re-lighting is simple with a butane torch. When they are used for hot sea water supply, internal fouling due to overheating of the stove can be avoided by using an indirect calorifier hot water tank. With this, a small quantity of fresh water circulates continuously through the stove.

Many types of oil and butane fired stoves, ranges and water heaters are available through chandlers for all purposes on yachts of any size. Special copper radiators are made for marine use which are shaped to fit below berths, and in lockers. Normal domestic radiators can rarely be squeezed into the small free spaces available and although cast iron domestic radiators can be used at sea for a cheap job, the more common pressed steel types should not be used at all.

There is no point in circulating sea water through radiators when an indirect system is used as the amount of fresh water wasted is negligible. Sea water could be used through copper marine radiators if necessary as long as the temperature is kept down. Two schematic diagrams for water supply systems appear in Figs. 90 and 91.

Some stoves and ranges are extremely heavy and must be securely bolted through the cabin sole to the bearers or to a bulkhead. When asbestos sheeting is used as a bulkhead lining behind a stove it should be spaced about 1 in. (25 mm.) away from

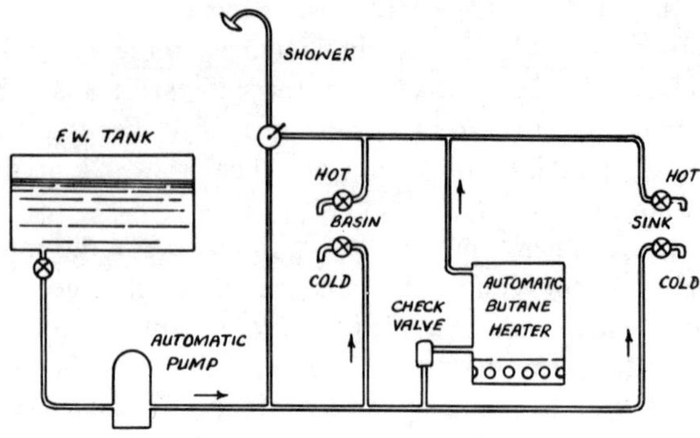

Fig. 90: Water supply heated by butane

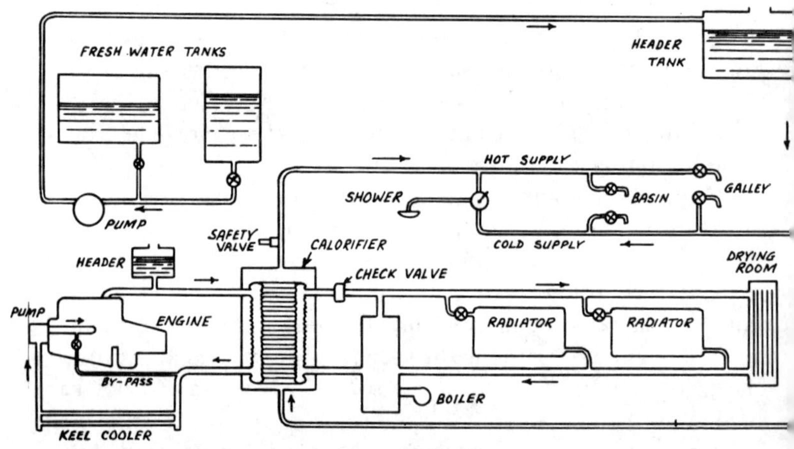

Fig. 91: Large water supply heated by engine

timber or other inflammable surfaces to provide an insulating air space. Similar treatment may be necessary to the deckhead directly over a stove. This also applies to the smaller primus and butane cooking stoves which are often situated in a confined space beneath the side decks on small craft. Where butane mantle lamps or wick oil lamps are used for cabin lighting (and there are still many craft without an electricity supply) *smoke bells* must be fitted on the deckhead above each lamp to prevent a fire.

Make sure the flexible hose connexion to a butane gas cooking stove in gimbals complies with all safety regulations. Build a proper stowage locker for gas cylinders, sealed except for the drainage pipe overboard. A bilge gas detector is a most satisfying precaution against possible explosions.

STOVE PIPES

Where small portable space heaters are used, such as the mantle reflector kerosene types, or the butane incandescent element or catalytic (producing heat with no flame) stoves, these, as well as all wick stoves, produce fumes and water vapour which can be troublesome in the confines of a small boat's cabin. When choosing a stove for permanent mounting and frequent use, choose one which exhausts up a flue through the deckhead.

Proper deck flanges can be obtained for securing the stove pipe at this point, in a variety of designs and sizes. The funnel pipe, which stands above deck level, is always made to unship at the flange so that it need not be rigged at sea unless the stove concerned is to be left working.

A good deck flange for yachts is the flush pattern with a lid to drop into its mouth when the funnel is unshipped. Above-deck funnels are usually made of galvanized steel about 30 in. (750 mm.) high. Stainless steel is a better material if available.

The length of flue from the stove to the deck flange should never be made from asbestos cement pipe as this can explode if overheated. Stove-enamelled cast iron is the best material, but stainless steel looks neat.

PLUMBING

Several different tubing materials can be used for yacht plumbing, polythene or vinyl plastics materials being the cheapest, copper the most expensive. Brass unions and fittings are best for both types of pipe, and these can cost more than the tube itself. Thin walled stainless steel tube is now readily available in the ½ in. (12 mm.) and ¾ in. (18 mm.) bores and this is at present cheaper than copper.

Stainless tube is worked in exactly the same way as copper and both these materials can be equipped with soldered fittings which are cheaper than the heavier compression fittings generally used with the plastics materials.

Moulded *Delrin* (nylon) fittings are gradually superseding metal for such items as skin fittings and taps (faucets) as well as for joining two lengths of plastics tubing together. These fittings are cheap but they are too soft to be used for moulding into a g.r.p. hull and they can be damaged if the nuts are over-tightened.

Stainless steel tube (with its polished external surface) is the smartest material where it has to be visible. The above mentioned plastics tubes cannot be used for hot water supply but nylon tube, although more expensive, is quite suitable.

To form sharp bends in polythene tubing, this should be submerged in boiling water (or wrapped with rag and boiling water poured over it) for a few minutes prior to forming the bend. On cooling, the shape will be permanently formed. To avoid kinking it would be advisable to insert a *plumber's spring* into the bore of the pipe attaching a cord to this if a long way from the end of the tube.

Tube bending jigs for copper and stainless steel pipe are available from tool hire stores. Without a machine, use a spring inside or outside the pipe. Alternatively, fill the pipe with dry sand and plug the ends before bending. For tight bends on small pipes, pour in molten solder temporarily. Note that the zinc coated steel tube commonly used for small-bore household heating installations is unsuitable for boat work especially where sea water supply is concerned.

Yorkshire fittings have solder (pronounced *sodder*) cast into each socket. This melts and fixes a joint as soon as heat is applied. To ensure success, scour the outside of the tube and the inside of the fitting thoroughly with steel wool or sandpaper (emery cloth is not suitable) and coat with *Baker's Fluid* (killed spirits of salts) or a proprietary paste flux. Note that soldering cannot be done while water is in a pipe.

Compression fittings are simple to use. The nut is slipped

onto the tube end, the annealed copper or nylon *olive* is then pushed on, the tube is inserted into the fitting until it comes to a stop and the nut is screwed tightly onto its thread. When one of these fittings has to be removed it may be necessary to fit a new olive before replacement.

Similarly, compression fittings are used with plastics piping, but in this case a small metal ferrule is thrust into the end of the pipe (perhaps first inserting the pipe end into boiling water to soften it) to create a rigid foundation for the olive. Certain types of connexions for these pipes are bonded on by a special adhesive.

When two fittings with metal threads are to be connected together, or when using standard galvanized steel water piping with steel or brass fittings, an important (though simple) technique is required to seal the threads against leakage. This is done nowadays by winding a layer of special PTFE (*Fluon* or *Teflon*) tape tightly around the male thread before screwing the parts together. If the threads are rough, tape can pick-up, so white liquid PTFE is then best. For slack threads, build up the tape thickness with overlapping turns.

The old method of sealing threads using a few strands of hemp laid in a special paste is still quite widely used and the materials required are always stocked by plumbers and builders merchants. The sealers used for gaskets on engines can also be utilized for sealing pipe joints, *Hermetite* being one of the most widely used in both the permanently soft and hardening varieties.

Additional plumbing details referring to water supply, engine fuel and exhaust pipes and flexible hoses, together with information on the overhaul and installation of yacht heads (toilets) are given in *Boat Maintenance*.

HEADS, BATHS AND BASINS

When choosing a yacht toilet, the question of cost may limit the range to one of the simple hand pump units used in ninety per cent of all small craft and produced by many makers in Britain and America. For inland water cruising, it may be essential to adopt either a chemical toilet or a standard marine type equipped with a chlorinator/macerator unit on the discharge end. For large power craft and motor/sailers electrically-operated yacht toilets may be chosen, but the price will then be higher.

Installation instructions are always available from the makers. Although the cost of seacocks and hoses is not normally included in the basic price, the majority of makers will supply these. Details of the seacocks to suit different types of hull (and the lengths of hoses normally required) are listed in their catalogues.

Correct siting of the seacocks in relation to the waterline is important to avoid contamination of the flushing water by the soil discharge. Also important is the creation of a loop well above the highest possible waterline with the soil pipe (between the toilet and the seacock) to reduce the likelihood of siphoning back which could cause flooding. Alternatively, a large non-return valve can be fitted into the soil pipe and some makers recommend this as an additional precaution.

Standard seacocks are not always applicable to every installation. It may be necessary to modify standard ones by extending the stem (or to fit an angled type seacock) to enable one to turn this off readily after use. Many craft have been sunk through faults with toilets or seacocks.

The level of lavatory basins and galley sinks is often close to the waterline and discharge by gravity through a skin fitting in the topsides is not always possible. When this is done, a seacock should be fitted to avoid flooding when the vessel is heeling or when she sits lower in the water on moorings due to rain water collecting in the bilges or perhaps through moving her into a fresh water dock.

Basins and baths can be emptied by means of a semi-rotary pump mounted in any suitable position, but for a shower bath, where the level of water in the sump must be kept low throughout the period of use, a suitable hand pump can be fitted to the bulkhead inside the shower compartment as indicated in Fig. 92. This operation is simplified considerably, of course, if an electric pump can be utilized for these duties.

A better idea (often used for big craft but also applicable to smaller ones) is to have an enclosed septic tank (made from

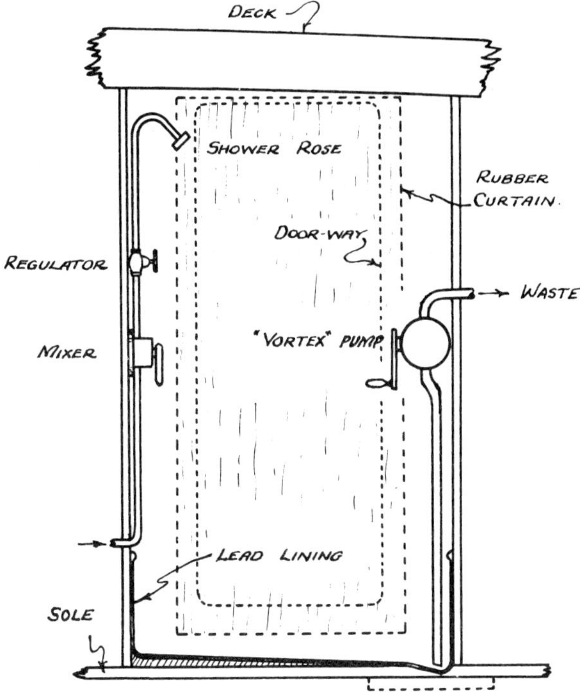

Fig. 92: Shower with hand extractor pump

g.r.p., p.v.c., or galvanized steel) in the bilges and lead all basins, sink and bath waste pipes into this. A large hand pump (or an electric unit) can be installed to empty the tank whenever required.

A simple float gauge can be mounted to a short stand pipe on top of the tank to indicate the level of the contents, but frequent emptying is advisable to prevent the formation of sludge. To simplify the cleaning of sludge from such a tank, two or more valves with hose connexions can be fitted to the top of it. Periodically, the deck wash hose (or a mains water hose from the shore if convenient) can be coupled to each valve in turn and water thrust vertically into the tank while the discharge pump is running. Too much sludge may clog the pump and so this job should be done more frequently than once a year.

Standard household lavatory basins can be used on large vessels, but chandlery firms stock a range of smaller sizes made for marine work in vitreous and stainless steel constructions.

To save space, corner basins can be fitted into cabins and tip-up units can be mounted on the bulkhead behind the toilet. A conventional tip-up basin is mounted inside a cabinet with dropping front. The basin has no waste hole. Instead there is a lip in the rim to allow the waste to be discharged into a funnel (fixed to the bottom of the cabinet) as soon as the lid is returned to the closed position. In Fig. 93 an idea is shown to enable the amateur to

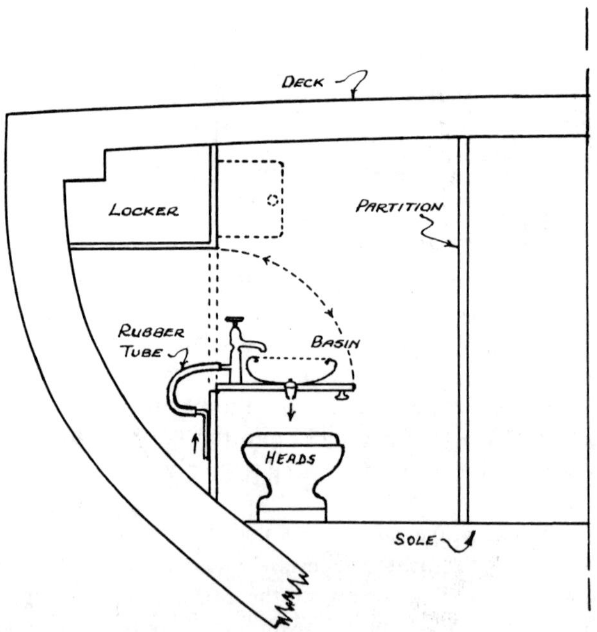

Fig. 93: Tip-up basin unit in the heads

fabricate his own tip-up unit by installing a standard stainless steel basin with plug hole. By locating this correctly, the waste from the basin can be discharged direct into the heads and pumped overboard from there.

Basins need not have anti-splash rims but this is a good feature to look for when choosing one. Galley sinks should never be of vitreous china due to the likelihood of breakage from falling objects. Stainless steel and Perspex (*Plexiglas*) are the most common materials, but it should be remembered that the plastics materials can be warped by boiling water and they tend to wear rough in time, making the surface difficult to keep clean.

On small craft, where the conservation of fresh water and hot water is important, most owners use a small circular bowl resting inside the galley sink for dish washing purposes. Such a bowl is readily emptied via the heads or directly overboard – to leeward!

A teak sink has certain advantages and is kind to crockery. The amateur handyman can save money by making a sink with oddments of teak from a boatyard fitted together in the form of a watertight box having all joints sealed with resorcinol glue. As the outside of such a sink is not normally visible, there is no need to dovetail the joints and simple external fillets glued and screwed into place are in many ways superior.

Small plastics bath tubs are made for use in trailer caravans, but showers occupy a minimum of space and if full headroom is not available a shoulder-high spray head can be adopted. Shower equipment can be fabricated at minimal cost by the handyman, but if finance is available it pays to buy a proper thermostatic control valve to eliminate the risk of injury by scalding.

A proper shower tray is expensive to buy, but the amateur can make his own quite easily by moulding in glass fibre or by forming an *in situ* lining using sheet lead with soldered joints as shown in Fig. 92. A home-made tray can be of the exact size to fit the available space. A firm foundation of timber packing underneath is essential and this should be laid with a fall towards the waste pipe. A standard domestic outlet fitting is satisfactory but there is no need for a trap beneath it unless the waste pipe leads direct to a septic tank. When the waste is discharged by a pump, there is no need for an outlet through the sole as the pipe can dip inside the tray. For cheapness a hand pump can be rigged similarly, concealed behind the bulkhead as shown in Fig. 92.

A teak grating standing inside a shower tray gives a warm feel and helps to raise one's feet above the level of water waiting to be pumped out. Teak gratings are simple to make. They have many uses on board a yacht and an attractive appearance.

There are two recognized ways of making teak gratings, the simpler (though less robust) method being illustrated in Fig. 94.

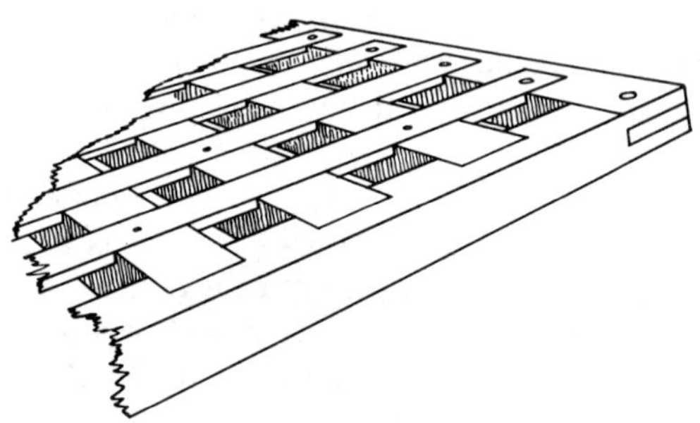

Fig. 94: Teak grating construction

Cutting the notches in the thicker pieces is best accomplished by sliding them across a correctly-set circular saw using the cross-cutting guide, but the job can be done equally well, though less quickly, by hand. If glue is used, only occasional screws (duly dowelled over on completion) are required through the joints. Care must be taken to keep the grating flat during assembly.

One of the greatest problems when making a shower cubicle is to seal the wall panelling against seepage of water which could cause hidden rot. One answer is to use a circular rubber curtain which completely surrounds the occupant, but when the more usual melamine-surfaced plastics materials are used as wall linings, these should be sealed in the corners and where they meet the shower tray by means of Polyseamseal or a similar white synthetic liquid rubber.

THE GALLEY

The galley compartment is usually lined with a washable material or melamine plastics fixed with impact adhesive, but a good layer of polyurethane enamel is cheaper and may be less liable to peel off. Furthermore, if the distaff side of the crew dislikes the colour this proves easier to change!

Worktops are usually melamine surfaced nowadays though scrubbed teak is in many ways more satisfactory, having a higher coefficient of friction. In any case there must be a *fiddle* or raised coaming along all edges to prevent crockery from sliding into the sink or onto the galley sole. An integral stainless steel pressing for sink and draining board eliminates the problem of sealing the sink unit to the surrounding worktop, this proving the weakness of many otherwise good installations.

Most galley fittings are obtainable from chandlery stores, but the essential racks for securing all crockery into readily accessible positions normally have to be made by the handy-man to match the sizes and numbers of plates and cups to be carried. A typical unit in polished mahogany is shown in Plate 35.

Whether the simplest form of alcohol stove is to be adopted, or a complicated butane gas cooker (perhaps even an electric range on some big conversions) great care is needed in the choice of these appliances to ensure that they will cope with the requirements of the owner and crew for the sort of cruising intended.

Cooking stoves on big vessels are rarely mounted in gimbals, but on lively small craft this is essential if any form of cooking is to be undertaken when at sea. Stoves of all sizes must have fiddles (guardrails) around the top to prevent accidents and to enable the cook to wedge his pots and pans on top of the stove without having to hold them there by hand.

Kettles and saucepans of aluminium should be avoided at sea and if stainless steel is too expensive, enamelled steel utensils are serviceable. A pressure cooker is more useful at sea than on shore as the contents cannot be spilled and much fuel is conserved. Note that the majority of pressure cookers are made of aluminium

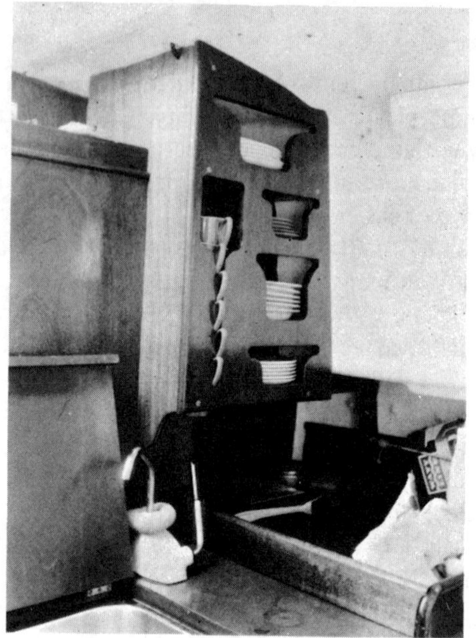

Plate 35: Mahogany crockery rack

but the Swedish stainless steel *Svensk* make is available in most parts of the world.

Although some yachtsmen of the salt-pork hard-tack variety scorn the use of a refrigerator, some form of cold storage arrangement is most useful for prolonged cruising. Low voltage electric refrigerators for yachts are readily available nowadays. If a butane gas model must be used, make sure this has a safety device to turn off the supply should the pilot jet become extinguished. Some of these absorption type refrigerators do not function properly at an angle of heel. On big power craft, refrigeration may be combined with a heat pump air conditioning system.

In parts of America where ice is available at all harbours, a simple ice-box is satisfactory for yacht cruising. To keep a small crew supplied for occasional weekends, large vacuum flasks or insulated containers are suitable if these are equipped with patent cooling packs prepared in the home refrigerator before leaving.

For extended cruising without refrigeration, a locker built into the bilges may be suitable for keeping canned beer while a louvred teak box on deck lined with zinc and with insulated top may prove cooler than any ordinary locker below decks. This rather old-world device can be improved by installing an evaporating cooler inside instead of the zinc lining. These coolers have porous walls and a container of water at the bottom. The water is drawn into the sides by capillary attraction and then evaporates producing a cooling effect.

Not all gadgets are successful, but the enthusiastic handy-man can derive much pleasure by keeping a notebook of all useful items of equipment he has observed on other people's boats or in yachting magazines. Having sorted out the useful ones from the playthings, he can design his own versions to suit his vessel and fit them into the most convenient places.

USING ELECTRICITY

Very few yachts nowadays have no electrical equipment at all, though many owners will confess that for complete relaxation on the water one should stick to wick lamps and a hand starting diesel engine, so that no electricity is required in any part of the ship!

Technical details of small craft electric wiring, charging, batteries and fittings, are given in *Complete Amateur Boat Building*. Firms such as the Onan Division of Studebaker Corporation in America and G. & M. Power Plant Ltd in England specialize in the supply of the complex equipment used nowadays on medium- and large-sized vessels. Their catalogues are a mine of information for the enthusiast who wishes to improve the electrical installation of his boat.

A complete book could be filled with the information necessary to describe all the possible equipment in current use, what circuitry to adopt for all conditions and what cable sizes are best. Many craft spend long periods of time alongside marina slips and docks where shore power is available. By making full use of this, noisy generators need not be run in harbour and many kinds of domestic appliances can be used on the boat, including power tools.

However, to make full use of shore power one should either have completely separate wiring throughout for the higher voltage, or a heavy duty converter (mains A.C. to low voltage D.C.) to feed the boat's circuits (by-passing the battery) plus a battery charger.

Mains A.C. on a boat can cause more serious electrolytic damage than D.C., especially with a metal hull, if stray current occurs undetected. When mains voltage as high as 240-v is used, this can be dangerous to crew members under moist conditions.

In America, 115–120 volt mains supply is more common, but even then D.C. circuitry is advisable. If a *Constavolt* converter (LaMarche Mfg. Co.) is fitted on board, this can feed any D.C. voltage between 6 and 230 (up to 60 amps) to the ship and it will also keep the batteries charged automatically.

If the boat's generator set is designed to deliver 120-volts A.C. (or whatever the normal shore voltage happens to be) both types of input can feed through the Constavolt, making no difference to the performance of the electrical appliances whether at sea or at a dock.

Although some appliances will work equally well on A.C. or D.C., some motors are not *universal* so special care is needed when choosing fans, air conditioners, refrigerators, vacuum cleaners, pumps, electric toilets, syrens, oil burners, record players, winches and power tools.

On small craft, lighting, fans and radio equipment can be supplied at 12-v or 24-v D.C. from the engine starter batteries.

On medium size craft there should be a separate bank of batteries for all auxiliary duties, but changeover switching should be incorporated to enable the auxiliary bank to be tapped for starting in an emergency. On big vessels there may be several separate circuits, perhaps at different voltages, the heavy loads (such as for cooking and space heating) being supplied direct from the generator set, eliminating the need for enormous batteries.

Certain modern generating sets are designed to start automatically whenever an appliance wired direct to them is turned on.

The higher the voltage adopted, the thinner the cables can be for a given wattage load and also the lower are the losses due to the resistance of long cable runs. Bigger batteries are not always necessary for higher voltages as in many instances the same number of cells connected together in parallel for a lower voltage supply merely need to be coupled in series to produce the same capacity with a higher voltage.

Before deciding what voltage to adopt, add up the wattages of all the appliances likely to be operating in unison for periods in excess of a few minutes and ask an electrician to advise you on the cable sizes and battery capacity likely to be required. He will need to know especially the wattages carried by any cables more than, say, half the length of the boat.

On a medium sized boat the following could be a typical list of wattages:

Navigation lights and searchlight/signalling lamp	100
Power windlass or capstan	250
Radio equipment	40
Water supply pump motor	150
Cabin lighting	180
Exhausting fans and blowers	80
Refrigerator	150
Outlets to take vacuum cleaner, kettle, cookery mixer and inspection lamp	900
Sound signal	60

This gives a total of 1910 watts. The engine starter (say 1800 watts) has been omitted and any engine ignition supply is normally catered for by the engine's own generator. Items of negligible wattage, such as an electric clock, may also be found on board.

For battery capacity calculation purposes one could assume a continuous load of about 1200 watts. Using 24-volt supply, the maximum current would be about 50 amps, necessitating the use of a 300 amp/hour battery. Using heavy duty 12-volt car batteries, this would mean having four units connected in parallel coupled in series with another four in parallel.

The greatest continuous load likely to be imposed, with all navigation lights working, some cabin lighting and certain fans, would be about 10 amps and this could be drawn for some 15 hours without affecting the battery voltage appreciably.

By increasing the voltage to 48 (nominally called 50) the current rating would be halved and the cables could be much thinner. The capacity of the batteries could be halved to 150 amp/hour and the same number of car batteries could be used, one bank of four connected in series being coupled in parallel to another bank of four connected in series. In America 32-volt equipment is easier to obtain than 50 volt.

Ordinary lead/acid batteries should not be charged at a higher amperage than the 10 hour rate, i.e. the amp/hour capacity divided by 10. For a 150 amp/hour bank this makes the maximum charging rate 15 amps. For the above instance, a $1\frac{1}{2}$ kilowatt generator powered by a $3\frac{1}{2}$ h.p. engine would be suitable, taking about 8 hours to recharge the batteries when in a fairly low condition, or about 4 hours in normal instances of partial discharge. A battery charge state indicator (or hydrometer set) is invaluable to prevent wasteful overcharging.

With a normal amount of cruising, it may be possible to use the main engine generator for all charging purposes, especially if this is one of the modern alternators with built-in rectifier which will produce a high output current even at relatively low speeds.

Nickel/iron (Nife) and nickel/cadmium batteries are more expensive than ordinary lead/acid types but they are almost indestructible and can be charged at a higher rate. With these, it may be possible to equip one of the main engines with a large generator operated via a clutch, enabling the batteries to be recharged very quickly with the main engine turning over at about one-quarter normal working speed.

This eliminates the need for a separate generator set and a main engine running at greatly reduced speed might make less noise than an auxiliary engine. Note, however, that a diesel or a petrol (gasoline) engine can be harmed if run under very light load for prolonged periods, so when a main engine is utilized for charging purposes only, the generator should be designed to absorb most of the engine's rated power at the chosen speed.

A simplified wiring diagram for the 48-volt installation described above is shown in Fig. 95, with typical cable sizes indicated.

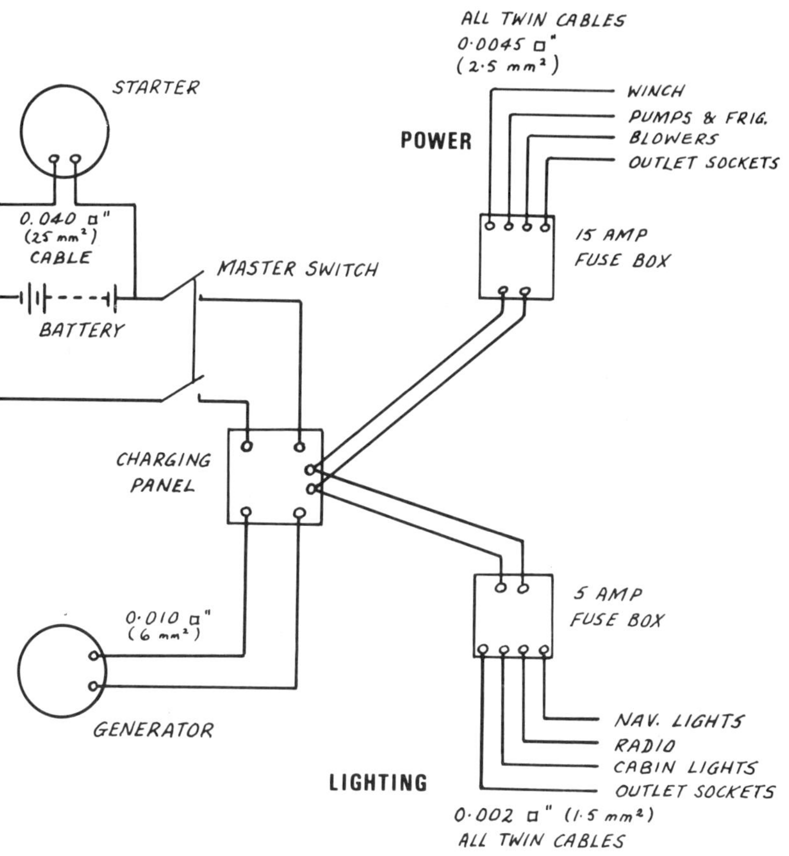

Fig. 95: Wiring diagram for 50-volt installaton

Charging panel details are given in *Complete Amateur Boat Building*.

The demands for electricity on a really big yacht (perhaps a motor fishing vessel conversion) can be very different from the above and a typical list of wattages is given below:

Air conditioner	400
Battery charger	800
Electric blankets (4)	200
Power tools	500
Cooking stove (range)	4000
Space heaters (2)	2000
Steam iron	500
Kettle	1000
Cabin lights	300
Navigation lights	200
Refrigerator/heat pump	400
Television	20
Water heater	1500
Oil burner	300
Toilets (2)	400
Bilge pump	500
Water pump	400
Radio equipment	100
Anchor windlass	1200
Cathodic protection	100
Syren	200
Vacuum cleaner	300
Toaster	800
Hairdryer	100

This makes a total of over 16,000 watts, giving 140 amps at 115-volts. All appliances are presumed to be fully on, but the electric motors are quoted at normal running wattages which can be exceeded considerably for a brief period on starting.

A more likely maximum load would be about 6500 watts, taking just under 60 amps. It may be a good idea to divide such a complicated circuit up into two parts (perhaps at different voltages) so that lighting and automatic pumps are operated from the batteries while all the heavy loads (especially cooking and other heaters) are operated direct from a generator set which starts on demand. To avoid having a huge generator to handle the total load, it may be wiser to adopt a smaller one with an overload cut-out which trips if too many appliances are operated in unison.

Running equipment from batteries which are being charged is best avoided as the charging voltage is often considerably higher than that of the cells. To obviate this problem some installations incorporate two identical banks of auxiliary batteries to avoid any interruptions of supply while charging is in progress.

Generator sets made for marine use are always fully suppressed to eliminate interference with radio equipment or televisions. Some makers can supply sound insulated booths to house their generator sets and with proper mounting and exhaust muffling the engines can be made tolerably quiet.

Details of ring-main and loop-in circuits for small boats are given in *Complete Amateur Boat Building*, but on large vessels separate two-wire circuits (preferably fused on both poles) should lead to each component requiring high current. It may be tempting to use a metal hull as an earth (ground) return for all wiring, as on an automobile. However this is not a good idea as electrolytic action might occur, especially if the insulation on one of the feeder cables broke down.

Three cable circuits incorporating an earth wire for protection against electric shock can lead to electrolytic trouble and are not necessary on most items of equipment working off 120-volts or less. A keel bolt may not always provide an effective ground, but a connexion to the sterntube is nearly always effective. To avoid stray currents causing trouble, each bank of batteries should be fitted with isolating switches, preferably of the double pole type. A test lamp with switch can be wired between each outgoing cable and earth. If either lamp will glow, leakage exists.

The rotation of a propeller shaft sometimes creates static electricity, especially when running in rubber bearings, or in metal bearings completely insulated with grease. This trouble may sometimes be overcome by fitting a small leaf of springy brass which rubs against the shaft and is wired to the sterntube.

Stiff and flexible cable for marine installations is nowadays usually sheathed and insulated with special plastics. Cables sheathed with lead or copper may lead to trouble if any leakage occurs. For maximum protection, cables can be enclosed in galvanized conduit, but provided the correct type of cables are used and properly clipped to battens, they can be left exposed or fitted with removable decorative covers.

Standard automobile cable is ideal for yacht wiring and is available in gauges suitable for most demands. All one needs to know to calculate resistance and current carrying capacity is the total cross sectional area of the metal.

In America, popular cable gauges are numbered 2, 4, 6, 8, 10 and 14. In Europe, gauges are in sq. mm., the common ones being 0.50, 0.75, 1.0, 1.5, 2.5, 4.0, 6.0, 10.0 and 16.0

The Onan technical leaflets provide useful tables showing the current capacity of the American cable gauges and the maximum length permissible to keep the voltage drop below the norm of 5%.

Excellent marine electrical fittings can be obtained from chandlery stores and although some of these parts are expensive, for safety reasons and reliability they are preferable to domestic lamp units, switches, junction boxes and outlet sockets. Proper weatherproof and corrosion-resistant fittings are essential above decks, especially for navigation lights. Special lights and sockets are made for connecting to shore power supplies at marinas and docks. When cruising extensively it may pay to keep adaptors for any different types of outlet known to exist. These can be made up quite simply in the form of short lengths of cable, each having a socket at one end to match the plug on one main lead, the other end having different types of plug to conform with all known shore outlets. If the intention is for the dock's own cable to come on board, reverse sets of adaptors (or shrouded terminals) may be necessary to enable this to be attached to one's own panel.

11

Cabin Sole, Bulkheads and Coamings

A standard hull bought for completion at home may already have her deck and cabin top whereas a conversion is sure to have large deck openings (or no deck at all) to let in the weather.

Some work below deck such as fitting an engine, an awkward bulkhead, or big tank, is much simplified with the minimum overhead obstruction in the way of decks or cabin top. However, if the cabin sole (floor) can be laid at an early stage, this platform will help to speed deck work as well as cabin fitments. If work must be done in the open air, every effort should be made to keep the vessel sheeted over during wet weather.

FLOORING

Considerable thought should be given to the method of laying a cabin sole, as this becomes a much seen and tested part of a yacht throughout the accommodation. In a big conversion this job can become quite complicated, demanding the use of drawings to indicate where different types of wood will be used, where tanks and pipes lie, and the positions of inspection hatches or removable panels to provide access to ballast, strum boxes and underfloor storage spaces. Even with a small conversion, a drawing is useful, as the position of the bearers (joists) can be shown and the quantities of timber measured off with fair accuracy.

Of the many possible combinations of materials available for flooring, the following are the most common:

(1) Clear pine, scrubbed, stained, or painted.
(2) Cheap pine, covered with Trakmark, rubber, or P.V.C.
(3) Plywood, covered as in (2).
(4) Scrubbed teak.

There is not much difference in price between the first three methods, but plywood is usually the quickest to lay. *Plydek* combines the simplicity of plywood with the appearance of laid teak. The veneered surface is not intended for hard wear, but should have ample life on the average yacht. Close boarded teak is ideal, but expensive. Thin teak strips on plywood look good but tend to squeak under foot. Cockpit soles are best payed like a main deck. Complete sealing is necessary for a self-draining cockpit.

All pine boarding used should have tongued-and-grooved edges. Although standard 6 in. × 1 in. (150 mm. × 25 mm.) flooring is suitable when permanently covered, the timber for Method (1) must not be wider than 4 in. (100 mm.). If this means having it specially cut, ensure that all the planks frequently walked upon are *rift sawn* (see Chapter 5) to prevent the surface from splintering.

Machining tongues on the edges of expensive timber like teak is wasteful, especially as narrow planks should be used. To obviate this, simply cut a groove along the centre of each edge, and insert *splines* as each board is laid. The splines should be made from offcuts of marine plywood with the outside grain running across the joint. Remember to get your offcuts in advance to ensure a snug fit. Splined joints can be secret nailed, and this is made easier by setting the spline grooves slightly higher than midway of the plank thickness. Many other types of hardwood can be used for a scrubbed floor, though teak is the best. Plank widths should be kept under 3 in. (75 mm.) for neat appearance, but 6 in. (150 mm.) planks with a knife cut up the centre can be made to have similar appearance.

Having arrived at the floor layout from the drawing, removable panels and access hatches should be made first as these, and their adjacent boards, will not require grooves. Having made the panels, the remainder of the flooring can be laid up to them, leaving $\frac{1}{64}$ in. (0.4 mm.) space all around for teak, and $\frac{1}{32}$ in. (0.8 mm.) for softwoods. Those areas of the sole which are nailed down permanently should be reduced to the minimum, for even beneath berths and cabinets screwed panels are useful when cleaning or painting the bilges. Where woodscrews are used to secure removable boards and panels flush brass screw cups (available from hardware stores) are ideal under the heads to prevent the wood from being chewed up after repeated removal.

Large inspection hatches should be made up with T & G or splined joints, screwed (or glued and nailed) to cross battens underneath. Bevel the outside edges slightly all around to ease replacement of the panels. Fit flush rings at each end to obviate having to prise them up with a screwdriver.

Having laid the fixed sole around a hatch, glue strips beneath the exposed edges forming rebates to support the hatch and prevent dirt from falling through. The end of each hatch will sit on one-half the width of a bearer.

Where sash cramps cannot be used to tighten the joints of the fixed sole boards, cramp chocks to the bearers and drive wedges between these and the board edge to produce the same effect. Where possible leave ventilation spaces where flooring ends along the inside of the hull.

On large yachts it may be a good idea to have a separate hatch in the floor leading to a wine and beer store in the coolest part of the ship. Another small hatch can have a shallow removable metal tray beneath it to receive all dust and dirt when the sole is swept. A boarded sole will probably need light planing on completion. Finishing with a power belt sander will ensure that all irregularities are smoothed out.

SOLE BEARERS

Yacht flooring does not need to be as rigid as the household counterpart and bearers set closer than 24 in. (600 mm.) interfere greatly with stowage and work in the bilges. Tongued or splined boarding $\frac{3}{4}$ in. (18 mm.) thick is generally adequate (irrespective of board width) but 1 in. (25 mm.) must be used with plain joints. Plywood should be at least $\frac{1}{2}$ in. (12 mm.) thick on small boats while $\frac{5}{8}$ in. (15 mm.) or $\frac{3}{4}$ in. (18 mm.) is preferable on big craft. Suggested bearer dimensions for 24 in. (600 mm.) spacing are shown in Table 3. A centrepost to the keelson or hog should always be devised where possible.

TABLE 3. CABIN SOLE BEARER SIZES

Bearer Length		SINGLE SPAN				WITH CENTRAL SUPPORT			
		Depth		*Thickness*		*Depth*		*Thickness*	
ft.	m.	in.	mm.	in.	mm.	in.	mm.	in.	mm.
2	0.6	2½	63	1½	38	1½	38	1	25
4	1.2	3	76	1½	38	2	50	1½	38
6	1.8	4	100	1½	38	2	50	1½	38
8	2.4	5	128	1½	38	2½	63	1½	38
10	3.0	6	152	2	50	3	76	1½	38
12	3.7	6½	164	2	50	3½	88	1½	38
14	4.3	7	176	2	50	4	100	2	50
16	4.9	8	200	2	50	4½	112	2	50
18	5.5	9	227	2	50	5	128	2	50

NOTE: Pine bearers at 24 in. (600 mm.) centres are assumed.
For 18 in. (450 mm.) spacing reduce depth by 10%.
For 30 in. (750 mm.) spacing increase depth by 20%.
Additional support is required under stoves, tanks, etc.

Having marked the approximate spacing of the bearers with chalk marks on the inside of the hull, two battens can be cramped together and set where the top of a bearer is to lie to determine the length. If the boat is set dead upright, a spirit level is handy to check athwartships, while a big square can be checked against the fore-and-aft line.

Use a carpenter's bevel to pick up the angles at the ends of each bearer so that very little adjustment with a plane should be needed when each bearer is offered up into position. If every third bearer is installed in this manner, the intermediate ones can be added to exact height while a fore-and-aft batten is laid across the top.

Wooden bearers are usually fixed at the ends by screwing into the boat's timbers, but where these are too weak it may be necessary to attach a separate chock to the planking alongside the bearer, or underneath the bearer secured to two timbers. In a plastics boat, glass the ends direct to the hull or fit brackets. The tops of bearers and framing in way of a cockpit sole hatch should be grooved with waterways piped to the pump well, especially if there is storage space beneath.

BULKHEADS AND PARTITIONS

On craft smaller than about 40 ft. (12 m.) in length each bulkhead can be a simple panel of marine plywood sunk into a post at the central door or passageway. In larger craft standard 4 ft. sheets may not be wide enough without scarfing and very thick plywood will be necessary for rigidity. It then becomes cheaper to use framing clad each side with thin plywood or T & G boarding (see Fig. 96). If required, the internal spaces can be packed with fireproof sound deadening material.

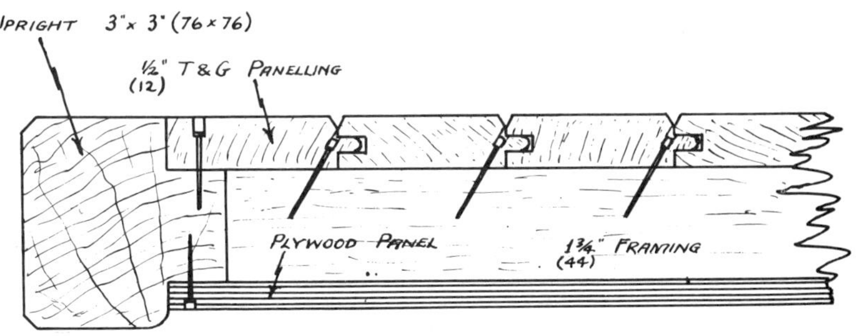

Fig. 96: Framed and clad timber partition

Stiff cellular plastics panelling materials are available with pleasing surface finishes. *Blockboard* is a cheaper substitute for this, also available with veneered, plastics, and enamelled surfaces, but as waterproof glue is not always used in this material it is not ideal for marine use.

Where plywood surfaces are to be varnished (or sprayed or French polished) the surfaces should be veneered, as normal mahogany plywood does not have a suitable grain for use in varnished joinery and imparts a cheap appearance. Enamelled plywood can be enhanced if surrounded with strips of varnished hardwood 2 in. (50 mm.) wide and $\frac{1}{4}$ in. (6 mm.) thick, glued and pinned on top. These also assist in hiding the gap which some amateurs leave when fitting bulkhead panels to the curve of a hull or deckhead!

It may be possible to use similar vertical strips to join two 4 ft. (1200 mm.) sheets of plywood and avoid making a scarf. When using T.G.V. boarding (see Fig. 96) this should be vertical and not wider than $2\frac{1}{2}$ in. (63 mm.). When of hardwood, 5 in. (125 mm.) or $7\frac{1}{2}$ in. (188 mm.) boards may be used with false V-joints cut into the surface. Brass panel pins can be used for secret nailing while *Gripfast* (*Anchorfast*) nails carefully driven flush with the surface can look pleasing on varnished work.

In the galley and toilet compartments, bulkheads, partitions and worktops can be faced with thin Melamine decorative plastics such as *Formica* and *Warerite*, held in place by impact adhesive. Elsewhere, washable vinyl coverings, thin self-adhesive tiles, and Melamine coated hardboard (such as *Laconite*) have their uses.

The interior hull surfaces of plastics and metal craft have a cold and depressing appearance but they may be painted or sprayed with attractive finishes or anti-condensation insulation materials.

SPILING TEMPLATES

Some sheets of old hardboard, packing material, or stiff cardboard are useful as templates to get the exact shape where bulkheads fit under side decks and around the curve of the hull.

Use a spiling block (see Chapter 3) or proceed as follows. Cut the template roughly to shape and hold it in position with temporary nails and battens. Get a stick of square wood (like a pencil but about 1 ft. [300 mm.] long) cut it square at one end, pointed at the other. Holding the point at each salient feature of the hull to be plotted, with the stick held flat on the template, draw pencil lines along each side of the stick and across the square end.

Later, with the template on top of the sheet of plywood to be cut, replace the stick exactly on each set of pencil lines in turn and plot where the point comes on the plywood. By joining up all these marks, an exact cutting line should result.

To plot certain positions more precisely, two 'bearings' can be taken, the lines being nearly 90° to each other. Note that if every contour of the carline, deckhead, and stringer is plotted, it may be impossible to get the shaped panel into position. This may necessitate leaving certain gaps, and the 2 in. (50 mm.) wide facia strips mentioned above then come into service. Even if the strips are not needed, it pays to fit small quadrant beadings all around, mitred at any sharp corners.

FRAMING AND FIXING BULKHEADS

Before fixing permanent partitions, the correct position can sometimes be verified by making a mock-up of certain fitments, such as a dinette, the galley, a settee berth, or the toilet, to ensure that the best use is made of the available space.

When cladding a bulkhead with $\frac{1}{4}$ in. (6 mm.) plywood a minimum frame spacing 15 in. (380 mm.) in either direction is desirable. With $\frac{1}{8}$ in. (3 mm.) hardboard the spacing should be 10 in. (250 mm.) or 30 in. (760 mm.) with $\frac{1}{2}$ in. (12 mm.) T & G. Fig. 97 shows a typical framework with another view in Fig. 96.

The end post (which should be 2 in. × 2 in. [50 mm. × 50 mm.] minimum) is fitted first followed by the framing which attaches it to the sole and deckhead. If the cabin is to be finished in hardwoods the post should be of the same timber, rebated to receive the cladding. For a painted finish, any good softwood would do. For lightness, the post and all interior framing can be of cedar, which should be not less than $1\frac{1}{4}$ in. × $1\frac{1}{4}$ in. (32 mm. × 32 mm.) sections. Should the rebate prove excessively deep for thin cladding, the exposed corner can be rounded off or chamfered.

The framing members can be connected by galvanized angle brackets with two galvanized or zinc plated screws in each arm as shown in Fig. 98a. These brackets are usually stocked by ironmongers and make a stronger job than morticing in such small

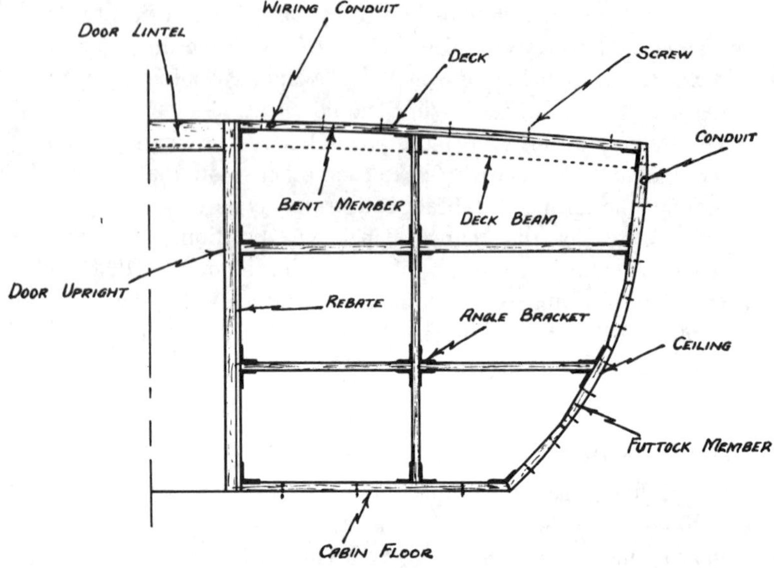

Fig. 97: Composite partition frame structure

timber. Framing attached to a sharply curved part of the hull can be made from a series of short pieces shaped to fit. On more gradual curves such as the under side of the deck, a single length of framing can be made to conform by cutting a series of nicks with a tenon saw half-way through the timber on the under side at intervals of about 1 in. (25 mm.). Both types of bend are pictured in Fig. 97.

Partitions can be constructed by exposing all the framing and letting panels into the spaces or, similarly, one side may be single boarded, with smart morticed and stop-chamfered framing showing on the other side. A typical joint in exposed framing is shown in Fig. 98b. Remember that although partitions may not be unduly strong, the fact that they may have to resist the shocks of gear or even members of the crew being flung against them under certain conditions should not be overlooked!

With a caulked deck, panelling underneath is usually unwise in case of leakage. Similarly, a fixed ceiling (or hull lining) restricts

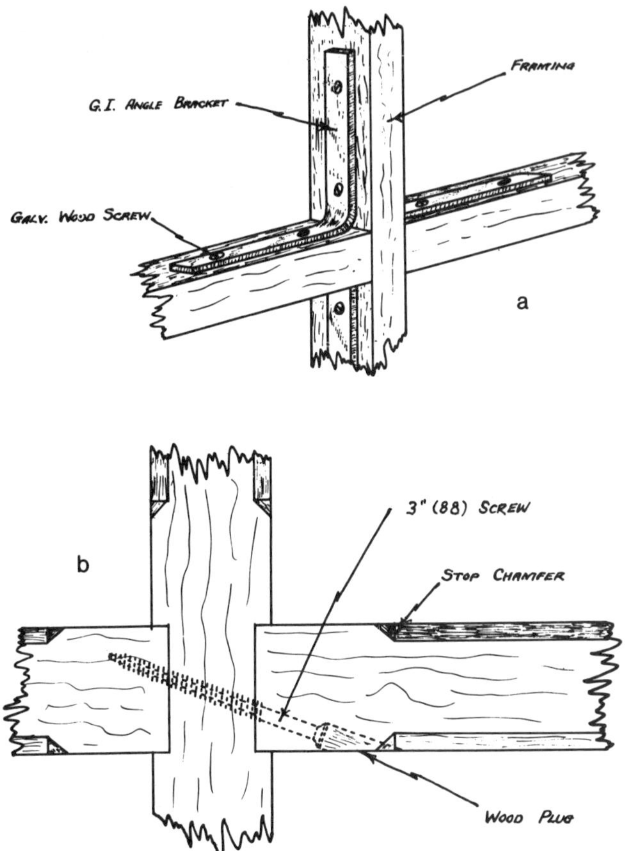

Fig. 98: Jointing systems for partition frames

ventilation and should be minimized in a wood-built yacht. Open spaced fore-and-aft battens, either varnished or painted, make suitable ceilings alongside the berths in small craft. Full panelling and hollow partitions are most useful to conceal plumbing and electrical wiring.

Where a bulkhead is installed in a plastics hull, the maker may have left wood block inserts moulded to the inner surface to facilitate fastening. If not, the strongest job results by roughing the whole surface and laying two or three pieces of glass tape properly impregnated with resin the whole way on both sides of the panel, and across the deckhead if this is of g.r.p.

If a framing similar to that in Fig. 97 is required, short blocks of timber can be shaped approximately and bonded firmly to the hull with thick epoxy resin. Failing this, or coupled with it, occasional thin stainless steel bolts can be used right through the hull with countersunk heads stopped over with resin putty. Unless the hull is white, it may have to be painted afterwards to camouflage such stoppings.

A plastics hull may have thin g.r.p. bulkheads built in. To prevent injury, stiffen the panels and improve appearance, padding (or mouldings of wood or plastics) should be fixed over exposed edges. Aluminium and P.V.C. extrusions are made which can be pressed over the edges of large rounded apertures through g.r.p. and plywood panels.

For fixing to interior g.r.p. panels and hollow box sections, self-tapping screws are suitable, but these should not be driven into the hull skin. Brackets of metal or preformed g.r.p. can be bonded to the skin quite readily by impregnating several layers of chopped strand mat around and over them.

For highly stressed attachments such as mountings for legs, deck fittings, and hand grips, special care is necessary when glassing in. Distribute the loads over a wide area by starting with a small patch of cloth, followed by ever increasing sizes until perhaps ten thicknesses are built up at the fitting, tapering out to one only at the periphery. See also plastics repairs in Chapter 4.

Attachments to a steel hull are normally made by welding or bolting. Magnets are useful for holding brackets in position for welding. Short separate runs of weld are normally adequate but note that brackets should be in the form of strips welded edgeways to the hull. If angled brackets are lap welded rust may occur where the two surfaces meet.

Where bulkheads consist of thin plywood boxed over a framework, it pays to glue chocks inside to take the fastenings for later fitments such as shelves, lockers, coat hooks, mirrors, lamps, or fire extinguishers. If a chock is forgotten, it may be possible to use standard toggle bolts. If through-bolts seem better the use of plated brass cap nuts may help appearance, or it may be possible to fix something useful on the opposite side of the bulkhead.

COACHROOF AND WHEELHOUSE

When completing a standard g.r.p. hull shell much work can be saved if the standard deck superstructure moulding is bought ready attached. On a large craft this part may cost nearly as much as the hull, so the impecunious amateur is more likely to fabricate all upper works himself. Even if the top moulding is attached, it will no doubt be necessary to cut out and fit all windows and portlights, hatches, ventilators, handrails, stanchions, footrails, chainplates, tank fillers, winch mountings, lightboards, chocks for deck gear, tabernacle and various other fitments.

Every practical yachtsman has his own favourite materials to work in. One may like to fabricate his own glass fibre coachroof, another may fancy panel beating in alloy (to produce a cabin top as shown in Plate 36 on a lifeboat conversion), or welding in steel as in Plate 37. Another might prefer a similar idea cold moulded from strips of wood veneer, but the majority no doubt go for the simple conventional construction shown in Plates 38 and 39 using coamings of teak or mahogany with deck beams between, and canvas covered tongued-and-grooved boarding on top.

An elliptical or deeply cambered roof section can be made by covering with two thin layers of plywood bonded together with resin glue. A superior deck can be made by sandwiching the beams between two panels of plywood, the spaces between being filled with blocks of rigid expanded foamed plastics material.

To ensure good appearance, superstructures should be designed with the following points in mind:

(1) The coamings, especially the fore-and-aft ones, should have a slight *tumblehome* (sloping inwards towards the top) to an extent of approximately 1 in. (25 mm.) in 8 in. (200 mm.) of height.

Plate 36: Cabin top in beaten aluminium alloy

Plate 37: Welded steel cabin top

Plate 38: Conventional framed timber cabin top

Plate 39: Covering a cabin top with canvas

(2) The coachroof top should have a camber greater than that of the existing deck. An elliptical section creates better headroom but might make the cabin top dangerous to walk on.

(3) Where the top meets the coaming there should never be a sharp angle, but a radius of at least 1 in. (25 mm.). This is not easy to make but is well worth any extra effort. At the front of a wheelhouse, the top should overhang like the peak of a cap, forming a visor as a protection against sun and rain.

(4) As well as the camber, there should also be a downward curvature at each end when viewed from one side. This may not be necessary where there is a companion hatch at one end to mask it, but especially towards a fore coaming the camber on the last two beams should be reduced to produce this effect.

(5) For seagoing craft any superstructure means weakness, so great strength should be built into it. One must admit that big windows are useful but, for ocean cruising they should be provided with shutters designed to bolt over the outside during storms.

A coachroof constructed in conventional manner is shown in Plate 38. Further notes on fitting the rebated corner posts are given in Chapter 12. The simpler corners shown in Fig. 99 can be adopted where there is tumblehome to the coachroof sides and also well rounded corners. In the illustration the fore coaming is shown vertical though equally well it could be sloping.

The order of work is as follows:

The two sides are shaped from teak or mahogany (using hardboard templates for preference) and these are cramped to the inside of the carlines. The curvature of the carlines should be taken up readily by the spring of the timber. Make the fore coaming from a template and fit the interior corner posts.

Now take the coamings off again, round off the top edges as shown in Fig. 99, rout the grooves just below this point to house the edges of the deck canvas, and fit the shelves to which the deck beams will be dovetailed and glued. Window or portlight openings can now be cut, all surfaces well sanded, and primed with varnish to stave off dirty marks while the job is being assembled.

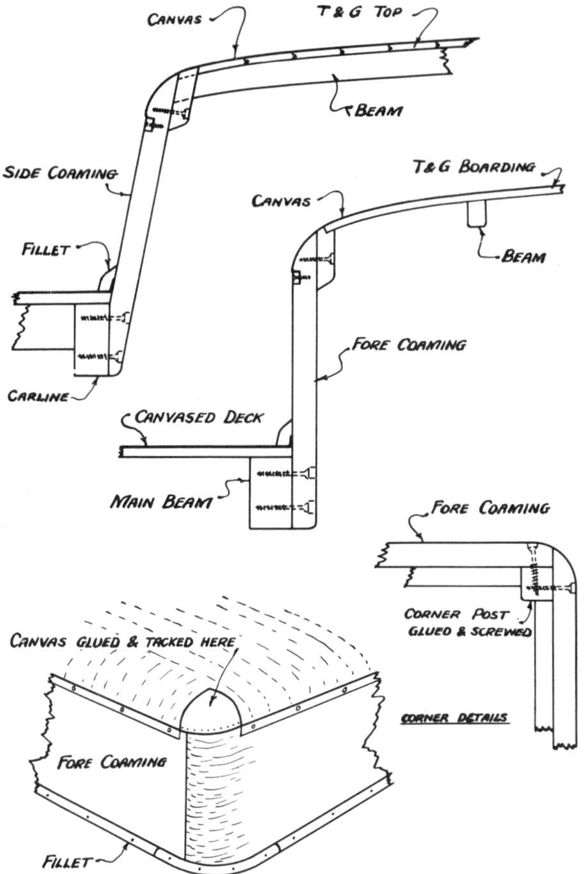

Fig. 99: Systems for coachroof construction

With the coamings permanently in place, fit the deck beams and the T & G boarding. Canvasing the top is not so easy as with the conventional square-edged coachroof, as separate pieces of canvas must first be glued in place over the rounded corners to allow the main piece of canvas to lie flat everywhere. The edges of the latter piece are housed in the grooves already mentioned and secured there by means of strips of hardwood screwed into place.

As soon as the main deck has been canvased, the quadrant moulding shown in Fig. 99 can be screwed on. Where this fillet curves around each corner it can be cut out of the solid and shaped up to match. For a larger radius such fillets could be steamed or laminated. To avoid this chore, the corners can be left square at deck level, rounding them on upwards as in Plate 38.

As described in Chapter 5, canvas makes the cheapest deck covering, but g.r.p. or Cascover avoids the need to house or cover the awkward canvas edges. These materials will conform to rounded edges and corners more easily than canvas and with g.r.p. a coloured roughened surface can be incorporated.

For canal cruisers, remember to check the permissible headroom before starting to design or construct a wheelhouse!

Instructions for using g.r.p. are given in *Complete Amateur Boat Building*. Marine stores sell kits for g.r.p. deck sheathing which come with full instructions for use. Glossy deck mouldings are dangerous when wet and should be either liberally covered with *Safety-Walk* (or similar) non-slip panels, or sheathed with resin/glass scrim cloth.

COAMINGS

When cabin top coamings are taller than about 9 in. (230 mm.) there is a great temptation to use plywood, which has certain advantages. However, varnished plywood looks cheap in large expanses and should either be teak veneered or enamelled. Plywood should only be slightly thinner than conventional solid timber coamings and one can get a good idea of the scantlings to use (as well as useful constructional details) by examining as many similar sized professionally built craft as possible.

If painted plywood is used, one can often fix a handsome varnished teak capping around the cockpit, built up as in Fig. 100a. The rail is shown laminated to enable it to take an upward curve towards the main bulkhead. If the cockpit coamings are attractively radiused at the after corners, the rail and the quadrant deck fillet may have to be cut out of the solid with a bandsaw or coping saw and then shaped up. To construct a radiused corner,

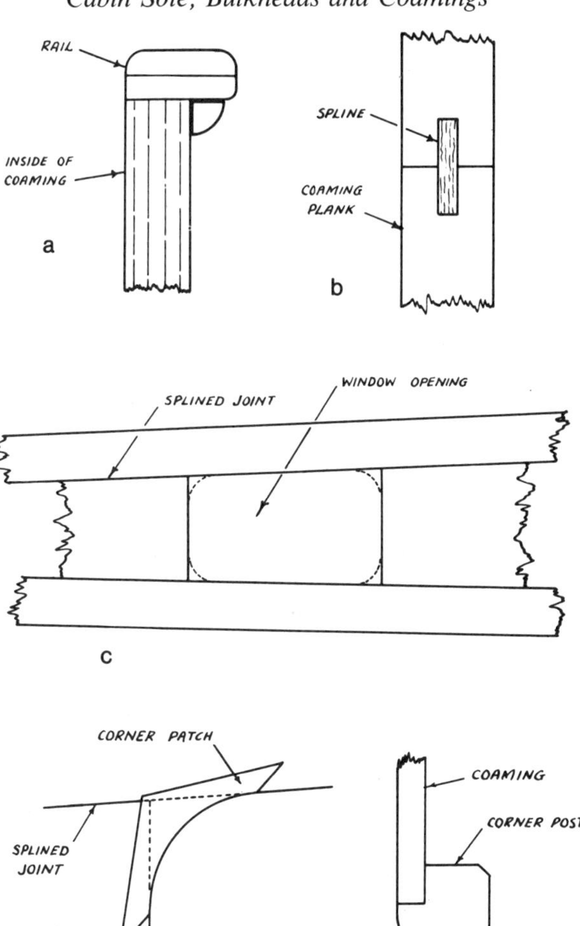

Fig. 100: Coaming details

$\frac{1}{8}$ in. (3 mm.) laminations the full height of the coamings are usually suitable for bending cold when gluing to a jig. The inner laminations can be of a cheaper type of hardwood if desired.

Where coachroof coamings rise to merge into a doghouse (see Fig. 2) or wheelhouse, and continue into the cockpit coamings or perhaps also into an after cabin, solid planking makes a much better job than plywood. It can be obtained in almost any length (whereas plywood is normally limited to 8 ft. (2400 mm.) unless scarf jointed) and wastage is minimized by joining comparatively narrow planks together with resin-glued splined joints (Fig. 100b) leaving openings for windows as in Fig. 100c.

As the corners of the window openings cannot be cut to an attractive radius without exposing the spline and leaving a feather edge, in high class work an insert of matching wood is glued into each corner after fabrication as shown in Fig. 100d, the grain running diagonally.

To avoid showing end grain at the coaming corners as in the simple construction shown in Fig. 99, rebated corner posts (Fig. 100e) make a superior job. These posts are not always easy for the amateur to make, as they must be vertical in way of the main deck beams and carlines, but sloping inboard above deck to permit the essential tumblehome of the coamings. With vertical coamings, one can use dovetails or the toothed and pinned skylight joints shown in Fig. 101.

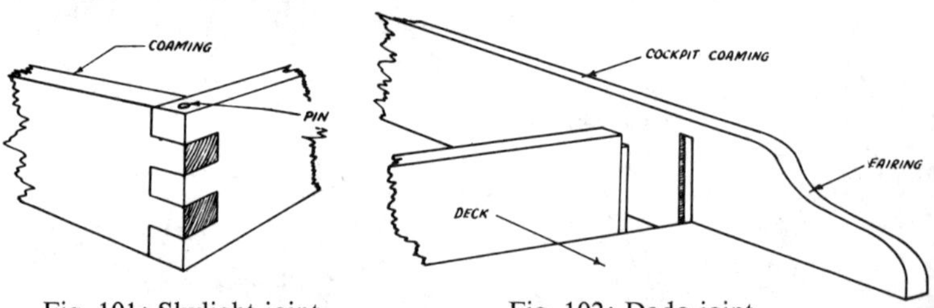

Fig. 101: Skylight joint

Fig. 102: Dado joint

An alternative at the after end of the cockpit is to use the glued stopped dado joints shown in Fig. 102. If unrebated corner posts are fitted for additional strength it might be a good idea to run these upwards and chamfer the tops neatly to use for belaying mooring warps.

Big wheelhouse sides cannot be made from horizontal boards planked together all the way up. It may be possible to extend coachroof coamings through to the wheelhouse doorway, but vertical stiles will then have to be mortised into this member to create a structure similar to the framed joinery described in Chapter 12. This will create openings for windows and doors while the lower spaces will be filled with wide panels.

When a wheelhouse is a separate box not connected to a coachroof (see Plate 40) a simple framing with rebated corner

Plate 40: A separate wheelhouse

posts can be planked over with narrow vertical T & G or narrow horizontal shiplap boarding.

Although teak is undoubtedly the best timber for coamings and all exposed trim, there are several other hardwoods at less than half the cost which are superior to the popular mahoganies. One of these, *Iroko* changes colour from yellow to teak brown on exposure to light, so although a layer of varnish after fabrication is a good idea to prevent the timber from getting dirty, in the case of Iroko priming should not be done too soon. *Afrormosia* and *Doussie* are also good alternatives to teak. Mahogany-type timbers such as Khaya, Sapele, Makore, and Utile often need staining to get boards to match each other and to produce a rich red colour. All the mahoganies are ruined if the varnish is allowed to peel off and a thick layer of wood must be planed off to bring back a good colour.

Remember, when building a wheelhouse over the engine compartment, it pays to incorporate a removable panel in the roof – big enough to lift an engine through. As this is not likely to be needed frequently, semi-permanent fixing is satisfactory, even to the extent of canvasing the roof outside in conventional manner.

Details of hatches and skylights are given in Chapter 12.

12

Useful Tips

The amateur who completes a yacht from a bare hull or carries out a conversion is likely to be handy at woodwork. If he is not accomplished at the start, he will soon get plenty of practice, and unless exceptionally ham-fisted, he should be quite proficient by the time the finer points of joinery come along.

The keen amateur can, with good instruction and by refraining from hurry, soon be able to match many a professional in workmanship. Although the amateur will have to think out every move most carefully and may take five times as long as the trained carpenter, the end product should be almost identical.

WINDOWS AND PORTLIGHTS

The front windows of a wheelhouse can prove quite a challenge for the amateur shipwright. They must slope gracefully and are often V-formation in plan, with either two or three lights. At least one should be hinged at the top to open wide in hot weather and a Kent clear view screen or marine type electric windscreen wiper is almost essential.

Toughened glass is almost universally used for big windows and these panes can be supplied to any shape if templates are sent to a glass works, perhaps via a garage or builder's merchant. The panes should be set with synthetic rubber caulking composition into a rebate in the timber frame and secured with metal bezels fabricated in brass, alloy, or stainless steel, screwed to the outside of the framing. In thick coamings it may be possible to make the rebates deep enough to allow a beading of matching hardwood to be screwed or pinned into place, but these are tricky to make or fit where the window corners are rounded.

Perspex (*Plexiglass*) is suitable only for very small windows as an impact can spring it out of the frame. Perspex is usually fitted to g.r.p. coamings (or thin plywood) on inland water and estuary craft using special rubber glazing strips. These are similar to the rubber seals on car windscreens. The strip must be ordered to match the thickness of the pane and the coaming. Instructions are supplied which include details of the margin required between the size of the pane and of the opening.

Decklights are discs of thick glass which can be rebated into deck or coamings, where they are sealed with glazing compound and secured by metal rings screwed down, or bolted. For a truly flush fitting it may be necessary to make a shallow rebate for the ring also.

Portlights are nearly all made to screw to the inside of coamings or hull planking and they have spigots which form lining sleeves right through the wood. Separate rings can be supplied to fit to the outside. For extra strength (and for metal and g.r.p. boats) through-bolts can be used, as the holes in the rings correspond with those in the portlight flanges. For ocean cruising yachts, portlights can be equipped with *deadlights*. These hinge across inside and seal the opening in case the glass should break.

Quadrilateral metal framed windows are popular for certain types of cruiser and complete ranges (custom built as well as in standard sizes) are made by several firms in Britain and America. Available in stainless steel, chromium plated brass, and anodized aluminium such windows are not cheap, but they might well put the finishing touch to a worthy conversion. Sliding windows allow good adjustment for ventilation in most weather conditions, whereas conventional portlights must be either open free or battened down.

VENTILATION

Adequate ventilation is extremely important on any type of decked boat, especially during the occasions when the craft is left locked up at moorings and when under way battened down in rough weather. Although rot can occur on a wooden vessel when damp and unventilated, internal condensation is even more likely to occur inside a steel, ferro-cement, plastics, or alloy craft, and this can lead to smells, damp clothing and engine troubles.

When a yacht is occupied, on moorings or under way, air tends to move forward from the main hatch. When left unoccupied (perhaps with the fore-hatch lodged open a little) air tends to move in the opposite direction.

The best ventilation system for small and medium-sized yachts is as follows:

(1) In general, fit intake cowl vents up for'ard with mushroom or extractor vents on the coachroof deckhead, at the main companion hatch and through the after deck.

(2) Use cowls that can be rotated to face the wind in hot weather. A Revon sprayproof cowl is shown in Plate 41. Sprayproof

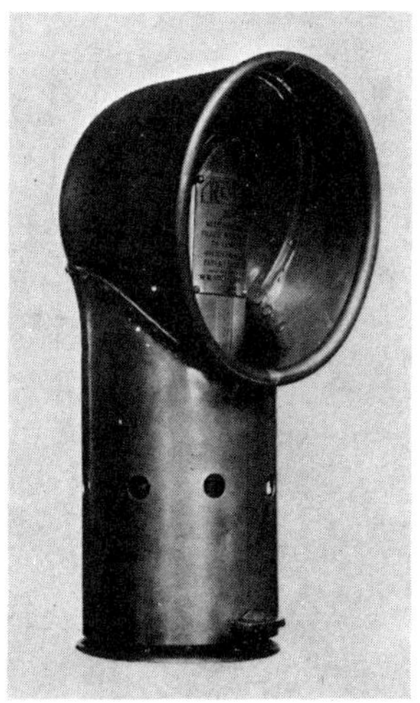

Plate 41: Revon sprayproof ventilator
Photograph by W. M. Still & Sons Ltd

ventilators can be made from ordinary cowls fitted to *Dorade* boxes (see Fig. 103) but do not site these over berths or the chart table as some water could get through under certain conditions. Use rubber cowls in preference to metal up to 6 in. (150 mm.) diameter as these prevent injury and snarl-ups with ropes.

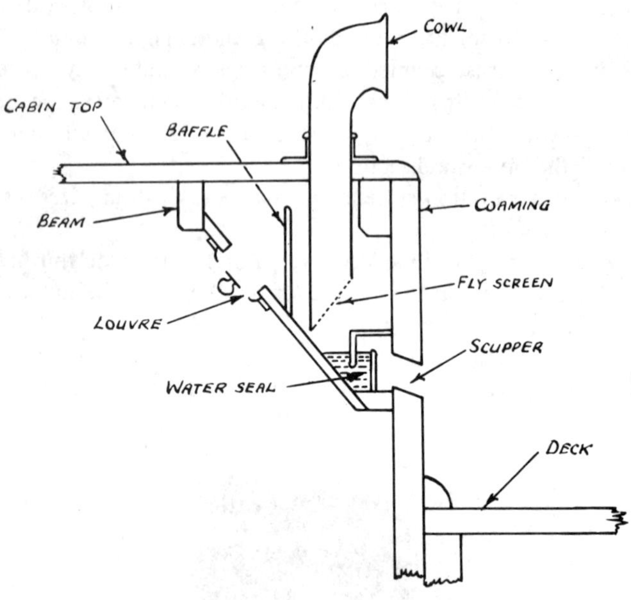

Fig. 103: Sprayproof Dorade box

(3) One for'ard vent should extend down to the bilges and this need not have an internal shutter to enable it to be closed.

(4) If the hull has a *ceiling* (lining) inside there must be apertures at the shelf to permit a free flow of air between the timbers.

(5) Keep the heads sweet by fitting an electric extractor vent in the deckhead with intake ports through the sole.

(6) Most motor cruisers have the engine compartment beneath the wheelhouse. Effective ventilation can be provided by means of half cowl shells fitted to the wheelhouse sides with ducts leading down to the engine. Electric extractor vents should then be fitted high up at the after end of the engine room.

(7) In the galley, an extractor fan through the deckhead (preferably over the stove) is a great boon to the cook and helps to keep cooking smells from the rest of the accommodation.

(8) Where funds (or adequate power) are not available to run extractor fans, venturi vents can be made as in Fig. 104 or a

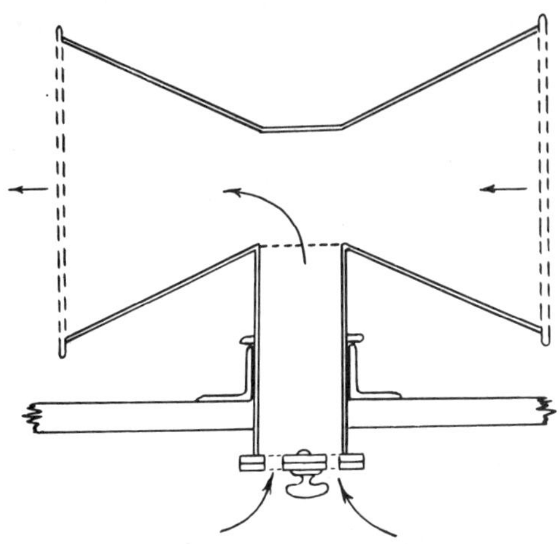

Fig. 104: Venturi extractor vent

commercial type, such as the Afco *Vacuvent* can be used. Failing this, ordinary cowls turned away from the wind work tolerably well.

(9) On craft with separate cabins, the doors should have louvres built into the panels and on bigger power craft air conditioning with ducts to each cabin is a welcome luxury. A reversible *heat pump* system is ideal on a large yacht as the surrounding water is always comparatively warm in winter and cool in summer. This can provide hot or cold air conditioning as well as refrigeration.

(10) Great care is necessary in siting the intake vent for an air conditioning plant. Most electric blowers are extractors which tend to keep spray out, but damage could be caused if much water is drawn in through the intake of a big air-conditioning fan.

(11) Remember to obviate having any compartment without some sort of ventilation. Lockers are especially susceptible unless the doors have louvres built in, or simply large holes at top and bottom. An oilskin locker is best made with no door as wet

Plate 42: Bridge and deckhouse on M.F.V. conversion

clothing may frequently have to be hung there awaiting an opportune moment for drying out. On big craft a drying room is often appreciated.

CABIN JOINERY

Of the numerous small yachts built nowadays some nine out of ten have cabin joinery of the simplest and cheapest variety. The amateur carpenter can score here by fitting really first class joinery in his boat, making cruising aboard her a pleasure and increasing her value considerably. The parts which can be improved in this way include cabin soles, bunk fronts and lee-boards, chart table, galley, drawers, saloon table, lockers, shelves, doors, hatches, skylights, cabinets and bulkheads.

Utile or Khaya are the most popular woods below decks. They can be French polished or catalyst sprayed to a fine finish.

Honduras mahogany is better but very costly, though it can often be obtained cheaply by demolishing certain types of secondhand furniture or shop counters. Teak has a more rugged appearance as it should have an oiled or waxed finish. Alternatively, any desired fancy hardwood may be used and some attractive effects can be produced by mixing light and dark coloured woods such as Opepe and Makore.

Most cabin fitments except tables incorporate large openings (especially for doors or drawers) and the first move is generally to frame up a *front*. A typical sideboard front is pictured in Fig. 105. The bottom rail is often made deep to allow a *plinth* to be attached. By fitting this to the inside of the rail a recess can be formed preventing the plinth from getting damaged by people's shoes. All the other members are plain battens (usually $\frac{7}{8}$ in. [22 mm.] thick) with mortices positioned as shown dotted in Fig. 105. If rebates are required for locker doors to close against,

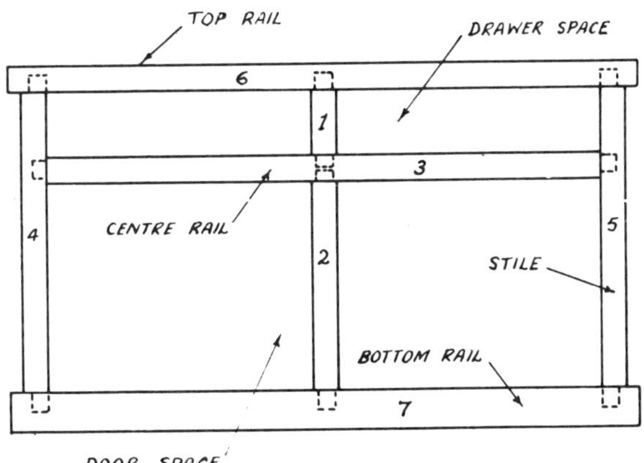

Fig. 105: Framed front for cabin fitment

separate strips can be glued behind. In oak joinery the mortices are often secured by driving small dowels right through, cut off flush or left proud.

Care is necessary to ensure that driving a dowel pulls the joint up tight. This is done by boring a hole straight through the mortice only, then inserting the tenon and marking this through the hole with a scriber or sharp pencil. The tenon is withdrawn, and when the dowel hole is bored through it, its centre is shifted about $\frac{1}{64}$ in. (0.4 mm.) towards the shoulder. The dowel end is chamfered to facilitate driving.

The method of erecting the front shown in Fig. 105 is quite simple. Parts 1 and 2 are glued and driven into 3, then 4 and 5 are attached, followed by 6 and 7. Four sash cramps are then applied to compress all the joints in unison but the assembly must be checked carefully with a big square and corrected by tapping diagonally before leaving to harden. If sash cramps cannot be borrowed (or made up with cramp heads) Spanish windlasses of Terylene cord can be used. If the mortices and tenons have been cut accurately the front should be dead flat after assembly.

Fronts are usually fitted between bulkheads or other furniture, but if used for a cabinet jutting out, sides of solid or panelled wood have to be fitted behind, flush to the end stiles, fixed inside with glued block fillets. A top is then added which should overhang slightly with rounded corners and fiddles set well in from the edges.

Cabinets and nests of drawers can be constructed without a front frame by making the sides to take the place of parts 4 and 5, the top to take the place of 6, a solid bulkhead for parts 1 and 2, and part 3 turned with its edge as the face. This method is used for bow-fronted cabinets.

DOORS AND PANELS

Small cabinet and locker doors can be made of solid wood with a $\frac{3}{16}$ in. (5 mm.) thick capping of the same wood glued on to mask the end grain. However, it is well worth the extra trouble to frame these up and fit a panel, as shown in Fig. 106a. The panel may be flat (made from veneered plywood to prevent shrinking and cracking); moulded from the solid as in Fig. 106b; or built up as in Fig. 106c.

The frame must be either rebated or grooved to receive a panel, the resulting mortice in each case being sketched in Figs. 107a

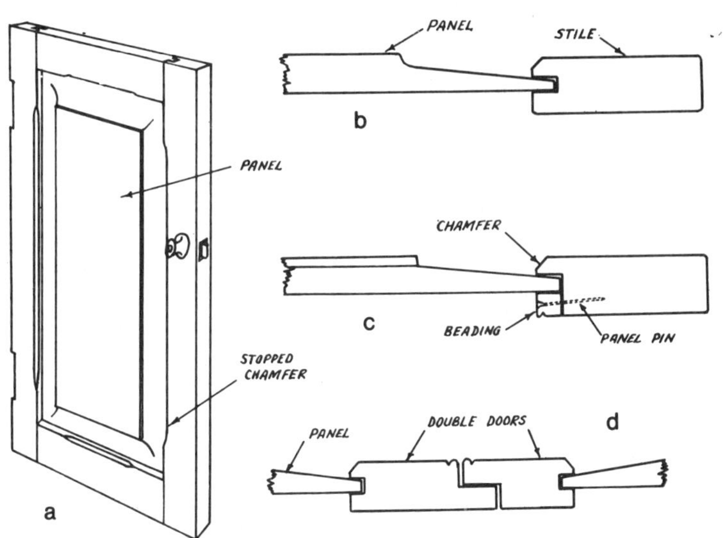

Fig. 106: Joinery panel construction

and 107b. If grooves are used, the panel must be inserted as the frame is assembled. With rebates, the panel is fitted later and secured with neat beads of wood glued and pinned inside. Cabinet door frames should be made the same thickness as the front.

Make ornamental *stopped chamfers* on the inner edge of each frame piece as seen in Fig. 106a. First cut these too short with square ends (using a rebate plane having a removable nose) then shape the scallop at each end with a chisel. Note that for double doors meeting against each other, one stile must be cut from wider stock than the other to allow for the rebate—see Fig. 106d.

A door which looks (to the inexperienced eye) almost identical to a framed and panelled door can be made by gluing strips of the correct wood on top of a sheet of veneered plywood the full size of the door. The false frame strips can be stop chamfered for realism. Thin capping glued to the edges of the door should be added to hide the plywood laminations.

Fitting a door into a front or frame is simple provided the door has been made about $\frac{1}{32}$ in. (0.8 mm.) too big all around and all

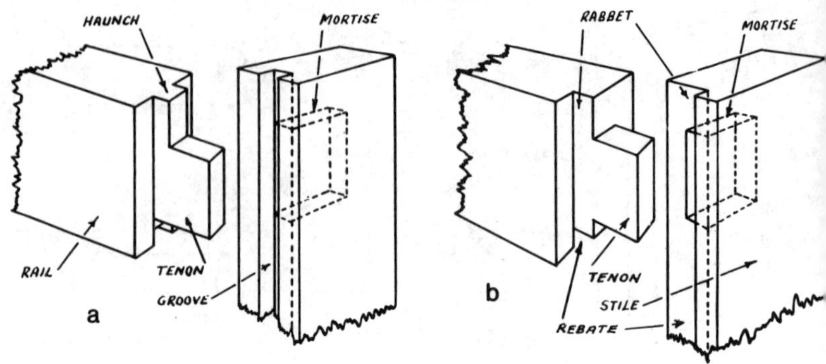

Fig. 107: Tenon and mortice joints

morticed joints are square. If you can reach inside, the shape can be scribed on to the door with a sharp pencil. If this cannot be done, plane the vertical edges until the door can be pushed into its frame at either top or bottom, then continue until the centre is also free.

Now plane the bottom edge to fit, checking this frequently by standing the door on the lower rail of the frame while the top of the door overlaps the top rail. Repeat this process for the top edge until the whole door sinks neatly into the frame. The clearance all around can be very small on well-made lockers and cabinets (with adequate allowance for paint or varnish) increasing to about $\frac{1}{16}$ in. (2 mm.) all around for a cabin door.

When fitting the hinges, recess them an equal amount into both door and frame, aligning the centre of the hinge pin with the face of the door. Plane a slight inward bevel on the vertical opening edge of the door to allow for the swing of the hinges. Although nylon (*Delrin*) hinges with stainless steel pins are cheap and readily available, brass hinges with brass pins are stiffer.

Locker and cabinet doors must have positive press button catches – ball and magnetic catches are useless on a boat. A cheap but effective spring catch fitted to the inside of a locker door can be tripped by passing one's finger through a neat hole in the door. Sliding doors of all sizes are useful in restricted spaces. Many types of track gear are available for operating sliding doors.

Plate 43: An excellent M.F.V. conversion

Some of these can corrode in sea air so all-nylon gear may be the best choice.

Cabin doors look best with two vertical panels at the bottom (see Fig. 108a) and a single louvred top panel. Instead of mortices, each joint can be secured by three or four dowels in a row. These should be blind dowels as in Fig. 108b but if you feel uncertain of the ability to mark out and bore identical holes in each pair of mating pieces (or you do not possess a Stanley dowel jig) the holes can be bored right through from the outside as in Fig. 108c while the joints are accurately cramped.

The holes can be hidden by cross-grained plugs, but the dowel lengths must be gauged to drive well below the surface. Remember that each dowel must be prepared with a chamfered nose and a shallow saw cut running the full length to allow surplus glue and air to escape on driving. When using resin glue, dowels should

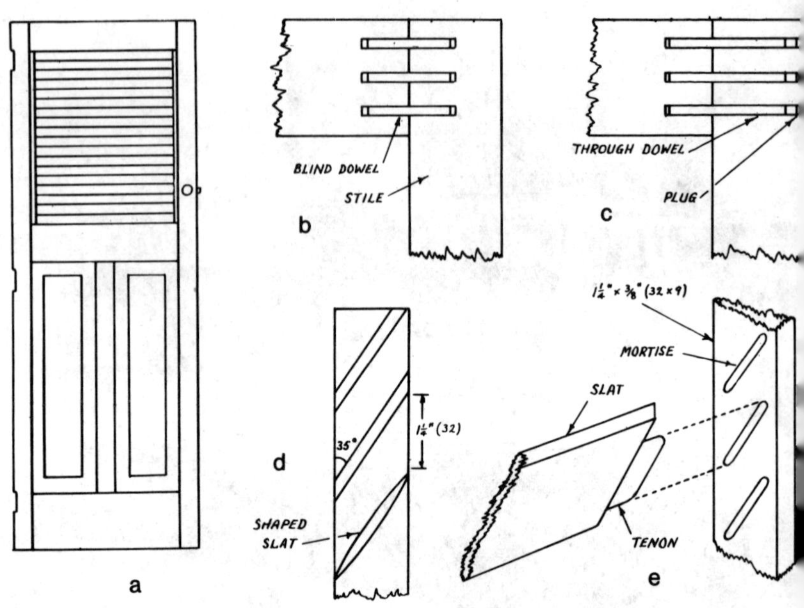

Fig. 108: Cabin doors and louvred panels

not be too tight; it should be just possible to turn them with the fingers when inserted.

The same rule applies to tenons which are resin-glued. Tenons are usually made one-third the thickness of the frame and they should be a nice push fit the narrow way but fairly tight the other way. If too tight the mortice may split. To avert this possibility, frame pieces with a mortice near the end are normally left 1 in. (25 mm.) too long (as in Fig. 105), the surplus to be trimmed off when the glue has hardened.

When using a gauge to scribe the lines for mortices, tenons and halved joints, remember to slide it against the outward face of both parts to ensure accuracy. Cut mortices first, then make the tenons to fit. Always use an electric drill with bench stand and machine vice to bore mortices before chiselling out – unless the proper equipment can be borrowed.

Louvred panels require some care to make neatly. The slats

should be set out as in Fig. 108e for a $1\frac{1}{4}$ in. (32 mm.) thick door but the intervals must be adjusted so that the top and bottom slats close up the space neatly. Do not attempt to mortice each slat into the door stiles. Instead, fit them into separate side pieces $\frac{3}{8}$ in. (9 mm.) thick, as indicated in Fig. 108d, so that the assembly just pushes into the opening left in the door. The slat edges can either be planed to a bevel flush with the door faces or, preferably, finished with feather edges – see Fig. 108d, bottom slat.

Simpler doors can be made where panels look out of keeping with the general decor. Flush doors with two skins of 4 mm. veneered plywood glued to simple $1\frac{1}{2}$ in. (38 mm.) thick framing are popular. The panel spaces can be packed with expanded plastics blocks (of the exact thickness) with improvements to stiffness and sound insulation.

Solid wood doors (preferably of 7 in. [180 mm.] wide boards splined together to mitigate warping) are ideal on small craft and for companion hatch doors. Simple vertical T & G doors strapped across on one side are cheaper but not quite so elegant.

DRAWERS

One rarely finds drawers in modern boats because open-fronted bins are cheaper and lighter. However, if you want comfort aboard and pleasant looking joinery, you will find drawers fascinating to make and they are ideal for stowing most forms of gear.

A typical drawer with the bottom panel removed is shown in Fig. 109. To get the right thicknesses for front, sides, and back, and the spacing of the dovetails, one should examine a few hand-made drawers in house furniture, remembering that some of these are made more delicately than might be advisable at sea. Plywood is ideal for all drawer bottoms and these should slide snugly into their grooves to be secured with a few screws or brass pins into the back. Note that when the sides are too thin to house grooves for the bottom, separate strips are glued on and rounded off to look like quadrant beading from inside the drawer.

If numbers of small or medium-sized drawers have to be made

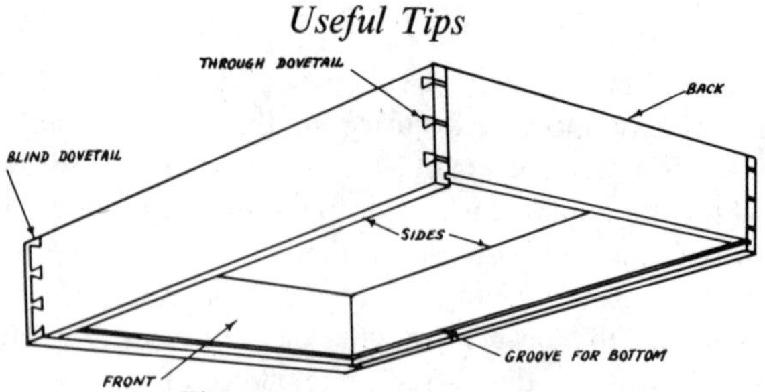

Fig. 109: Drawer construction

quickly, dovetails need not be used, as rebated joints fixed with resin glue and brass panel pins (or Gripfast nails) are quite satisfactory.

Ordinary drawers must have press button catches or gravity turn-buttons to keep them shut, but the neatest yacht drawers are made to lift about $\frac{1}{4}$ in. (6 mm.) before they can be pulled out. Making these is an interesting exercise for the handyman. To hide the gap at the top which is necessary to allow for the lift, one can fit false fronts overlapping all around, as shown in Fig. 110.

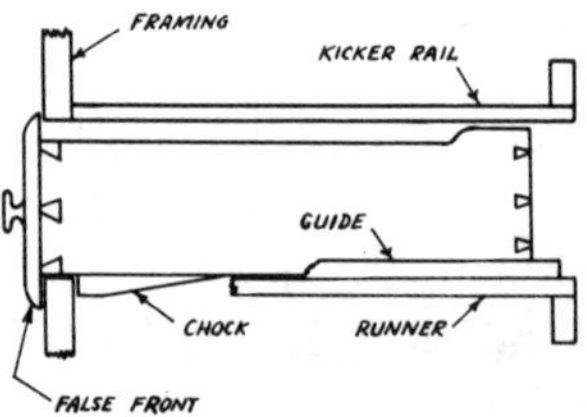

Fig. 110: False front on lifting drawer

Once a drawer has been made to slip neatly into its opening, the runners, guides, kicker rails and stops must be carefully installed so that the drawer slides smoothly when pushed at one side only, with very little play in either direction. Again, examine a few pieces of furniture if not certain how the parts are fitted.

Making dovetails takes time but is merely a question of careful marking out, sawing and chiselling. The dovetails in the drawer sides are cut first. These are then clamped over the mating pieces while the shapes are marked off with a knife or sharp pencil.

When there is to be a false front as in Fig. 110, the dovetails are simple to cut, but when they must not show on the front face (as in Fig. 109) this is called a *blind dovetail* and involves fewer saw cuts and more chiselling.

SKYLIGHTS AND HATCHES

Skylights are used mainly on large flat-decked yachts. The familiar traditional shape is still used for teak construction while the lids of sliding hatches are often of varnished wood even on modern plastics boats. Fore hatches are now commonly made as translucent g.r.p. mouldings.

Skylight coamings are normally deep, fixed to the inside of the beams and carlines, but where an existing and rather small deck opening must be utilized on a conversion, the coamings can sit on deck. The corners are usually dovetailed or toothed and pinned as shown in Fig. 101.

Conventional skylights are made with internal gutters under the hinges, discharging through weep holes at the ends, but leakage is still a strong possibility if green seas come aboard. Rubber seals can be used, but a simpler form of skylight which can be made completely tight with rubber is shown in Fig. 111.

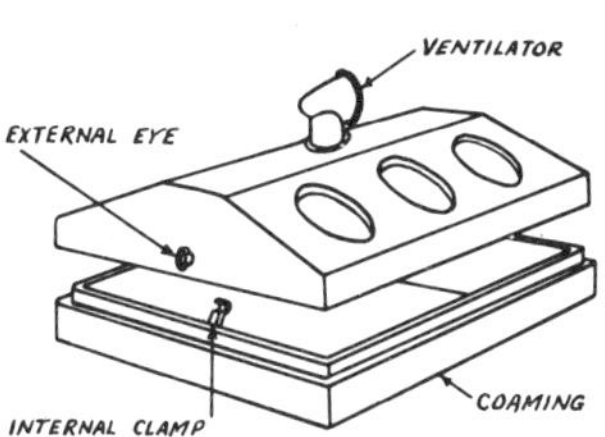

Fig. 111: Waterproof skylight

The top can be lifted right off in hot weather and fixed alongside with special clips. A sprayproof ventilator can be fitted on top if necessary.

Normal skylights have rectangular toughened glass lights protected by grids of metal bars. An alternative is seen in Fig. 111 and the circular lights can be standard decklights with metal bezels. If a traditional hinged top is preferred, the standard hinges and stay fittings made by *Simpson-Lawrence* and other makers can be ordered through any chandler.

As with all yacht joinery work it pays to inspect as many similar professionally made items as possible before sketching out one's own ideas.

A simple fore hatch is illustrated in Fig. 112, and one of the

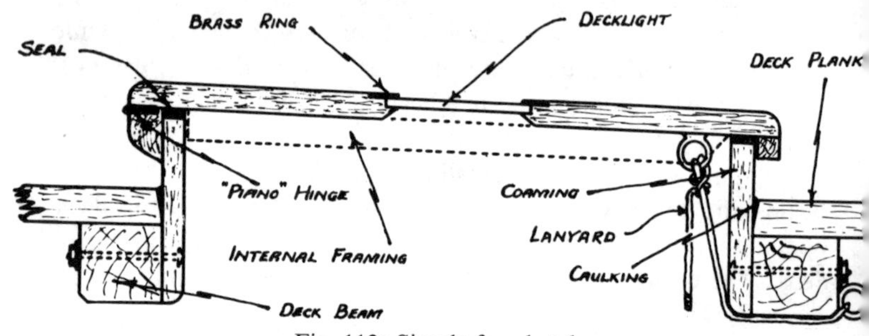

Fig. 112: Simple fore hatch

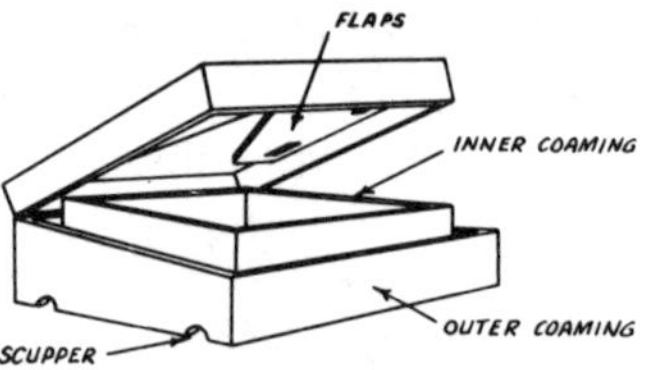

Fig. 113: Maurice Griffiths double coaming hatch

Maurice Griffiths double coaming types in Fig. 113. Always make a hatch top sloping or cambered to drain off rain water. Triangular side flaps hinged to the inside of the lid are invaluable. These can be lowered to support the lid partly open for ventilation and it may be wise to arrange for the hatch to be locked from the inside in this position as well as completely shut.

The minimum internal size of a rectangular fore hatch should be 20 in. (500 mm.) athwartships and 18 in. (450 mm.) fore-and-aft, but on a small fore deck the shape can with advantage be made trapezoidal as in Plate 38. On large craft a ladder may be fitted under the fore hatch, but on small boats a single step (perhaps hinged) can often be attached to a partition nearby to assist clambering up and down.

On big craft a companion hatch as shown in Fig. 114 can be

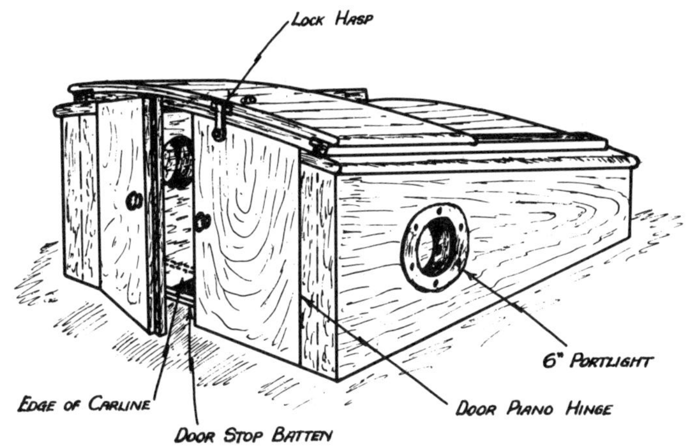

Fig. 114: Companion hatch on large yacht

used to great advantage, but horizontal washboards sliding in vertical grooves are more often fitted instead of hinged doors. With a lot of spray about, the bottom washboard can be left permanently in place.

Small yachts usually have a sliding companion hatch on top of the coachroof as shown in Fig. 115. The way such a hatch is built up may be analysed as follows.

(1) The hatch sides (a) are fixed to the required height and length, the top edges planed to the correct bevel and a capping piece (b) is glued and screwed to the top, ending about 1½ in. (38 mm.) from the after end to allow the washboards to drop into place.

(2) The three or four beams (c) for the sliding hatch lid are sawn to the required camber from solid timber, or laminated on a jig, with a lug (d) formed at each end to run under the side capping piece (b). The endmost beams should be about ½ in. (12 mm.) deeper than the intermediates, as in Fig. 115 (vi).

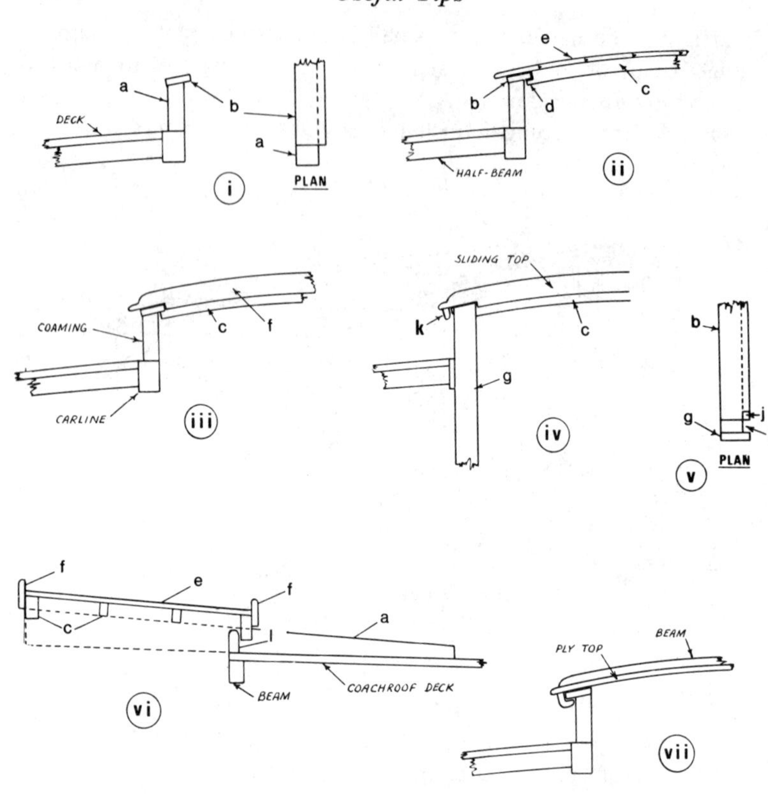

Fig. 115: Sliding companion hatch on coachroof

(3) The lid planking (e) is then glued and screwed to the beams. This can be of T & G splined teak or mahogany to be varnished on completion.

(4) A facia piece (f) is cut from solid timber and fastened to each end of the lid to hide the end grain of the planking, the after one also forming a handhold above the planking to facilitate closing the hatch, and an anti-spray rebate behind the top washboard.

(5) A facia piece (g) is fixed to each side to mask the slider groove and to form a groove (h) for the washboards.

(6) A batten (j) is glued to the side coaming to complete the rebate for the washboards to slide in. This batten must end

just below the lid beams, as the aftermost beam must just pass over it to stop against the top washboard.

(7) A moulding (k) may be fixed below the outside edges of the lid planking to further waterproof the structure.

(8) If there is no decking at the for'ard end over which the lid slides when opened, this must now be laid. Where the lid slides over a cabin top this decking will already be in place.

(9) A batten (l) must be fixed across the after end of the decking to make a seal against the foremost lid beam when the hatch is closed. As the aftermost lid beam is also $\frac{1}{2}$ in. (12 mm.) deeper (see Item 2) this will stop against the batten also when the lid is fully open.

(10) A decklight can be fitted into the hatch top but is not necessary in a coachroof companion where there are scuttles or windows already in the side coamings.

Note that a simpler type of lid can be made as in sketch vii of Fig. 115. The lid is of marine plywood and the beams are fitted to the top of the lid – unsightly but effective!

The slides should be made quite slack to eliminate jamming, but not too loose athwartships or the lid will not slide when pushed from one side only.

We live in an age when all property must be locked and barred at all times. Yachts are no exception, so the locking system should be made as simple yet as secure as possible. On most yachts only the main hatch is locked from the outside, any other access places being bolted from the inside. A companion hatch with doors (as in Fig. 114) can have a good quality brass rim lock, making opening and closing much simpler than wrestling with the slippery brass padlock used on most yachts. When a padlock must be used, fit a hasp and staple of the thief-proof variety with no screwheads visible. In any case bolts are preferable to woodscrews to make levering off with a jemmy more difficult.

Hasps frequently cause trouble when left flapping about. This can be obviated by fitting a second staple enabling the hasp to be locked back to this when the ship is occupied. On a companionway, by hinging the hasp to the top washboard instead of to the sliding lid, the hasp will fall to safety when unlocked and it will be unshipped with the washboard.

MISCELLANEOUS JOINERY

Once the above mentioned essential joinery items have been installed and the vessel is in commission at last, the keen yachtsman who has been smitten with joinery disease will no doubt continue to think up new items in teak or mahogany to whittle away at through the winter months of many years to follow.

Amongst these not so urgent items one might include teak gratings for the cockpit floor, shower compartment, or oilskin locker (see Chapter 10); a boarding ladder; folding saloon table; helmsman's seat; bookshelves; tool boxes; wine cabinet; nest of drawers and various racks to hold the hand-bearing compass; magazines; international code flags; binoculars; log book; note pad; thermos flasks; glasses; flares and charts.

Most racks, the treads of step ladders, and shelves set one above the other, should be notched into the side members with the stopped dado joint shown in Fig. 102 in high class work, so that the notching is not visible from the front.

The cabin table should be the *pièce de résistance* of the amateur joiner and should demonstrate his ingenuity and skill fully. The top and flaps are all important. End grain should be masked by mitring in filler pieces as shown in Fig. 116a, unless the top is framed all around like a flush panel.

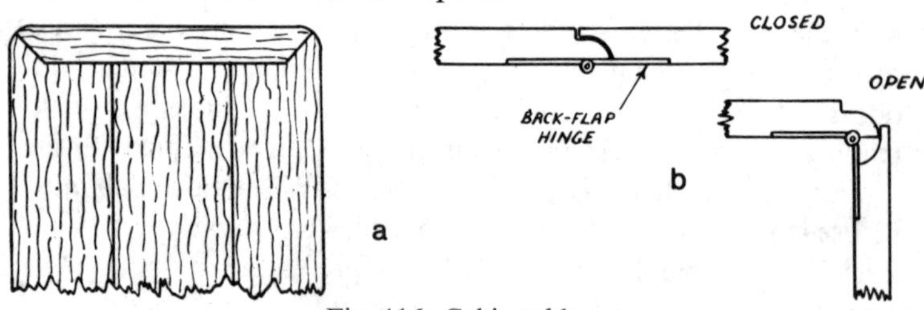

Fig. 116: Cabin table

A very wide table top is less likely to crack or twist if spline jointed from several boards under 8 in. (200 mm.) in width. Brass piano hinges are worth their cost for neat appearance but if you want to feel really proud of your table, use the knuckle joint shown in Fig. 116b with standard brass backflap hinges.

BERTHS

A whole book could be written describing the various ways to install yacht joinery, but the amateur can avoid mistakes by examining several existing boats of differing quality and type, not forgetting to jot down copious notes and measurements.

Settees, dinettes and cockpit seats are generally best made about 16 in. (400 mm.) high above the sole, but the thickness of any cushion, padding, or mattress must be deducted to get the joinery height. Bunk mattresses laid on plywood bases are often 3 in. (75 mm.) thick nowadays, but 4 in. (100 mm.) is more comfortable.

When rubber (*Pirelli*) webbing is used instead of a bunk board, even a 2 in. (50 mm.) mattress proves comfortable. Remember, however, that rubber webbing puts an enormous inward load on the sides and ends of a berth frame and two plywood baffles (hollowed on top to provide clearance when a heavy body depresses the webbing!) between bunk front and hull skin, are usually essential to avoid the use of heavy beams or angle steel reinforcement for the frame.

A bunk front of $\frac{3}{8}$ in. (9 mm.) plywood will take all the downward load of a traditional slatted, boarded, or $\frac{1}{2}$ in. (12 mm.) plywood bunk top. When the front has no drawers in it, access to the useful locker space formed is best provided by a large lift-out flush hatch trepanned out of a plywood top panel. With a webbing top, locker access without drawers must be via lids or open bins through the front panel.

Remember, plywood is acceptable for many parts in good quality boat accommodation, but it must be joinery quality veneered waterproof plywood. The amateur can save money by veneering standard marine plywood himself after cutting out each panel.

DINGHY CONVERSIONS

Many an enthusiast of modest means thinks about building a small two-berth power or sailing cruiser by converting an open 14 ft. (4 m.) or 16 ft. (5 m.) pulling boat.

The best results are obtained by choosing a tight, heavy, beamy

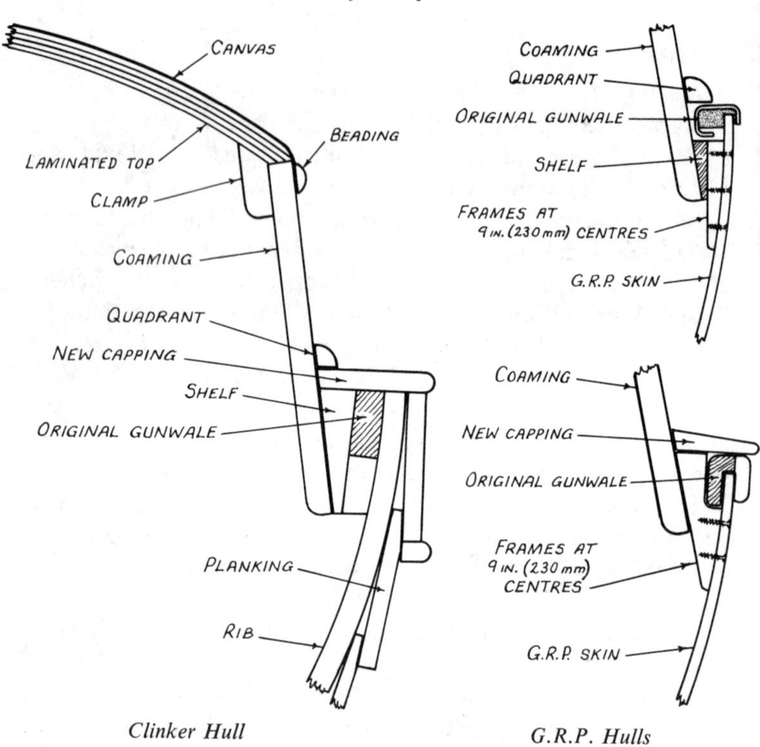

Clinker Hull *G.R.P. Hulls*

Fig. 117: Cabin structure for small open boat

hull, or by stowing inside ballast in a g.r.p. hull to improve stability. Adequate buoyancy is always a wise safety measure. A drop keel takes up too much space inside, but twin bilge keels are easy to fit. Generally, it proves best to adopt a modest lugsail rig for off-the-wind sailing, which will not cause the boat to heel greatly. Then install a good outboard motor for windward and harbour work.

To reduce tophamper weight, a low full-width cabin top and small foredeck is all you need add. A hatch through the coachroof for'ard of the mast is useful to facilitate anchoring and mooring. A one-piece cabin-top/foredeck unit in glass fibre helps to reduce weight and eliminate leaks. If timber is preferred, aim for well-cambered prefabricated cold moulded decking which needs little support from beams.

Whether deck beams are fitted or not, you will no doubt need to strip off an old gunwale capping, plant a new shelf inside the old gunwale (angled to receive tumblehome on the coachroof sides), then fit new cappings where required – see Fig. 117.

With a berth each side of the cabin about 8 in. (200 mm.) above sole level, good sitting headroom should just be available without resorting to an unsightly tall cabin top.

The cockpit should have coamings standing at least 4 in. (100 mm.) above gunwales, with seating about the same distance below gunwales.

A rudder with tiller or wheel steering is essential for sailing, necessitating a motor attachment to one side of the transom. For pure power boating, a pair of small outboard motors ensure better safety and easier detachment for stowage than a single motor.

TABERNACLES

With the advantages listed on page 147, amateurs often prefer to fit a tabernacle to secure a mast on deck.

A galvanized steel tabernacle (page 172) is normally through-bolted to chocks above and below the deck, well braced to extra strong beams and with a central tubular galvanized steel strut or bulkhead in the cabin connecting deck to keel.

However, there are advantages for some amateurs in making the tabernacle entirely in timber. Two heavy planks called *soldiers* are used, forming horns to support the mast and passing through the deck partners to terminate at a keel chock, or forming part of a drop keel case.

The partners consist of a pair of carlines joining the two main beams (see Fig. 118), spaced so that the soldiers may be bolted straight against them. A big chock is set between the soldiers to fill the gap, standing slightly above deck level. Lamination is often best to build up the considerable depth needed.

It pays to make the top surface of the chock slope downwards towards the bow for drainage, then bevel the base of the mast to

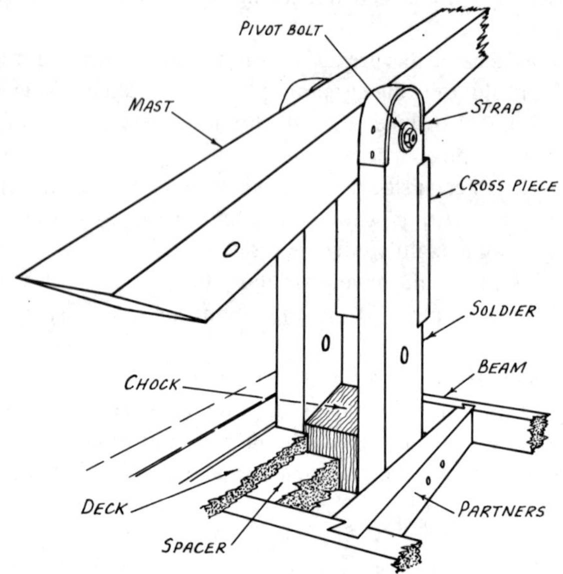

Fig. 118: Timber tabernacle construction

match. When the mast is raised (pivoting on the top tabernacle bolt) the heel then shuts tightly against the chock, relieving the bolts of full downward thrust.

After deck laying, caulk all tabernacle seams to prevent water getting below.

Soldier scantlings would be 7 in. (180 mm.) × 1¾ in. (44 mm.) with ¾ in. (18 mm.) mast bolts for the design in Fig. 4, and 5 in. (130 mm.) × 1¼ in. (32 mm.) with ⅝ in. (16 mm.) bolts for the Fig. 33 boat.

Bore the big bolt holes while the soldiers are cramped together, taking pains to drill dead at right angles to the faces.

The horns of the tabernacle above deck must be braced together with a single cross-piece. Fasten this across the after edges of the horns only and end it well below the top pivot bolt position. Get this wrong and you will never be able to hinge the mast down!

POLISHING GRP

Polishing (burnishing) a g.r.p. hull is only possible where there is a good smooth gel coat. It will not help to bring back the original colour where this has faded or become mottled, but it will improve the appearance of a matt weathered hull.

On a repaired surface, first rub down wet with 240 grit paper followed by 400 grit, to ensure smoothness. Then use the rubbing pastes made for car bodywork.

Avoid coarse compounds. Start with medium, preferably used on soft rag covering a fleece mop spun by an electric drill. Then change to fine paste and finish off with car or boat wax.

Bibliography

Although several of these titles may be out of print it may well be possible to obtain them from libraries.

Boat Carpentry, by H. Garrett Smith (Van Nost. Reinhold).
Boat Maintenance, by M. Verney (Kaye & Ward).
Boatbuilding and Repairing with Fiberglass, by M. Willis (International Marine).
Boatbuilding with Steel, by G. Klingel (International Marine).
Complete Amateur Boat Building, by M. Verney (John Murray).
The Complete Book of Boat Maintenance and Repair, by D. Kendall (Doubleday).
Designer's Notebook: Ideas for Yachtsmen, by I. Nicolson (Adlard Coles).
Every Man His Own Shipwright, by J. Bell (Chantry).
Fiberglass Kit Boats, by J. Wiley (International Marine).
Fibreglass Boats: Fitting Out, Maintenance and Repair, by H. duPlessis (Adlard Coles).
Fitting Out a Moulded Hull, by F. Green (Hollis & Carter).
Gaff Rig, by J. Leather (Adlard Coles).
Glass Fibre Yachts: Improvement and Repair, by C. Jones (Harrap).
Hints and Gadgets for Small Craft Owners, by H. Williams (Brown, Son and Ferguson).
Inboard Motor Installations in Small Boats, by G. Witt (Sincere).
Lifeboat into Yacht, by M. Verney (Yachting Monthly).
Lifeboats and Their Conversion, by C. Lewis (Witherby).
Make Your Own Sails, by Bowker and Budd (Macmillan).
Marine Engines and Boating Mechanics, by D. Wright (David & Charles).
Marine Conversions, by N. Warren (Adlard Coles).
Marinize Your Boat, by I. Nicholson (Stanford).

Modern Marine Electricity, by P. Smith
Modifying Fiberglass Boats, by J. Wiley (International Marine).
Motor Boat and Yachting Manual, by T. Cox (E. Stanford).
Naval Conversions, by C. Evans (Witherby).
New Boats for Old, by C. Davies (Faber).
Offshore, by J. Illingworth (Adlard Coles).
Power for Yachts, by T. Cox (Stanford).
The Repair of Wooden Boats, by John Lewis (David & Charles).
Sails, by J. Howard-Williams (Adlard Coles).
Small Boat Conversion, by J. Lewis (Hart-Davis).
Small Craft Engines and Equipment, by E. Delmar-Morgan (Adlard Coles).
Small Steel Craft, by I. Nicholson (Adlard Coles).
Vintage Boats: Restoration & Preservation, by J. Lewis (David & Charles).
Your Boat's Electrical System, by C. Miller

Index

Page numbers printed in italics refer to plates